GROUNDED DESIGNS FOR ONLINE AND HYBRID LEARNING SERIES

GROUNDED DESIGNS FOR

ONLINE AND HYBRID LEARNING

DESIGN FUNDAMENTALS

EDITED BY ATSUSI "2C" HIRUMI

International Society for Technology in Education
EUGENE, OREGON • WASHINGTON, DC

Grounded Designs for Online and Hybrid Learning Series
Online and Hybrid Learning Design Fundamentals
Edited by Atsusi "2c" Hirumi

© 2014 International Society for Technology in Education

Production Editor: *Lynda Gansel*
Production Coordinator: *Emily Reed*
Copy Editor: *Kathy Hamman*
Proofreader: *Ann Skaugset*
Indexer: *Wendy Allex*
Cover Design: *Tamra Holmes*
Book Design and Production: *Kim McGovern*

Library of Congress Cataloging-in-Publication Data

Online and hybrid learning design fundamentals / edited by Atsusi "2C" Hirumi.
    pages cm. — (Grounded designs for online and hybrid learning series)
  Includes bibliographical references and index.
  ISBN 978-1-56484-335-7 (pbk. : alk. paper)
  1. Computer-assisted instruction. 2. Blended learning. 3. Distance education.
  I. Hirumi, Atsusi. II. Title.
  LB1028.3.O5514 2013
  371.334—dc23
                                                                2013026944

First Edition
ISBN: 978–1–56484-335-7 (paperback)
ISBN: 978–1–56484-485-9 (e-book)

Printed in the United States of America

Cover Art: © fotolia.com/radoma
ISTE® is a registered trademark of the International Society for Technology in Education.

About ISTE

The International Society for Technology in Education is the premier membership association for educators and education leaders committed to empowering connected learners in a connected world. Home to the ISTE Conference and Expo and the widely adopted ISTE Standards for learning, teaching, and leading in the digital age, the association represents more than 100,000 professionals worldwide.

We support our members with professional development, networking opportunities, advocacy, and ed tech resources to help advance the transformation of education. To find out more about these and other ISTE initiatives, visit iste.org.

As part of our mission, ISTE works with experienced educators to develop and publish practical resources for classroom teachers, teacher educators and technology leaders. Every manuscript we select for publication is carefully peer reviewed and professionally edited.

About the Editor and Authors

Editor and contributor **Atsusi "2c" Hirumi** is an associate professor in the Instructional Design and Technology program at the University of Central Florida (UCF). Born in New York, Hirumi spent most of his formative years growing up in Nairobi, Kenya, where he went to middle school and high school at the International School of Kenya. He earned a bachelor's degree in science education at Purdue University, a master's degree in educational technology at San Diego State University, and a doctorate in instructional systems at Florida State University. He earned tenure and promotion to associate professor at the University of Houston-Clear Lake (UHCL) before moving to the University of Central Florida in 2003.

Since 1995, Hirumi has centered his teaching, research, and service on the design of online and hybrid learning environments. At UHCL and UCF, Hirumi led efforts to transform entire certificate and master's degree programs in Instructional Design & Technology for totally online and hybrid course delivery. He has also worked with universities, community colleges, K–12 school districts, medical centers, and the military across North America, South America, and the Middle East to establish online and hybrid training programs, courses, and degree programs. For the past five years, Hirumi has focused his research and development on using story, play, and game to evoke emotions and spark the imagination to enhance experiential learning. He is currently working with colleagues to examine the neurobiological foundations for experiential learning and to develop, test, and refine the Inter*PLAY* instructional theory to guide the design of experiential learning landscapes.

Based on his work, Hirumi has published 28 refereed journal articles, 16 book chapters, and has made more than 100 presentations at international, national, and state conferences on related topics. He also recently edited the book *Playing Games in Schools: Video Games and Simulations for Primary and Secondary Education* published by ISTE (2010). Awards include the Army Training DL Maverick Award for leadership in distance learning, the Texas Distance Learning Association award for Commitment to Excellence and Innovation, the WebCT Exemplary Online Course Award, the University of Houston-Clear Lake Star Faculty Award, the Phi Delta Kappa Outstanding Practitioner Award, the ENRON Award for Innovation, and a second place Award for Excellence for an electronic performance support system designed to help faculty develop and deliver interactive television courses.

Dedication

This first book in the series is dedicated to my parents, Dr. Hiroyuki and Kazuko Hirumi. Mom and Dad—Thank you for supporting and encouraging me throughout life, and for teaching me to work hard, to always finish what you started, and to play and enjoy life along the way.

Chapter Authors

Rhonda H. Atkinson has a doctorate in curriculum and instruction and more than 30 years of experience in higher education as a faculty member and administrator at Louisiana State University, the University of Central Missouri, and Polk Community College. She is currently a professor at Valencia College in Orlando and teaches undergraduate courses in education as well as courses for the Educator Preparation Institute in both hybrid and completely online formats. She is the coauthor of numerous textbooks in reading and study strategies for college learners and has developed literacy curricula for the workplace, health education, nutrition, after-school programs, and English as a second language.

Tom Atkinson has a doctorate in educational leadership and research from Louisiana State University and more than 30 years in higher education, specializing in designing, producing, delivering, and evaluating instruction.

Michael Corry is an associate professor of educational technology leadership and director of the Center for the Advancement of Research in Distance Education (CARDE) at The George Washington University in Washington, DC. Corry is also heavily involved with The George Washington University Online High School. For more than 12 years he was the director of the Educational Technology Leadership (ETL) program and closely involved with the course design, delivery, and management of this pioneering program delivered via distance education. Corry's research interests include distance learning theory, policy, and practice; faculty and teacher development; the integration of technology into K–12 and higher-education settings; instructional design; and human-computer interaction. He has written and edited numerous publications and presentations, including the book *E-Learning Companion: A Student's Guide to Online Success* (Houghton Mifflin/Wadsworth, 2005, 2007, 2010, 2013) and *Distance Education: What Works Well* (Haworth Press, 2003). Corry holds a doctorate from Indiana University in instructional systems technology. Corry previously taught at Indiana University, as well as at the high school level in Utah, and was an information systems consultant for Andersen Consulting/Accenture.

Tracy McKinney is a postdoctoral research associate at the University of Illinois at Chicago LEND program. She serves as the administrative coordinator for the Illinois Act Early team. McKinney's academic credentials include a doctorate from the University of Central Florida, a master's degree in special education from Virginia Commonwealth University, and a bachelor's degree in deaf education from the University of North Carolina at Greensboro. She is a board certified behavior analyst who has more than 15 years of experience working with students with autism in a variety of social contexts, including work in the United States, Japan, and Belgium and within the U.S. military system. Her work has ranged from implementing developmental screening protocols to providing direct service and family support. McKinney's research interests include autism, technology discrete trial teaching, and parent and teacher preparation.

Damon Regan is a doctoral candidate specializing in instructional technology at the University of Central Florida. Regan started out building PCs and networking them together during high school. After being introduced to the web in 1995, he built many websites and web applications and programmed databases for businesses and the U.S. government. In 2004, he began working with the Advanced Distributed Learning (ADL) Initiative on its implementation of the Sharable Content Object Reference Model (SCORM) and various research projects involving simulations, assessments, and distributed learning content repositories. After a short stint working with a small company that developed automated metadata to tag software and tools for creating e-learning content, he rejoined ADL and managed a software project to develop open source 3-D repository software. Regan is currently leading the Department of Defense Learning Registry project, which is a joint open government effort between the Department of Education and the Department of Defense to create an infrastructure for exchanging learning data among websites offering educational resources.

Carrie Straub earned a doctorate in special education at the University of Central Florida as a Trustee's Fellow and currently serves as director of research for TeachLivE, a classroom simulator used for innovative teacher preparation. Her achievements in the areas of research, teaching, and service attest to her commitment to encouraging youth with special needs in face-to-face and online learning environments. Straub was a special education teacher for eight years in a rural boarding school, founded a school for twice exceptional students, and has experience co-teaching with general educators in K–12 distance education courses for students with special needs. She is currently researching cognitive strategy instruction in writing for students with learning disabilities in synchronous online environments. Her research in the area of online instruction for adolescents with special needs highlights the importance of high quality instruction for a growing number of students with special needs required by state law to take online classes in the K–12 setting.

Ryan Watkins is an associate professor at The George Washington University in Washington, DC. He is a coauthor of *E-Learning Companion: A Student's Guide to Online Success* (Houghton Mifflin/Wadsworth, 2005, 2007, 2010, 2013); *The Handbook for Improving Performance in the Workplace* (Wiley, 2010); *Performance by Design: The Systematic Selection, Design, and Development of Performance Technologies* (HRD Press, 2006); and *75 E-Learning Activities: Making Online Courses Interactive* (Pfieffer, 2005). In addition, he has coauthored two books on educational planning and more than 90 articles on instructional design, strategic planning, needs assessment, distance education, and performance technology. Watkins is an active member of the International Society for Performance Improvement (ISPI) and was a vice president of the Inter-American Distance Education Consortium (CREAD). In 2005 Ryan was a visiting scientist with the National Science Foundation.

Jana Willis is an associate professor in the Departments of Instructional Technology and Teacher Education at the University of Houston-Clear Lake (UHCL). She received a bachelor's degree in literature from UHCL with secondary teacher certification in English and computer science. She received a master's degree in instructional technology from UHCL and a doctorate in educational psychology with an emphasis in educational technology from Texas A&M University. Willis designs, develops, and implements online and hybrid courses. She guides faculty and preservice/inservice teachers in effective uses of technology in the curriculum. Her research interests include instructional and educational technology in online/hybrid environments, technology integration, electronic portfolios, critical thinking in online/hybrid environments, and project- and problem-based learning and instructional design as they impact student success. Scholarly works include international, national, and regional refereed and non-refereed journal articles, edited book chapters, and professional conference presentations. She contributes to her field through editorial service on national and international journals, review of conference proposals, and member/committee involvement in state, regional, national, and international organizations.

Contents

Introduction to the Series

Over the past decade, the number of K–12 students enrolled in an online course has increased exponentially: from 40,000 to 50,000 in 1999–2000 to more than 2 million in 2009–2010 (iNACOL, 2012). All 50 United States and the District of Columbia now offer K–12 students online learning opportunities (Watson, Murin, Vashaw, Gemin, & Rapp, 2010), and it is expected that e-learning in K–12 education will continue to expand over the next decade. Some even suggest that e-learning may encompass half of all of K–12 schools in the United States by the year 2020 (Christensen, Johnson, & Horn, 2011). e-Learning is also expanding outside the United States. As reported by Barbour and Kennedy in Chapter 4 in the third book in the series, *Online and Hybrid Learning Trends and Technologies,* many countries around the world, such as Mexico, Canada, Australia, New Zealand, Singapore, South Korea, and Turkey, are also offering K–12 students a variety of e-learning opportunities. Apparently, e-learning, encompassing both totally online as well as hybrid coursework, is not just another fad; it is now a primary mechanism for education, training, and professional development across the United States and abroad.

The problem is that while technology continues to increase access to learning opportunities, it may not enhance the quality of the learning experience. Let me explain. In business and industry, quality is often measured by the amount of variance demonstrated by a product or service around a set standard: the smaller the variance, the higher the quality; the greater the variance, the lower the quality. High-quality coffee, for example, is served at the same hot temperature with the same rich flavor each time it's served. In contrast, low-quality coffee may be too hot one time, too cold the next, too dark, and then too light, and so on. Let me give you a more technology-related example. Back before personal computers, people sent their newsletters, posters, and brochures to professional print shops for design and production. Then, desktop publishing came along, and many people thought they could generate their own high-quality print materials. Not! Homemade posters, newsletters, and brochures varied greatly in quality because the average person was not professionally trained in areas such as graphic arts, page layout, and copyediting. Technology increased capacity (a lot more people were able to generate print materials) but decreased quality (due to greater variance in the visual appeal and readability of the materials).

A similar phenomenon is occurring with e-learning. Learning management systems, such as Blackboard, Moodle, and Saba, along with software applications, such as Dreamweaver, Captivate, HTML5, and Adobe CS6, are making it easier for people to generate and post online instructional materials to facilitate e-learning, but easier does not mean better. Technology is again increasing capacity (this time with many more people designing and delivering online and hybrid coursework) but may be decreasing the overall quality of the learning experience.

A great deal of variance can be found in the quality of e-learning materials and e-learning experiences now being offered online. Few educators are given the time and training to learn how to use what may be a whole new set of computer applications necessary to facilitate e-learning. Even fewer are given the resources required to rethink their coursework and redesign their instructional materials to facilitate effective e-learning. This explains why many e-learning programs continue to mimic traditional teacher-directed and correspondence models of distance education. With limited time, training, or resources, educators have little recourse but to continue to do what they know best, which, for the majority, still means using traditional teacher-directed methods. Teacher-directed methods rely heavily on self-instructional text or lecture-based materials, which often fail to promote meaningful interactions among students and between students and the instructor, particularly online.

This three-book series, Grounded Designs for Online and Hybrid Learning, is written primarily for educators and instructional designers creating online and hybrid learning environments. While the examples are primarily geared to K–12 educators, if you teach in a college or university setting or design training programs for business and industry, I think you will find that the fundamental principles and processes covered in these books may also offer valuable insights into the design of online and hybrid learning environments across settings.

The three books in the series are based on three basic premises. To increase quality (reduce variance) and design effective, efficient, and engaging online and hybrid courses, we should (1) ground the designs of our coursework on research and theory; (2) follow a systematic design process to align basic elements of instruction (namely, objectives, assessments, and instructional strategy); and (3) think and, whenever possible, act systemically to ensure that all necessary components of the educational system are aligned and work together to facilitate e-learning.

Grounded Design

Grounded design is defined as "the systematic implementation of processes and procedures that are rooted in established theory and research in human learning" (Hannafin, Hannafin, & Land, 1997, p. 102). Grounded design articulates and aligns theory with practice to optimize learning. Regardless of your underlying educational values and beliefs, grounded design provides a method that you can follow in a variety of settings.

To facilitate the method, Hannifin, et al. (1997) posit four criteria for grounded design:

1. The application of a defensible theoretical framework clearly distinguishable from other perspectives,

2. The use of methods that are consistent with the outcomes of the research conducted,

3. The ability to generalize beyond one particular instructional setting or problem, and

4. Iterative validation through successive implementations.

Adhering to these criteria will give you a solid foundation for designing coursework, as well as improving your methods and materials over time. However, grounding the design of your lessons and coursework does not necessarily guarantee that your students will achieve targeted outcomes in an effective, efficient, and engaging manner. Before and after you design your course to facilitate e-learning, you'll need to complete a number of tasks.

Systematic Design

To create an online or hybrid learning environment, you may or may not follow a systematic design process. Those who follow a systematic process use the results of one task as input for subsequent tasks. For instance, an educator or instructional designer following a systematic process may use: analyses to identify essential skills and knowledge; the skills and knowledge to generate, cluster, and sequence objectives; the objectives to define and align learner assessments; the objectives and assessments to formulate an instructional strategy; and the strategy to select tools and technologies for facilitating achievement of the objectives.

Systematic design is vital for a number of reasons:

- ▸ It provides clear linkages among design tasks. The resulting alignment among instructional objectives, strategies, and assessments is essential for facilitating learning in online, hybrid, as well as conventional classroom learning environments.

- ▸ It begins with an analysis of the target learners and desired learning outcomes. Such analyses are necessary for proper planning and decision making. Without it, key instructional components may be missing or misaligned.

- ▸ It is based on a combination of practical experience, theory, and research. Key design decisions are informed by what is known about human learning, instruction, and emerging technologies to avoid haphazard investments in unsubstantiated fads or opinions.

- ▸ It is empirical and replicable. To increase return on investment, instruction is designed to be used more than once with as many learners as possible. The costs associated with systematic design are worth the investment because the resulting materials are reusable.

- ▸ It is generalizable across delivery systems. The resulting materials may be used to support the delivery of instruction in conventional classrooms, hybrid, and totally online learning environments.

There are also a number of limitations associated with systematic design. For instance, systematic design takes time and expertise—vital resources that may be spent on other projects. Educators and instructional designers are rarely given enough time and support to go through the entire systematic design process in a rigorous fashion. Interim products (e.g., paper-based design documents) are not very flashy and may not capture the attention of key stakeholders who are important for supporting you and your efforts.

Many also associate systematic design with ADDIE (analysis, design, development, implementation, and evaluation), a well-known model for producing training and educational programs. ADDIE has been used successfully by the military and corporations across the United States and around the world for decades. Variations of ADDIE (e.g., Dick, Carey, & Carey, 2009; Smith & Ragan, 1999) continue to be adopted by educators and instructional designers to produce training and educational programs in a systematic fashion for the reasons mentioned earlier. Critics of ADDIE, however, now argue that it is too linear, too time consuming, too resource intensive, and too inflexible, and that it fails to accommodate changes in learner needs and instructional materials during development and delivery. Critics also point to poorly designed instructional materials, said to be based on the ADDIE process, that are ineffective, inefficient, and not engaging. Yet, experienced instructional designers realize that more often than not, ineffective, inefficient, and unappealing instruction and instructional materials result from inappropriate or inadequate applications of ADDIE (e.g., people cutting corners due to the lack of time, training, or resources) rather than inherent problems with the model itself. ADDIE also does not have to be applied in a linear fashion, which is a common myth; spiral and other iterative models of ADDIE are widespread.

Experts now advocate agile approaches to design, such as the successive approximation model (SAM) that further accentuates the iterative and collaborative nature of design (Allen, 2012). Figure I.1 depicts what Allen refers to as the extended successive approximation model (SAM2) for projects that require significant content or e-learning development and more advanced programming.

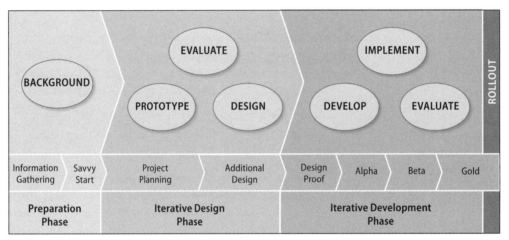

FIGURE I.1 ▶ The three-phase extended successive approximation model or SAM2 *(This figure is reprinted from Allen, 2012, with permission from ASTD Press.)*

Whether you use ADDIE, SAM, or other processes, it is important to keep in mind that a singular focus on generating tangible products, without sufficient planning or testing, may result in a false sense of economy. The impact of poorly designed instruction may not be evident until would-be learners are asked to perform key tasks for which they are not prepared. Dissatisfied learners may drop out and warn others to avoid your program. The bottom line is that you should use a process that ensures the alignment of objectives, assessment, and instructional strategies and leads to the development of instructional materials that consistently result in desired learning outcomes on time and within budget. Systematic design (as discussed in this book and advocated in the second and third books in this series, *Online and Hybrid Learning Designs in Action* and *Online and Hybrid Learning Trends and Technologies*) helps ensure alignment of fundamental instructional elements and reduces variance without inhibiting creativity if applied in an appropriate manner. Nevertheless, grounded and systematic design may still not be sufficient for ensuring that your students achieve targeted learning outcomes.

Systemic Thinking and Action

Well-designed instructional materials and coursework are essential but not necessarily sufficient for facilitating e-learning. In an online environment, an instructor may not be readily available to fill in gaps and make up for inadequacies in the instructional materials. Students may not be able to drop what they are doing and see an advisor to address a logistical issue. If any students cannot readily register for and access coursework, acquire materials, submit assignments, obtain feedback, see an advisor, access technical support, and otherwise navigate the training or educational system, it doesn't matter how good the instruction, these students may not learn. In fact, students have told me that they would prefer online programs with high-quality student services and mediocre course materials than programs with mediocre student services and high-quality coursework.

Systematic design is not sufficient for establishing effective and efficient online and hybrid programs. You must also think systemically; in other words, you must view e-learning as part of a larger system that consists of a set of interrelated components that must all be aligned to achieve a common goal. Figure I.2 depicts nine functional components of an e-learning system that must work together to facilitate student achievement (Hirumi, 2000, 2010; Harmon & Hirumi, 1996; Hirumi & Harmon, 1995). It further highlights three key components of the system addressed directly by this book series: instruction, curriculum, and assessment.

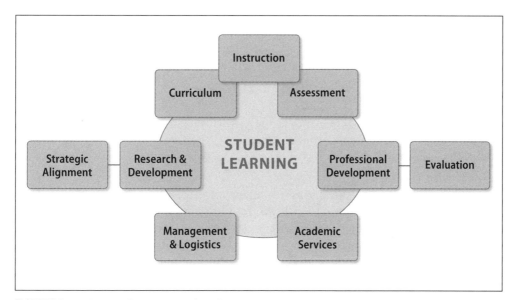

FIGURE I.2 ► Functional components of an e-learning system

The nine functional components are (1) strategic alignment, which aligns the mission, strategic plans, and tactical plans of the e-learning system with the mission and strategic plans of the larger educational institution, organization, or system; (2) research and development, which facilitates the integration as well as the dissemination of new knowledge and information generated outside and within the system; (3) curriculum, which specifies and organizes learning outcomes; (4) instruction, which guides the deliberate arrangement of events, including tools and techniques, for facilitating achievement of specified learning outcomes; (5) assessment, which defines the methods and criteria for determining whether students achieve the curriculum outcomes; (6) management and logistics, which bring together the human and physical resources necessary to support the system, including plans, policies, procedures, and budgets; (7) academic services, which cover a wide range of support for students, such as (but not limited to), admissions, registration, fee payment, financial aid, and academic advising; (8) professional development, which ensures all system stakeholders have the skills and knowledge necessary to fulfill their roles and responsibilities; and (9) evaluation, which aggregates assessment data and gathers additional information to improve the effectiveness and efficiency of the overall system and its components. Addressing each system component in detail is well beyond the scope of this book series. Rather, the three books in this series focus on the instructional components of the system, covering different instructional strategies, tools, and techniques for facilitating e-learning, which, in turn, necessitate some discussion of curriculum and assessment.

Contents and Organization

Based on the three basic premises listed in the first section of this Introduction, I wrote and solicited chapters from practitioners in the field and organized the chapters into three books to help you ground the design of your online and hybrid learning environments. This, the first book in the series, *Online and Hybrid Learning Design Fundamentals,* covers basic tasks and a systematic process for designing high-quality online and hybrid coursework. In Chapter 1, I bring to light the importance of defining objectives and aligning learner assessments to the objectives as key precursors to grounded design. Then, in Chapter 2, I present a framework for designing and sequencing meaningful e-learning interactions and posit five steps for grounding the design of your instruction in research and theory. Next, I asked Damon Regan to write Chapter 3 to help you reduce production time and cost by introducing you to vast, searchable repositories of content information and sharable content objects for existing instructional materials that may help you bring your designs to life. Chapter 4 considers the various technologies you may use and integrate to facilitate the delivery of your course. Here, Jana Willis distinguishes the application of Web 2.0 from prior technologies and touches on emerging applications for facilitating e-learning. The book then turns its attention to students. In Chapter 5, Ryan Watkins and Mike Corry discuss what it takes to prepare students for success in online learning environments. Carrie Straub and Tracy McKinney then interpret laws that govern the education of students with special needs and provide examples of how online instruction can be universally designed, using the Web Accessibility Initiative guidelines in Chapter 6. Rhonda Atkinson and Tom Atkinson conclude our treatment of design fundamentals in Chapter 7 by discussing how e-learning meets ISTE's NETS for teachers and students and how quality guidelines for distance learning can further optimize your time and effort.

As I applied the systematic design process characterized in this book, I learned that it is difficult to design different types of learning environments if you haven't seen or experienced one yourself. The second book in the series, *Online and Hybrid Learning Designs in Action,* illustrates how you can apply eight different instructional strategies—based on cognitive information processing, inquiry, experiential, and game-based theories of teaching and learning—to ground the designs of your online and hybrid coursework. *Online and Hybrid Learning Designs in Action* represents the heart of the series, providing you with concrete examples of how online and hybrid lessons may look and feel, based on the application of different instructional approaches.

The third book in the series, *Online and Hybrid Learning Trends and Technologies,* looks further at aspects of e-learning that I have found both useful and interesting for designing online and hybrid learning environments. Like the other two books, this third book also focuses on the instructional component of the e-learning system, looking primarily at e-learning trends and technologies, such as managing large classes, creating podcasts, the educational uses of virtual worlds, and the development of virtual schools in North America and around the world.

Taken together, the three books have been written to give you useful tools, techniques, and insights for designing online and hybrid e-learning environments. The books are based on 15-plus years of experience designing and developing my own online and hybrid courses, as well as more than a dozen years helping others in K–12 and higher education, business, and industry across the United States, Canada, Mexico, South America, and the Middle East to establish and improve e-learning. The books are also based on the skills, knowledge, and insights of my colleagues, who have many years of experience both teaching and learning online. If you think that a systematic and systemic approach, grounded in research and theory, may help you create high-quality online and hybrid courses, I encourage you to read on and use this book series to design rich, engaging, and memorable learning experiences for your students. In addition, if you do use one of the strategies included the series, or if you know of and use other strategies grounded in research and theory to design an online or hybrid learning environment, please let me know. I would love to hear about it. The more we can bring grounded practice and systematic design to light, the more I think we can do to increase the quality of e-learning experiences and improve education for our children.

References

Allen, M. (2012). *Leaving ADDIE for SAM: An agile model for developing the best learning experiences.* Alexandria, VA: ASTD Press.

Christensen, C., Johnson, C., & Horn, M. (2011). *Disrupting class, expanded edition: How disruptive innovation will change the way the world learns.* New York, NY: McGraw-Hill.

Dick, W., Carey, L., & Carey, J. O. (2009). *The systematic design of instruction* (7th ed.). Upper Saddle River, NJ: Pearson.

Hannafin, M., Hannafin, K., & Land, S. (1997). Grounded practice and the design of constructivist learning environments. *Educational Technology Research and Development, 45*(2), 101–17.

Harmon, S. W., & Hirumi, A. (1996). A systemic approach to the integration of interactive distance learning into education and training. *Journal of Education for Business, 71*(5) 267–71.

Hirumi, A. (2000). Chronicling the challenges of web-basing a degree program: A systems perspective. *The Quarterly Review of Distance Education, 1*(2), 89–108.

Hirumi, A. (2010, November–December). *21st century e-learning systems: The need for systemic thinking and change.* Invited keynote presentation at the 2nd Annual International Conference on e-Learning and Teaching, hosted by the Iran University for Science and Technology, Tehran, Iran.

Hirumi, A., & Harmon, S. W. (1995). The design and implementation of a system for infusing computer technology into teacher education. *Journal of Technology and Teacher Education, 2*(4), 265–284.

International Association for K–12 Online Learning (iNACOL). (2012). *Fast facts about online learning.* Retrieved from wwwl.inacol.org.

Smith, P. L., & Ragan, T. J. (1999). *Instructional design* (2nd ed.). Upper Saddle River, NJ: Prentice-Hall.

Watson, J., Murin, A., Vashaw, L., Gemin, B., & Rapp, C. (2010). *Keeping pace with K–12 online learning: An annual review of policy and practice.* Evergreen: CO: Evergreen Education Group.

CHAPTER 1

Aligning Learning Objectives and Learner Assessments

An Essential Precursor for Grounded Design

Atsusi "2c" Hirumi

BEFORE YOU SELECT AND APPLY an instructional strategy to ground the design of your online or hybrid learning environment, it is important to define measurable learning objectives and align learner assessments to the objectives. Alignment of these two basic elements of instruction is essential to and a key precursor to grounded design. No matter how good your instructional strategy is or how much time, effort, or money you put into designing and developing your instructional materials, if learner assessments are not aligned to the learning objectives, students may not do well because they may not know what's expected of them or they may spend a lot of time learning and demonstrating their efforts in ways that are not assessed. For this chapter, I delineate the terms used to state objectives, emphasizing the need to communicate expectations clearly, rather than arguing the virtues or drawbacks of using certain terms. I then characterize basic methods used to assess student learning, including conventional multiple-choice, true/false, fill-in-the-blank type tests, along with product and performance checklists and analytic and holistic assessment rubrics. I spend the remainder of the chapter illustrating how a learner assessment alignment table may be used to ensure alignment between objectives and assessments in a lesson on off-world (that is, on the moon) health and wellness.

Training and education programs consist of three basic elements: (1) objectives, (2) strategies, and (3) assessments. While the actual terms used to refer to these elements may differ, the alignment of these elements is fundamental to high-quality instruction. Whether the instruction is delivered online, in conventional classrooms, or in hybrid learning environments, the method used to assess student learning must be aligned to specified learning objectives, and the instructional strategy must be aligned to facilitate achievement of the objectives and the assessments of student learning. For instance, if your objective is to teach learners how to list 50 states, your assessment should ask learners to list 50 states, and your instructional strategy should give learners guidance and practice in listing 50 states. If the objective is to teach learners how to solve quadratic equations, your assessment should ask learners to solve quadratic equations, and your strategy should give learners guidance and practice in solving quadratic equations. Sounds like common sense, right? Such alignment, however, is not as prevalent as you may think.

How many times have you taken a test and wondered where the heck a question or answer came from? How often have you completed an assignment and were unsure what the teacher was looking for and how it was going to be graded? Have you ever put a lot of time and energy into a project but did not receive the grade you felt you deserved? One of the primary reasons for defining objectives is to help learners focus their attention on what's important, but many students have been conditioned to ignore objectives because subsequent tests or assignments are not aligned. To make things worse, students are often presented with fuzzy objectives or are not given a clear set of explicit assessment criteria to guide their efforts. To design effective, efficient, and engaging online and hybrid learning environments, you must start with a clear set of concrete and measurable objectives, and you must define valid learner assessments that are aligned with those objectives. You may then select and apply an instructional strategy that supports the achievement of your objectives and is congruent with your assessments as well as with your educational beliefs and values.

This chapter focuses on defining and aligning learning objectives and learner assessments. All the chapters in this first book of the Grounded Designs for Online and Hybrid Learning series concentrate on how to select and apply an instructional strategy to ground the design in online and hybrid learning environments. A good or even a great instructional strategy, however, may not be sufficient to facilitate learning if objectives, assessments, and strategies are not properly aligned. Problems due to the lack of alignment may be further amplified in online and hybrid learning environments if the teacher is not always readily available to clarify students' expectations and to help them make sense of complex or confusing subject matter.

I begin the chapter by characterizing learning objectives and alternative learner assessment methods. I then detail steps for completing a "learner assessment alignment table" that may help you define and align learning objectives and learner assessments as an important precursor to the application of a grounded instructional strategy to design online or hybrid learning environments.

Learning Objectives

Learning objectives are probably one of the most well-known components of training and educational programs. Most, if not all, of you have seen or read objectives in textbooks, state and national standards, or other types of training and curriculum materials, and many of you have probably written objectives as part of your jobs. For decades, teachers and instructional designers have been trained to write objectives to account for their instruction and to communicate what students are expected to learn.

Clear and unambiguous statements about what learners are expected to know and be able to do as a result of instruction were initially labeled "behavioral objectives" by Robert Mager in 1961. Although behavioral objectives are prevalent in K–12 and higher education, as well as in business and industry, some argue that breaking down instruction into such small, discrete details may cause students to "lose sight of the forest for the trees" and miss out on what's really important about the learning experience. The relationships among objectives and between objectives and greater educational goals are not always clear. The term "behavioral" is also associated with behavioral learning theories and traditional teacher-directed instructional methods, which are no longer favored in training and education. In addition, there are those who say that presenting learners with concrete objectives limits learning to what and how the instructor wants students to learn, rather than allowing students to construct knowledge, derive meaning, and demonstrate what they learned based on their individual needs and interests.

Educators have addressed concerns with behavioral objectives in a number of ways. Some focus on what students should be able to do (rather than know) and have replaced the term behavioral objectives with performance, learning, or instructional objectives to communicate desired results. Following the outcomes-based education movement championed by William Spady in the 1990s, others now prepare "outcome" statements to describe what students should be able to do as a result of instruction. Outcome statements may be transitional in nature, focusing on desired results from a traditional subject-related academic perspective, or transformational in nature, addressing cross-curricular outcomes such as critical thinking, problem solving, and interpersonal communications, which reflect the complexities of real life and students' future roles as productive citizens.

Many still do not agree on what to call statements about what students should know and be able to do as a result of instruction. However, most do agree that students learn best when they know what is expected of them (Angelo, 1995). Communicating clear expectations is particularly important in online and hybrid learning environments, when learners are physically separated from the instructor or may not be able to receive immediate attention from the instructor. Of equal importance to e-learning is the possible need to clearly communicate desired learning objectives to others involved in the design, development, delivery, and evaluation of online programs, including instructional designers, media specialists, programmers, graphic artists, administrators, copy editors, parents, or other caregivers.

It's beyond the scope of this chapter to review all the arguments for and against the derivation, presentation, and use of learning objectives. There are also many free, readily accessible online resources on how to write clear and measurable objectives. Thus, I will limit the remainder of my discussion on objectives to noting where they come from and how they are used to determine appropriate learner assessment methods.

Learner Assessment Methods

As depicted in Figure 1.1, there are two fundamental forms of learner assessments: norm-referenced tests (NRTs) and criterion-referenced tests (CRTs). Norm-referenced tests compare an individual's score to the scores of a larger population or norm group. In contrast, CRTs measure student achievement of an explicit set of objectives or criteria. Educators and instructional designers typically do not prepare NRTs. Norm-referenced tests are written by professional test writers, measure general ability levels (e.g., Stanford-Binet), and require very large populations to validate. So, I'll focus the remainder of this section on distinguishing criterion-referenced tests.

Criterion-referenced tests are important in testing and evaluating students' progress and for providing information about the effectiveness of the instruction. Dick, Carey, and Carey (2009) note three basic purposes for implementing CRTs:

1. To inform the instructor how well learners achieved specified objectives,

2. To indicate to the instructional designer exactly what components worked well and which ones need revision, and

3. To enable learners to reflect on and improve their own performances.

There are two basic types of CRTs (1) conventional assessments, and (2) performance-based assessments. Conventional CRTs use multiple-choice, true/false, fill-in-the blank, and short answer items to measure students' acquisition of knowledge. In contrast, performance-based CRTs use either checklists or assessment rubrics to assess students' ability to apply knowledge. Figure 1.1 shows the holistic and analytic elements of assessment rubrics as parts of performance-based CRTs.

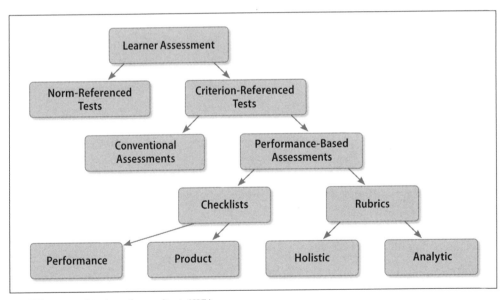

FIGURE 1.1 ▶ Criterion-referenced tests (CRTs)

Conventional versus Performance-Based Assessment Methods

Conventional learner assessment methods are relatively easy to score; when designed properly, they can provide a reliable and valid means for assessing students' acquisition of skills and knowledge. As advocates point out, conventional tests can be mass-produced, administered, and scored, and they provide the quintessential sorting criterion—a score that has the same meaning for every student who takes the same test. Conventional CRTs offer empirical support for the sorting function of schools.

However, in the mid 1980s, it became apparent that if all schools do is rank students, those in the bottom third of the distribution may find it difficult to contribute to society. These students were labeled "at risk" of dropping out of school. Further, employers began to note that grade-point averages and class ranks failed to assure that newly hired employees could read, write, work in teams, solve problems, or bring a strong work ethic to the job. Colleges, wanting to provide programs to meet specific student needs, required more information than just comparative achievement scores. These forces brought many educators to realize that schools must do more than sort students. Educators began to explore the potential of alternative performance assessments.

Advocating the use of performance-based CRTs is not to say that conventional CRTs are inappropriate. However, the exclusive use of conventional CRTs may be insufficient for measuring learners' abilities to apply skills and knowledge. Table 1.1 illustrates some of the basic differences between conventional assessments and performance-based assessments.

TABLE 1.1 ▶ Comparison of Conventional and Performance-Based Assessments

CONVENTIONAL ASSESSMENT	PERFORMANCE-BASED ASSESSMENT
Used to rank and sort students	Used as an integral part of learning
Measures students' ability to acquire and recall skills and knowledge	Measures students' ability to apply skills and knowledge
One-dimensional and episodic—only tests skills and knowledge at specific time and place	Multidimensional and over time—tests development of skills and knowledge across situations

Conventional CRTs are often used to sort students. Students who score 90–100% are considered exceptional ("A" students) and are ranked higher than students who score 80–89% ("B" students) and so on. Conventional CRTs are also good at measuring students' acquisition of skills and knowledge, frequently asking students to recall skills and knowledge that they studied during a lesson. Conventional CRTs are considered one dimensional and episodic, measuring students' ability to memorize and recall information at a specific time and place. Of course there are exceptions. Some educators use conventional CRTs as an integral part of learning and give students the opportunity to complete multiple-choice tests to monitor progress toward specified objectives.

Some conventional CRTs also require students to apply skills and knowledge to derive the correct solutions to problems. I depict common applications of both approaches to illustrate key points.

Educators are now using performance-based assessment methods that focus on measuring students' abilities to apply rather than recall information. Recent applications carry labels such as authentic assessment, alternative assessment, exhibitions, and student work samples. Performance assessments, however, are not new. They are not radical inventions recently discovered by critics of traditional testing. Rather, they are a proven method of evaluating human characteristics that have been the focus of research in educational settings and in the workplace for some time (Berk, 1986; Linquist, 1951).

Performance assessments call for students to demonstrate what they are able to do with their knowledge. Performance assessments allow observation of students' behaviors, ranging from individual products or demonstrations to work collected over time. These types of instruments typically do not involve conventional "test" items. Instead, instruments for performance assessments have two basic components: a clearly defined task and explicit criteria for assessing the performance or product. The defined task includes clear directions to guide learners' activities. The assessment criteria are also used to guide peer, teacher, and learner self-evaluations. It is important that the criteria focus on specific behaviors described in the objectives that are both measurable and observable. The challenge is to make assessments more reliable, cost-effective, and able to meet measurement standards.

Aligning Learner Assessment Methods

The alignment of learner assessments to well-defined and measurable learning objectives is a necessary precursor to the design of any form of instruction or training. In other words, if your assessments are not aligned to your objectives, learners may not do well on specified outcome measures no matter how effective your instructional materials are.

This section details the parts of a learner assessment alignment table, column by column. Table 1.2 depicts a sample of a completed learner assessment alignment table that uses a small, yet illustrative, sample of skills derived from a goal analysis completed for an instructional unit that was designed to teach high school students how to regulate health and wellness (see Table 1.10 for the full table). The design of the health and wellness lesson is depicted in Chapter 7 of the second book in the series, *Online and Hybrid Learning Designs in Action,* describing and illustrating the application of the Inter*PLAY* instructional strategy. I recommend completing the table in a similar manner to ensure alignment of learner assessment to specified objectives for each unit or lesson contained in a course. With time and practice, you may not have to fill in all of the columns or may not even need to use the table at all.

TABLE 1.2 ▶ Components of a Learner Assessment Alignment Table

SKILL/ STANDARD	LEARNING OBJECTIVE	CLASSIFICATION OF OBJECTIVE	ASSESSMENT METHOD	ASSESSMENT ITEM OR CRITERIA
Manage mental and physical well-being of colonists on the moon	**TO.** Given the mission to sustain health and wellness, manage the mental and physical well-being of colonists on the moon	Problem Solving	Posttest Rubric at end of lesson	**Performance Indicators for Distinguished Level:** Checked health metrics during every challenge Consistently maintained colonists' physical and mental/behavioral health above 90% on the metrics Noted abnormalities at least 90% of the time Distinguished between physical and/or mental/behavioral health problems with at least 90% accuracy Correctly classified 90% of the symptoms of problems Correctly identified 90% of the causes of problems Distinguished between individual problems and system problems with at least 90% accuracy Selected appropriate solutions for 90% of the problems encountered
Monitor health-care instruments	**EO 1.** Given graphical representations of instrument readings, monitor readings and address all checklist items	Rule	Practice test Checklist during lesson	**Checklist Items:** Monitors health metrics daily: temperature, blood pressure, heart rate, nutrition, and physical strength Distinguishes between a normal and abnormal reading Records readings accurately in proper documents Records readings in proper format Monitors instruments to catch problems before altered by the system Turns off the health monitor alert within one minute of receiving it

Column 1 lists the skills or standards to be addressed by a lesson or unit of instruction. Column 2 contains the measurable learning objectives associated with each skill or standard. Column 3 classifies each objective according to a published learning taxonomy. Column 4 defines the method that will be used to assess each objective, and Column 5 specifies the actual assessment item(s) or criteria that will be used to assess each objective.

I use this table to teach novice instructional designers and teachers how to specify learning objectives and ensure alignment between learner assessments and the objectives. For the purposes of this chapter, I'll focus on specifying and aligning learning objectives and learner assessments for one instructional unit.

Column 1—List Skills or Standards

Where do objectives come from? Typically, educators derive objectives from national or state standards, curriculum frameworks, instructional goal statements, textbooks and/or other pre-existing instructional materials. Those tasked with creating training or professional development opportunities may also derive objectives from published standards or by conducting goal, subordinate skills, task, or other forms of instructional analysis. Others have written extensively about how to derive instructional goals and objectives (e.g., Dick, Carey, & Carey, 2009; Mager, 1997; Anderson & Krathwohl, 2001). You can also find many good resources on identifying instructional goals and objectives by searching the web using key terms, such as "preparing objectives." So, I will begin my treatment of the alignment process by assuming you have a particular course in mind, along with a set of related standards, skills, or objectives to be covered in the course.

Begin the alignment process by listing the standards or skills associated with one lesson or one unit from your course in the first column of the learner assessment alignment table. Column 1 in Table 1.3 lists a subset of skills specified for the lesson on health and wellness referred to earlier to illustrate how the table is used to align learner assessment with learning objectives. If you already have a set of learning objectives specified for a lesson or unit, you can skip Column 1 and start by filling in Column 2.

TABLE 1.3 ▶ Learner Assessment Alignment Table with Sample Skills

SKILL/ STANDARD	LEARNING OBJECTIVE	CLASSIFICATION OF OBJECTIVE	ASSESSMENT METHOD	ASSESSMENT ITEM OR CRITERIA
Manage mental and physical well-being of colonists on the moon				
Monitor health-care instruments				
Classify types of problems				
Identify probable cause(s) of abnormalities				
Match solution(s) to problems				

Column 2—Define Objectives

To complete Column 2, you may either transform the skills listed in Column 1 into learning objectives by adding condition(s) and degree (as depicted in Table 1.4) or list pre-existing objectives to be covered in an instructional unit. For the purposes of this chapter, I use the term *terminal objectives* (TO) to refer to what learners should be able to do at the end of the instructional unit and *enabling objectives* (EO) to refer to what learners must know and be able to do to achieve or otherwise demonstrate the terminal objective.

TABLE 1.4 ▶ Learner Assessment Alignment Table with Sample Learning Objectives

SKILL/ STANDARD	LEARNING OBJECTIVE	CLASSIFICATION OF OBJECTIVE	ASSESSMENT METHOD	ASSESSMENT ITEM OR CRITERIA
Manage mental and physical well-being of colonists on the moon	**TO.** Given the mission to sustain health and wellness, manage the mental and physical well-being of colonists on the moon			
Monitor health-care instruments	**EO 1.** Given graphical representations of instrument readings, monitor readings and address all checklist items			
Classify types of problems	**EO 2.** Classify the given symptoms as either physical or mental/behav-ioral with at least 90% accuracy			
Identify probable cause(s) of abnormalities	**EO 3.** Given a health-care guide and a patient exhibiting symptoms of an illness, identify probable cause(s) for abnormal health with 90% accuracy			
Match solution(s) to problems	**EO 4.** Given a physical or mental/behav-ioral problem, match potential solution(s) to the problem with 90% accuracy			

Note that each objective consists of three basic elements: (1) a condition, (2) a criterion, and (3) a behavior. As an educator or instructional designer, you have probably had considerable experience preparing objectives and have access to resources to help you write good objectives, so I will simply highlight a few key points related to each element.

The condition describes the situation under which the students are expected to perform the behavior. Conditions may include particular "givens," such as tools and information, environment, or circumstance. Examples of condition statements include the following:

► Given an environmental problem …

► When confronted by a potential assailant …

► Given a thermostat …

► Given wet and rainy conditions …

Keep in mind, objectives should not contain condition statements such as, "Given an instructional unit …" or "After reading the assigned book chapter …" or "Given a practice assignment …". Objectives should not state how the learner will acquire or develop the specified skill or knowledge. Rather, it should state typical and authentic conditions under which the learners will be expected to perform the skill or demonstrate their knowledge. In this way, students contextualize the objective; that is, they achieve understanding and transference of knowledge.

The criteria are specified as the acceptable level of achievement desired. They tell the learner how they are expected to perform. For example:

► Percent of correct responses

► Within a given time period

► In compliance with criteria presented by the instructor

The criteria are often omitted from objectives, which is acceptable when the instructor communicates expected levels of performance to students or does not deviate from standard procedures or protocols. For example, it is acceptable not to include criteria in your objectives if you publish and give students online access to an assessment rubric or a performance checklist (aligned to your objectives) prior to and during instruction. The key point to keep in mind: it is crucial to communicate your expectations. A list of objectives, an assessment rubric, or a performance checklist communicates to students what they are expected to know and do. The criteria stated in your course's objectives communicate the degree to which students are expected to know or perform each objective.

The third and most essential element of an objective is the specification of the expected behavior: what students are expected to know and do. I hesitate to use the term "behavior" because some people immediately associate it with behaviorism and behavioral learning theories, and automatically disregard whatever is being said because such views are considered out-of-date and related to traditional, teacher-directed forms of instruction. Rather than arguing whether or not we should specify behaviors, I will concentrate on what's important—*to communicate expectations*—and will refer to this critical element of an objective as the "action verb."

To communicate expectations clearly, the action verb should be measurable. If an objective cannot be measured, how will you know if it was ever achieved? Some verbs and modifiers should not be used in objectives because they are not measurable, for example:

has awareness of	has knowledge of
shows appreciation for	shows interest in
is familiar with	knows
is capable of	learns
is conscious of	memorizes
comprehends	understands

Another key to presenting students with well-written objectives is to ensure that they are prepared for appropriate levels of learning. Again, much has been written and posted about writing objectives, including lists of measurable action verbs that are classified according to various learning domains, so I will simply refer to a table of measurable action verbs provided in Supplement 1.A to this chapter and discuss one more important issue about writing objectives.

I know many educators who prefer to use a phrase, such as "learners will demonstrate an understanding of …" or "learners will demonstrate knowledge of …," in place of a concrete, measurable verb in their objective or outcome statements. Consistent with the outcomes-based movement and the use of portfolio assessments, they argue that there may be many different ways a person can apply and demonstrate skills, knowledge, and understanding of a topic and that presenting students with behavioral objectives limits their understanding of the topic and basically spoon-feeds the answer to them. When the instructor uses a phrase such as "will demonstrate knowledge of …," students are challenged to consider the different ways a person "in real life" may utilize knowledge, and then they must use higher-order thinking skills to select and apply an appropriate way or ways to demonstrate their understanding and achievement of the objective.

While I do agree that there are often many different ways of applying knowledge and demonstrating an understanding of a topic, I can only support the use of the phrase "demonstrate knowledge of …" or "demonstrate an understanding of …" under one condition: when the teacher spends sufficient time with students to discuss, reflect, and clarify what it means to demonstrate knowledge or demonstrate understanding of a topic. I agree that challenging students to use higher-order thinking skills to consider how they can and should demonstrate their knowledge can be very beneficial, but only if the teacher and students actually go through the process of thinking and reflecting on the issue *and* the process of clarifying expectations. Too often I've seen students left frustrated, confused, and in doubt, wondering, "What does that mean?" only to fail if they don't guess correctly what the teacher's expectation actually was.

In a totally online learning environment, the issue of communicating clear expectations is particularly important because it often takes considerably more time and effort to clarify vague statements and requirements. If you feel compelled to use statements such as "demonstrate knowledge of …" or "demonstrate an understanding of …" to communicate learning objectives in an e-learning environment, you must be prepared to spend significant amounts of time online negotiating and clarifying what such statements mean and helping students determine appropriate ways of demonstrating their knowledge and understanding. If you are not prepared to spend hours online clarifying your expectations, then stick with the use of concrete, measurable action verbs when writing objectives. (See examples of these verbs in Supplement 1.A.)

Column 3—Classify Objectives

It is important to classify objectives to (a) help select appropriate learner assessment methods and (b) ensure your lesson is addressing appropriate levels of learning. A number of taxonomies have been published for distinguishing and classifying learning objectives. Bloom's (1956) taxonomy is perhaps the most well-known by educators for classifying objectives. Anderson and Krathwohl (2001) have since revised this taxonomy. As suggested by the taxonomies listed in Table 1.5, considerably more work has been done delineating learning objectives associated with the cognitive domain compared with the affective or psychomotor domains. It is also important to keep in mind that the comparisons in Table 1.5 illustrate general ideas, not the specifics of each taxonomy.

The particular taxonomy you use to classify your learning objectives does not really matter. The key is to distinguish the nature of your objectives to inform and make proper decisions regarding the specific methods you use to assess students' achievement of each objective. You should also ensure that your lesson is addressing appropriate levels of learning. If you classify your objectives and find that most or all are at the verbal information or concept learning level, you may want to reconsider and revise your objectives to ensure you are also covering higher-order thinking skills within lessons and across your course. Conversely, if you only specify higher-order learning objectives, you may want to consider defining objectives that target the acquisition of key verbal information, concepts, and principles that are necessary to perform higher-order skills. Table 1.6 shows the classification of each of the sample objectives for the health and wellness lesson in Column 3, based on Gagné's (1985) taxonomy of learned capabilities.

TABLE 1.5 ▶ Published Taxonomies for Classifying Learning Objectives

Tripartite (Hilgard, 1980)	Gagné (1985)	Bloom (1956)	Revised Bloom Anderson & Krathwohl (2001)		Anderson (1981)	Merrill (1983)	Reigeluth & Moore (1999)	Krathwohl, Bloom & Masia (1964)	Simpson (1972)
Cognitive	Verbal Information	Knowledge	Factual Knowledge / Conceptual Knowledge / Procedural Knowledge / Meta-Cognitive Knowledge	Remember	Declarative Knowledge	Kinds of	Memorize Information		
	Concepts	Comprehension		Understand			Understand Relationships		
	Procedures & Rules	Application		Apply		How to	Apply Skills		
	Problem Solving	Analysis		Analyze	Procedural Knowledge	What Happens			
	Cognitive Strategies	Synthesis / Evaluation		Evaluate			Apply Generic Skills		
				Create					
Affective	Attitudes							Receiving / Responding / Valuing / Organization / Characterization	
Psycho-motor	Motor Skills								Perception / Set / Guided Response / Mechanism / Complex Response / Adaptation / Origination

TABLE 1.6 ▶ Learner Assessment Alignment Table with Sample Classifications of Learning Objectives

SKILL/ STANDARD	LEARNING OBJECTIVE	CLASSIFICATION OF OBJECTIVE	ASSESSMENT METHOD	ASSESSMENT ITEM OR CRITERIA
Manage mental and physical well-being of colonists on the moon	**TO.** Given the mission to sustain health and wellness, manage the mental and physical well-being of colonists on the moon	Problem Solving		
Monitor health-care instruments	**EO 1.** Given graphical representations of instrument readings, monitor readings and address all checklist items	Rule		
Classify types of problems	**EO 2.** Classify the given symptoms as either physical or mental/behavioral with at least 90% accuracy	Concept		
Identify probable cause(s) of abnormalities	**EO 3.** Given a health-care guide and a patient exhibiting symptoms of an illness, identify probable cause(s) for abnormal health with 90% accuracy	Concept		
Match solution(s) to problems	**EO 4.** Given a physical or mental/behavioral problem, match potential solution(s) to the problem with 90% accuracy	Concept		

The terminal objective (TO) in Table 1.6 is considered problem solving because it involves the "process by which the learner discovers a combination of previously learned rules and plans their application so as to achieve a solution for [a] novel problem situation" (Gagné, 1985, p. 178). The first enabling objective (EO 1) is classified as a [procedural] rule because students must "respond to any instance of a class of stimulus situations with an appropriate instance of a class of performances" (Gagné, 1985, p. 118). In other words, students must complete a series of well-defined steps (class of performances) to monitor instruments (class of stimulus situations) and demonstrate the specified behavior. The remaining enabling objectives (EO 2–4) are considered examples of concept learning because students must learn the shared characteristics of health and wellness problems plus their causes and solutions in order to demonstrate the specified skills. The proper classification of specified learning objectives is important because it helps you determine appropriate assessment methods.

Column 4—Determine Assessment Methods

To determine learner assessment methods, you must make two important decisions; you must decide (1) when you are going to assess learners and (2) how you are going to measure students' achievement of specified objectives. Dick, Carey, and Carey (2009) distinguish four uses for criterion-referenced testing: (1) as an entry-behavior test, (2) as a pretest, (3) as a practice test, or (4) as a posttest.

Entry-behavior tests and pretests are given prior to instruction. Entry-behavior tests measure students' prerequisite skills and knowledge. These are the skills and knowledge students must have prior to instruction because they are essential but not taught during the instruction. If it is essential that your students have certain prerequisite skills or knowledge to successfully initiate or otherwise complete a lesson, you should consider preparing an entry behavior test. Of course, you should also be prepared to help remediate students who do not do well on the test in such cases. Pretests measure learners' prior skills and knowledge of objectives that are to be taught during the instruction. Pretests are typically given when educators and/or educational researchers are interested in determining learners' gain scores or are planning to individualize the instruction. If you need or want to quantify skills or knowledge students gained from a lesson or if you are prepared to adapt and individualize the instruction based on students' scores, then you may want to specify pretests.

Practice tests and posttests are given during and after instruction. Practice tests help learners monitor and assess their progress toward specified objectives. On the whole, it's very helpful to give students an opportunity to practice and test their knowledge during a lesson, especially if you do so without attaching any punitive consequences for their work if they do not meet requirements. I recommend giving students the option of completing self-scored practice tests and practice activities for developing and refining the skills whenever possible. I also allow students to submit drafts, and I provide feedback based on published criteria so they can improve their work at least once before submitting their assignments for a grade. Posttests measure students' achievement of specified learning objectives after the instruction. Posttest scores provide a measure of proficiency that may be necessary for students to earn a grade and progress to the next lesson, class, or grade level. Posttests are also useful in helping identify areas of the instruction that may not be working and need revision. In most cases, it is probably important for you to specify the use of posttests to assess the degree to which students achieved specified objectives.

In addition to specifying when you are going to assess student learning, you must also specify the type of CRT that will be used to assess student learning. It is the alignment between the type of CRT and the specified learning objectives that is critical to student learning and serves as the foundation for this chapter. The type of assessment instrument and assessment items used to measure students' achievement of specified objectives should be based on the nature of the learning objectives.

As described earlier, types of CRTs include conventional (e.g., multiple-choice, true/false, fill-in-the-blank) and two forms of performance-based CRTs (checklists and assessment rubrics). To select and align appropriate types of learner assessment, look at the action verbs and the classification of specified objectives. In general, I recommend use of the following tests:

▶ Conventional criterion-referenced testing to assess learning of verbal information and concepts. In other words, use multiple-choice, true/false, fill-in-the-blank, and matching type tests to assess student learning when there is one correct answer or one correct method for deriving the correct answer;

▶ Performance or product checklists to assess a student's ability to follow procedures, apply rules, and demonstrate psychomotor skills. In other words, use checklists when there is one correct way to complete an assignment (e.g., prepare a report that contains certain items that are addressed in specific ways) or one proper way do something (e.g., a relatively simple procedure for performing a task); and

▶ Holistic or analytic assessment rubrics to assess a student's ability to solve problems and apply cognitive strategies. In other words, use assessment rubrics to assess learning when there may be more than one correct answer and/or more than one correct way to derive the correct answer.

Table 1.7 notes the recommended assessment method and types of assessment items based on Gagné's (1985) taxonomy of learning domains.

TABLE 1.7 ▶ Alignment between CRTest Assessment Methods, Types of Tests, and Learning Domains

METHODS	TYPES OF TESTS	LEARNING DOMAINS
Conventional Assessments	Multiple-Choice	Verbal Information
	Fill-in-the-Blank	Concepts
	True/False	
	Matching	
Performance-Based Assessments	Performance or Product Checklists	Procedures Rules Motor Skills
	Holistic or Analytic Assessment Rubrics	Problem Solving Cognitive Strategies

Table 1.8 depicts the methods specified for assessing the sample learning objectives identified for the instructional unit on health and wellness. Column 4 notes both when and how each objective is to be assessed.

TABLE 1.8 ▶ Learner Assessment Alignment Table with Sample Assessment Methods

SKILL/ STANDARD	LEARNING OBJECTIVE	CLASSIFICATION OF OBJECTIVE	ASSESSMENT METHOD	ASSESSMENT ITEM OR CRITERIA
Manage mental and physical well-being of colonists on the moon	**TO.** Given the mission to sustain health and wellness, manage the mental and physical well-being of colonists on the moon	Problem Solving	Posttest Rubric at end of lesson	
Monitor health-care instruments	**EO 1.** Given graphical representations of instrument readings, monitor readings and address all checklist items	Rule	Practice Test Checklist during lesson	
Classify types of problems	**EO 2.** Classify the given symptoms as either physical or mental/behavioral with at least 90% accuracy	Concept	Practice Tests and Posttest Conventional CRTs during and at end of lesson	
Identify probable cause(s) of abnormalities	**EO 3.** Given a health-care guide and a patient exhibiting symptoms of an illness, identify probable cause(s) for abnormal health with 90% accuracy	Concept	Practice Tests and Posttest Conventional CRTs during and at end of lesson	
Match solution(s) to problems	**EO 4.** Given a physical or mental/behavioral problem, match potential solution(s) to the problem with 90% accuracy	Concept	Practice Tests and Posttest Conventional CRTs during and at end of lesson	

As you can see from Table 1.8, an assessment rubric was specified as a posttest to measure students' achievement of the terminal objective (row 1). The terminal objective requires problem solving where there may be more than one correct answer or more than one correct way to regulate mental and physical well-being that will be assessed at the end of the lesson. Row 2 specifies the use of a [performance] checklist as a practice test during the lesson to help students assess their progress toward Enabling Objective (EO) 1. Monitoring readings from health-care instruments requires the application of a relatively simple [procedural] rule. Thus, a checklist provided during the instruction was felt to be a valid and efficient method to help students monitor and assess their abilities to perform the objective. Enabling Objectives 3–5 all require students to learn and apply a number of basic concepts. Since learning the concepts was also vital to achieving the terminal objective, I specified the use of conventional (multiple-choice, true/false, fill-in-the-blank) practice tests during the lesson to help students assess their progress toward meeting EOs 3–5 as well as posttests after the lesson to assess students' achievement of EOs 3–5.

Column 5—Define Assessment Items or Criteria

After you've selected appropriate learner assessment methods, attention must be placed on preparing well-written assessment instruments to ensure alignment. Instruments and related assessment items or assessment criteria vary. First, let's take a look at how to align the appropriate conventional CRT item to specified learning objectives. Then, we'll look at the formatting and alignment of performance-based checklists and assessment rubrics.

Conventional CRT assessment items. Conventional CRTs may consist of multiple-choice, true/false, matching, and fill-in-the-blank type items. Depending on the specified action verb, the objectives that ask students to match, list, describe, or perform require different item formats and responses. If the objective asks students to "match," matching and/or multiple-choice items are probably appropriate. Table 1.9 lists the basic types of criterion-referenced test items and matches them to related objectives (sample skills). As you can see from the table, there are no strict guidelines or rules for determining the type of test items. A particular type of test item may be used to assess a variety of skills, and specific skills may be assessed using different types of test items.

TABLE 1.9 ▶ Alignment between Item Types and Learning Objectives

TYPE OF CRT ITEMS	RELATED OBJECTIVES (SAMPLE SKILLS)
Multiple-Choice	identify, recognize, select, distinguish, solve, locate, choose
True/False	identify, recognize, select, choose
Matching	match, identify, recognize, select, distinguish, locate
Fill-in-the-Blank	state, identify, discuss, define, solve, develop, locate, construct, generate

However, to properly align learner assessments to specified objectives, you should make sure that the behavior required to answer the test item matches the behavior specified in the objective. If the objective states that the learner should recall a fact, then the test item (such as a fill-in-the-blank question) should ask students to state or define, that is, recall the fact. If the objective states that learners are to distinguish between two or more concepts, then the test item (such as multiple choice) must ask students to distinguish between two or more concepts. Such alignment between assessments and objectives is an essential characteristic of high-quality instruction in general and vital to e-learning when an instructor may not be readily available to clarify requirements and expectations.

Performance or Product Checklists. Product and performance checklists represent one form of performance assessment that is appropriate for measuring learners' ability to follow relatively uncomplicated procedures, perform relatively simple psychomotor skills, or generate relatively straightforward work samples. In other words, checklists are appropriate when there is typically one correct way of applying a procedure, performing a psychomotor skill, or deriving a correct answer. Figure 1.2 presents a template for either a product or performance checklist.

Product/Performance:			
CRITERIA	**MEETS CRITERIA?**		**COMMENTS**
	Yes	No	
Checklist item 1			
Checklist item 2			
Checklist item 3			
Checklist item…			
Checklist item N			

FIGURE 1.2 ▶ Template for product or performance checklist

As suggested by the template, if you prescribe the use of a checklist, you are to define the checklist items. If you are assessing students' ability to follow a procedure (e.g., fixing a flat tire), the items would consist of the basic steps necessary to complete the procedure (e.g., locate jack, set up jack, lift car, unscrew bolts, etc.). If you are assessing a psychomotor skill (e.g., putting a golf ball) the checklist would consist of key points in the performance of the skill (e.g., checking the slope of the green, identifying the putting line, positioning the putter, positioning the feet, etc.). If you assess the development of a work sample (e.g., research report), checklist items would consist of key components of the specified product (e.g., problem statement, hypothesis, method, results, etc.). Again, the key is to make sure that the behavior(s) necessary to complete the checklist items are consistent with the behavior specified in the related objective to ensure alignment.

Assessment Rubrics. To create and align assessment rubrics to specified learning objectives, you must take into consideration both the scoring criteria and scoring method. The scoring criteria contain both descriptors and a scale that defines the range of performance. The descriptors: (a) communicate the standards for the product or performance, (b) are derived from the stated performance objectives, (c) link the curriculum and assessment, and (d) provide for student self-assessment. The scale consists of the quantitative values that correspond to the descriptors. Figure 1.3 depicts the descriptor and related scale for various levels of leaping ability.

Performance Standard: Leaping Ability	
Score	**Descriptor**
4	Leaps tall buildings in a single bound
3	Leaps short buildings in two or more bounds
2	Leaps short buildings with a running start
1	Barely leaps over a port-o-potty
0	Falls flat on face while playing hopscotch

FIGURE 1.3 ▶ Scoring criteria for assessing leaping ability

The scoring methods for assessment rubrics may be either analytic or holistic. The analytic method provides a score for specific work samples, such as a research paper or book report. If you were to apply the analytic method, you would create an assessment rubric for each expected work sample and compare each sample to its related rubric to assess student achievement. More importantly, the assessments may serve as a diagnostic tool to provide students with profiles of their emerging abilities to help them become increasingly independent learners. Figure 1.4 provides an example of an analytic assessment rubric for a research paper.

Distinguished (90–100 pts)	Establishes and maintains clear focus and purpose with awareness of audience.
	Depth and complexity of ideas supported by rich, engaging, and pertinent details.
	Clear and consistent evidence of analysis, reflection, and insight.
	Complete synthesis of readings.
	Exceeds minimum number of required references.
	References indicate substantial research.
	Careful, suitable, and explicit organization with clear beginning, middle, and end, and well-formed topic and transition sentences.
	Grammatically correct with few to no errors.
	Information presented in clear, professional, and well-formed manner.
Proficient (80–89 pts)	Focuses on a purpose yet lacks sufficient awareness of audience.
	Depth of idea development supported by relevant details.
	Evidence of analysis, reflection, and insight.
	Evidence of synthesis of readings. Use of references indicates sufficient research.
	Logical organization but not explicit enough. Contains beginning, middle, and end but may lack or use inadequate topic and/or transition sentences.
	Few errors in grammar and sentence structure relative to length and complexity.
	Information presented in a professional manner with few errors in formatting.

Developing	Limited awareness of audience and/or purpose.
(<80 pts)	Minimal idea development, limited and/or unrelated details.
	Few and insufficient references.
	Random or weak organization.
	Incorrect or lack of topic and/or transition sentences.
	Incorrect and/or ineffective wording and/or sentence structure.
	Errors in grammar (e.g., spelling, punctuation, capitalization).
	Information presented in a professional manner with errors in formatting.

FIGURE 1.4 ▶ Sample analytic assessment rubric for a research paper

Figure 1.5 presents an alternative format used to present what is labeled as an assessment rubric by a common learning management system. As you may have noticed, it is formatted in the same way as a product checklist depicted in Figure 1.2. I included it here to illustrate how the same term, in this case an assessment rubric, may be used in practice to refer to similar but different assessment methods. It also illustrates how a product checklist and a rubric may be used to assess the same assignment and achievement of similar objectives.

CRITERIA	RATINGS		POINTS EARNED (100 pts Total)
	Full Marks	No Marks	
Establishes and maintains clear focus and purpose with awareness of audience.	10 pts	0 pts	
Depth and complexity of ideas supported by rich, engaging, and pertinent details.	20 pts	0 pts	
Clear and consistent evidence of analysis, reflection, and insight.	10 pts	0 pts	
Complete synthesis of readings.	10 pts	0 pts	
Exceeds minimum number of required references.	10 pts	0 pts	
References indicate substantial research.	10 pts	0 pts	
Careful, suitable and explicit organization with clear beginning, middle and end, and well-formed topic and transition sentences.	10 pts	0 pts	
Grammatically correct with few or no errors.	10 pts	0 pts	
Information presented in clear, professional, and well-formed manner.	10 pts	0 pts	

FIGURE 1.5 ▶ An alternative format for evaluating performance criteria using an assessment rubric

Holistic scoring methods differ from analytic techniques in that they provide one general score for a compilation of work samples rather than individual scores for specific work samples. They focus on more general proficiencies or performance standards and allow students to select different work samples to demonstrate achievement of the standards. If you were to apply the holistic method, you would define performance standards for a particular program, course, or unit of instruction. For example, for an introductory computer course, you may define performance standards related to basic operations and use of productivity tools, multimedia tools, and telecommunication tools. You would then create an assessment rubric for each standard. For example, Figure 1.6 presents a sample of a holistic assessment rubric for the use of productivity tools, such as Microsoft Office.

PERFORMANCE STANDARD	PERFORMANCE LEVELS		
	Novice User	Intermediate User	Advanced User
Use of Productivity Tools	Evidence of little to no knowledge of the availability or the basic functions and features of various productivity tools. Evidence of little to no knowledge of instructional strategies for integrating productivity tools with instruction. Requires significant amounts of help to select, locate, run, and use productivity tools.	Uses basic features of word processing application to create word-processed document. Uses basic features of database management program to create and manipulate a database. Uses basic features of spreadsheet application to create and manipulate a spreadsheet. Uses basic features of graphics program to create and manipulate an image.	Uses advanced features of word processor, database management program, spreadsheet, and graphics applications. Combines use of word processor and database to create personalized form letters by using mail merge function. Combines word processor with graphics to create documents that contain both text and graphics (i.e., desktop publishing).

FIGURE 1.6 ▶ Sample holistic assessment rubric for instructional unit on the use of productivity software

When applying holistic assessment rubrics, students are often asked to prepare a portfolio of their work. Student portfolios, in turn, typically contain (a) performance standards with related assessment rubrics, (b) work samples that demonstrate achievement of the targeted goals and objectives and student's ability to apply the skills and knowledge, and (c) student narrative that describes how the work samples demonstrate achievement of specified criteria and reflect on their experience. The use of portfolio assessments to assess student learning are detailed in many other books and online.

Next, I will concentrate on defining assessment items and criteria for assessment rubrics, checklists, and conventional CRTs that are aligned to specified objectives. Table 1.10 completes the learner assessment alignment table for the sample instructional unit on off-world health and wellness.

TABLE 1.10 ▶ Learner Assessment Alignment Table with Sample Assessment Items or Criteria

SKILL/ STANDARD	LEARNING OBJECTIVE	CLASSIFICATION OF OBJECTIVE	ASSESSMENT METHOD	ASSESSMENT ITEM OR CRITERIA
Manage mental and physical well-being of colonists on the moon	**TO.** Given the mission to sustain health and wellness, manage the mental and physical well-being of colonists on the moon	Problem Solving	Posttest Rubric at end of lesson	**Performance Indicators for Distinguished Level:** Checked health metrics during every challenge Consistently maintained colonists' physical and mental/behavioral health above 90% on the metrics Noted abnormalities at least 90% of the time Distinguished physical and/or mental/-behavioral health problems with at least 90% accuracy Correctly classified 90% of the symptoms of problems Correctly identified 90% of the causes of problems Distinguished between individual problems and system problems with at least 90% accuracy Selected appropriate solutions for 90% of the problems encountered
Monitor health-care instruments	**EO 1.** Given graphical representations of instrument readings, monitor readings and address all checklist items	Rule	Practice Test Checklist during lesson	**Checklist Items:** Monitors health metrics daily: temperature, blood pressure, heart rate, nutrition, and physical strength Distinguishes between a normal and abnormal reading Records readings accurately in proper documents Records readings in proper format Monitors instruments to catch problems before altered by the system Turns off the health monitor alert within one minute of receiving it
Classify types of problems	**EO 2.** Classify the given symptoms as either physical or mental/behavioral with at least 90% accuracy	Concept	Practice Tests and Posttest Conventional CRTs during and at end of lesson	Classify each problem under the correct category: 1. dehydration 2. loneliness 3. malnutrition 4. dementia **Physical** **Psychological** dehydration loneliness malnutrition dementia

(Continued)

TABLE 1.10   ▶   *(Continued)*

SKILL/ STANDARD	LEARNING OBJECTIVE	CLASSIFICATION OF OBJECTIVE	ASSESSMENT METHOD	ASSESSMENT ITEM OR CRITERIA
Identify probable cause(s) of abnormalities	**EO 3.** Given a health-care guide and a patient exhibiting symptoms of an illness, identify probable cause(s) for abnormal health with 90% accuracy	Concept	Practice Tests and Posttest Conventional CRTs during and at end of lesson	A team member comes to you complaining of dizziness and an upset stomach. What is a possible cause? **a.** dehydration **b.** loneliness **c.** radiation sickness **d.** sun sickness An astronaut comes to you after a long mission complaining of loss of physical strength. What is a possible cause? **a.** the flu (influenza) **b.** laziness **c.** infection **d.** muscle loss Energy levels for the five research team members are low as they head out for a long mission. What could be the reasons? Select all that apply. **a.** all five are lonely **b.** they all skipped breakfast **c.** their suits are malfunctioning **d.** they are sleep deprived
Match solution(s) to problems	**EO 4.** Given a physical or mental/behavioral problem, match potential solution(s) to the problem with 90% accuracy	Concept	Practice Tests and Posttest Conventional CRTs during and at end of lesson	Which would be an appropriate treatment solution for bone loss? **a.** bed rest and good nutrition **b.** good nutrition and resistive exercise **c.** resistive exercise and bed rest **d.** call home Which would be an appropriate treatment solution for loneliness? **a.** call home **b.** send an email **c.** put up photos of loved ones **d.** all of the above

The fifth and final column of the learner assessment alignment table depicted in Table 1.10 specifies the criteria and items for assessing the objectives specified for the instructional unit on health and wellness. Let's begin by examining the assessment criteria and items specified for the terminal objective (TO) and the first enabling objective (EO 1). Column 5 for Row 1 lists descriptors for distinguished levels of performance for the terminal objective. In other words, students who exhibit such characteristics would have done an exceptional job regulating the colonists' mental and physical well-being. To generate the rubric that would actually be used to assess students' achievement of the terminal objective, similar sets of descriptors should then be specified for proficient and developing levels of performance. The checklist for assessing EO 1 (Column 5 for Row 2) lists the steps necessary for learners to properly monitor health-care instruments. After verifying alignment by making sure each item is directly related to the procedure and that the items, when combined, adequately cover the procedure, they may be added to a checklist template to generate the actual assessment instrument.

Column 5 for Rows 3–5 contains the assessment items specified to assess EOs 2–4. As you can see, the behavior required to complete each assessment is consistent with the behavior specified in each related objective. For example, both the objective and the assessment items for EO 2 ask learners to classify given problems as either physical or mental/behavioral problems. EO 3 and the corresponding multiple-choice items both ask learners to identify probable causes for an illness, given related symptoms. And the assessment items specified for EO 4 ask students to match solutions to problems as stated in the objective. Note how more than one assessment item (or criterion) may be required and specified to properly measure the achievement of one objective. The number of items and criteria will depend on the scope of the objective.

By delineating the assessment criteria and items along with the objectives in the table, you can make sure that the behaviors necessary to demonstrate achievement of each criteria or item are consistent with the behaviors specified in each related objective. After verifying the alignment of learner assessments to the learning objective, you can ask students to compile criteria and items listed in Column 5 to generate the assessment instruments for the lesson or unit.

A holistic assessment rubric, a performance checklist, and a conventional multiple-choice (practice) CRT, specified for the sample lessons depicted throughout Chapter 1, are provided in Supplement 1.B.

References

Anderson, J. R. (1981). *Cognitive psychology and its implications* (3rd ed.). New York, NY: W. H. Freeman.

Anderson, L. W., & Krathwhol, D. R. (2001). *A taxonomy for learning, teaching and assessing: A revision of Bloom's taxonomy of educational objectives.* New York, NY: Addison Wesley Longman.

Angelo, T. (1995). Reassessing (and defining) assessment. *The AAHE Bulletin, 48*(2), 7–9.

Berk, R. A. (Ed.), (1986). *Performance assessment: Methods and applications.* Baltimore, MD: Johns Hopkins University Press.

Bloom, B. S. (Ed.), (1956). *Taxonomy of educational objectives: The classification of educational goals. Handbook I: Cognitive domain.* New York, NY: Longman.

Dick, W., Carey, L., & Carey, J. O. (2009). *The systematic design of instruction* (7th ed.). Upper Saddle River, NJ: Pearson.

Gagné, R. M. (1985). *The conditions of learning and theory of instruction* (4th ed.), New York, NY: Holt, Rinehart and Winston.

Hilgard, E. R. (1980). The trilogy of mind: Cognition, affection and conation. *Journal of the History of the Behavioral Sciences, 16,* 107–117.

Krathwohl, D. R., Bloom, B. S., & Masia, B. B. (1964). *Taxonomy of educational objectives: The classification of educational goals.* (Handbook II: Affective domain). New York, NY: Longman.

Linquist, E. F. (1951). Preliminary considerations in objective test construction. In E. F. Linquist (Ed.), *Educational measurement* (pp. 4–22). Washington, DC: American Council on Education.

Mager, R. F. (1961). *Preparing behavioral objectives for programmed instruction.* San Francisco, CA: Fearon Publishers.

Mager, R. F. (1997). *Preparing instructional objectives: A critical tool in the development of effective instruction.* Atlanta, GA: The Center for Effective Performance.

Merrill, M. D. (1983). Component display theory. In C. M. Reigeluth (Ed.), *Instructional design theories and models: An overview of their current status* (pp. 279–333). Hillsdale, NJ: Lawrence Erlbaum.

Reigeluth, C. M., & Moore, J. (1999). Cognitive education and the cognitive domain. In C. M. Reigeluth (Ed.), *Instructional-design theories and models: A new paradigm of instructional theory* (pp. 51–68). Mahway, NJ: Lawrence Erlbaum.

Simpson, E. (1972). *The classification of educational objectives in the psychomotor domain: The psychomotor domain.* (Vol. 3). Washington, DC: Gryphon House.

Supplement 1.A
Action Verbs for Preparing Measurable Objectives

TABLE 1.A.1 ▶ Measurable Verbs for Generating Objectives Based on Gagné's Taxonomy

Verbal Information Names, labels, facts or a collection of propositions	Acquire Arrange Define Distinguish Duplicate Identify	Label List Match Memorize Name	Order Recall Recognize Repeat Reproduce
Concepts A set of objects, symbols, or events grouped on the basis of shared characteristics that can be referenced by a name or symbol	Classify Describe Discuss Distinguish Explain Express Identify	Interpret Locate Recognize Rephrase Report Represent Restate	Review Select Sort Tell Transform Translate
Rules Relational rules (principles) and procedural rules (procedures)	Apply Classify Demonstrate Develop Dramatize Employ Generalize Illustrate	Interpret Inventory Operate Organize Practice Prepare Reconstruct Relate	Schedule Set up Sketch Solve Transfer Use
Problem Solving Learned principles, procedures, verbal information, and cognitive strategies combined in a unique way within a domain to solve original problems	Analyze Appraise Assemble Calculate Compose Construct Contrast Create Criticize	Deduce Derive Design Detect Diagram Estimate Examine Experiment Formulate	Hypothesize Plan Produce Question Synthesize Test Validate

(Continued)

TABLE 1.A.1 ▶ *(Continued)*

Cognitive Strategy Internally organized skills whose function is to regulate and monitor the utilization of concepts and rules	Agree	Choose	Modify
	Appraise	Compare	Predict
	Argue	Contrast	Rate
	Assess	Decide	Select
	Assume	Defend	Support
	Attack	Evaluate	Synthesize
	Challenge	Judge	Value

TABLE 1.A.2 ▶ Measurable Verbs for Generating Objectives Based on Bloom's Taxonomy

KNOWLEDGE LEVEL	COMPREHENSION LEVEL	APPLICATION LEVEL
Acquire	Classify	Apply
Arrange	Demonstrate	Classify
Define	Describe	Demonstrate
Distinguish	Discuss	Develop
Duplicate	Distinguish	Dramatize
Identify	Explain	Employ
Label	Express	Generalize
List	Identify	Illustrate
Match	Interpret	Interpret
Memorize	Locate	Operate
Name	Recognize	Organize
Order	Rephrase	Practice
Recall	Report	Prepare
Recognize	Represent	Reconstruct
Repeat	Restate	Relate
Reproduce	Review	Schedule
	Select	Sketch
	Sort	Solve
	Tell	Transfer
	Transform	Use
	Translate	

(Continued)

TABLE 1.A.2 ▶ *(Continued)*

ANALYSIS LEVEL	SYNTHESIS LEVEL	EVALUATION LEVEL
Analyze	Arrange	Agree
Appraise	Assemble	Appraise
Calculate	Collect	Argue
Categorize	Compose	Assess
Classify	Construct	Assume
Compare	Create	Attack
Contrast	Derive	Challenge
Criticize	Design	Choose
Deduce	Document	Compare
Detect	Formulate	Contrast
Diagram	Manage	Decide
Differentiate	Modify	Defend
Discriminate	Organize	Estimate
Distinguish	Plan	Evaluate
Examine	Prepare	Judge
Experiment	Produce	Predict
Inventory	Relate	Rate
Question	Set up	Score
Test	Synthesize	Select
	Tell	Support
	Transmit	Validate
	Write	Value

Supplement 1.B

Assessment Instruments for Instructional Unit on Health and Wellness

TABLE 1.B.1 ▶ Holistic Assessment Rubric for Regulating Mental and Physical Health Off-World

PERFORMANCE LEVELS	PERFORMANCE INDICATORS
Distinguished Performance Ready for Off-World Deployment (90–100%)	• Checked health metrics during every challenge • Consistently maintained physical and mental/behavioral health above 90% on the metrics • Noted abnormalities at least 90% of the time • Distinguished between physical or mental/behavioral health problems with at least 90% accuracy • Correctly classified 90% of the symptoms of problems • Correctly identified 90% of the causes of problems • Distinguished between individual problems and system problems with at least 90% accuracy • Selected appropriate solutions for 90% of the problems encountered
Proficient Performance Candidate for Off-World Deployment (80–89%)	• Checked health metrics during most challenges • Consistently maintained physical and mental/behavioral health above 80% on the metrics • Noted abnormalities at least 80% of the time • Distinguished between physical or mental/behavioral health problems with at least 80% accuracy • Correctly classified at least 80% of the symptoms of problems • Correctly identified at least 80% of the causes of problems • Distinguished between individual problems and system problems with at least 80% accuracy • Selected appropriate solutions for at least 80% of problems encountered
Developing Performance Training for Off-World Deployment (<80%)	• Checked health metrics during some challenges • Was unable to consistently maintain physical and mental/behavioral health above 80% on the metrics • Noticed abnormalities less than 80% of the time • Distinguished between physical or mental/behavioral health problems with less than 80% accuracy • Correctly classified less than 80% of the symptoms of problems • Correctly identified less than 80% of the causes of problems • Distinguished between individual problems and system problems with less than 80% accuracy • Selected appropriate solutions for less than 80% of the problems encountered

TABLE 1.B.2 ▶ Performance Checklist for Monitoring Health-Care Instruments

CHARACTERISTIC	MONITORS INSTRUMENTS?		COMMENT
	YES	NO	
Monitors instruments daily for • temperature • blood pressure • heart rate • nutrition • physical strength			
Distinguishes between a normal and an abnormal reading			
Records readings accurately in proper documents			
Records readings in proper format			
Check instruments to address problems before alerts			
Turns off the health monitor alert within one minute of receiving it			

TABLE 1.B.3 ▶ Conventional Multiple-Choice Practice Test

QUESTION	DISTRACTORS/ANSWERS
1. Presented with four graphics of the oxygen gauge showing varying oxygen levels, select the normal reading.	a. 17% *b. 21%* c. 25% d. 30%
2. A team member comes to you complaining of dizziness and an upset stomach. What is a possible cause? Select all that apply.	a. radiation sickness b. loneliness *c. dehydration* d. sun sickness
3. Several crew members complain that John has excessive body odor. Who might help solve the problem?	a. John b. team psychologist c. chaplain *d. all of the above*
4. Crew members complain that regolith is irritating their feet. What is regolith?	*a. moon dust* b. cleaning fluid c. foot powder d. alcohol wipes
5. Energy levels for the five research team members are low as they head out for a long mission. What could be the reason(s)? Select all that apply.	a. all five are ill b. they ate too much c. their suits are malfunctioning *d. they are sleep deprived*
6. Which of the following would not be considered a physical problem?	a. labored breathing b. loss of muscle strength *c. loneliness* d. upset stomach
7. Which of the following would be considered a health and wellness problem?	a. damaged space suit b. unexplained anger c. loneliness *d. all of the above*
8. Radiation exposure is most likely to be _____.	a. an individual problem b. a system problem *c. both* d. none
9. _____ is an example of an individual problem.	a. irritability b. bone loss c. muscle loss *d. all of the above*

TABLE 1.B.3 ▶ *(Continued)*

QUESTION	DISTRACTORS/ANSWERS
10. Which would be an appropriate treatment solution for bone loss?	a. bed rest and good nutrition *b. resistive exercise and good nutrition* c. both d. none
11. Which would be an appropriate treatment solution for loneliness?	a. exercise *b. send an email* c. sleep d. all of the above
12. Which of the following would not be considered a mental/behavioral problem?	a. loneliness b. unexplained anger *c. damaged space suit* d. boredom
13. What are the causes of bone loss in space?	a. no load due to low gravity b. poor muscular performance c. hormonal changes *d. all of the above*
14. What is the best and only countermeasure for loss of muscle strength (muscle atrophy)?	*a. exercise* b. sleep c. drugs d. calling home
15. What are the potential risks involved with exposure to ultraviolet radiation?	a. bone loss b. loss of sleep *c. damage to eye* d. muscle loss
16. Which of these problems can be characterized as acute radiation syndrome?	a. vomiting b. diarrhea c. bleeding *d. all of the above*

CHAPTER 2

Applying Grounded Strategies to Design and Sequence e-Learning Interactions

Atsusi "2c" Hirumi

IN CONVENTIONAL FACE-TO-FACE classroom environments, key interactions that affect student attitudes and achievement often occur spontaneously in real time, based on a good teacher's intuition. For such key interactions to occur as an integral part of e-learning, they must be carefully planned and managed. Published taxonomies reveal a plethora of interactions that may be used to facilitate e-learning. However, relatively little has been done to clarify the relationships between e-learning interactions and classroom learning interactions or to provide practical guidelines for designing and sequencing them. In this chapter, I present a framework that delineates three levels of planned e-learning interactions, along with five steps for applying the framework to help educators and instructional designers ground the design and sequencing of key interactions on research and theory and create effective and engaging online and hybrid coursework. A compilation of grounded instructional strategies is included along with examples illustrating the application of the framework for designing new, as well as improving existing, online and hybrid coursework.

I have found that teachers and other subject matter experts, given the time and resources, can either codify their knowledge or find relevant textbooks, articles, and websites to present students with content information and facilitate learning. With some HTML programming and graphic design help, they can also make the content information readily accessible and aesthetically appealing. Preparing and organizing content information for online or hybrid courses can be an arduous task, much like putting together a textbook, but it can be done. Learning management systems, such as Blackboard, Moodle, and CourseBuilder, also make it easier to put course content online. So, why do experienced educators and instructional designers often find it difficult to transform successful classroom teaching materials into effective e-learning programs? What is it about e-learning that makes the transition from traditional classroom education and training to emerging online and hybrid delivery systems so challenging?

In traditional classroom settings, key interactions that affect learners' attitudes, motivation, and behavior often occur spontaneously in real time. Good educators read body language, interpret verbal and nonverbal cues, tell stories, clarify expectations, facilitate activities, promote discussions, elaborate concepts, render guidance, and provide timely and appropriate feedback—all as they present content information in a clear and engaging manner. Educators can also make up for flaws in design or lack of content by using their charisma to gain and sustain learners' attention and their knowledge and expertise to shed light on complex content matter. In short, good educators facilitate many different types of interactions in a real-time classroom setting, and they often do so spontaneously, based on their intuition.

During e-learning, communications are predominately asynchronous and mediated by technology. Opportunities to interact in real time are relatively limited. Furthermore, with little time, tools, or training, educators have little choice but to revert to what they know best, namely, teacher-directed, instructor-led methods. Educators assigned to design and teach an online course may post some multimedia content, add bulletin board discussions, schedule chat sessions, facilitate a few webinars, and/or otherwise use email to call their courses "interactive." However, as most experienced distance educators and students would attest, the use of interactive technologies does not ensure that meaningful interactions will occur. In reality, many, if not most, online courses still mimic correspondence mail models of distance education, where students are tasked with reading and completing a list of prescribed assignments to earn course credit with relatively limited opportunities to interact with an instructor, other learners, or additional human resources (e.g., practitioners in the field) in meaningful ways. Key interactions that occur spontaneously and often intuitively in traditional classroom environments must be carefully planned and sequenced as an integral part of e-learning. Educators and instructional designers may need help in designing totally online and hybrid coursework to facilitate such vital interactions.

e-Learning Interactions

What do we know about e-learning interactions? What can and what should we do to plan and facilitate meaningful e-learning interactions? Over the past 20 years, much has been written about interactions and interactivity in distance education and training. A quick search on Google reveals numerous definitions, examples, and frameworks for creating and classifying e-learning interactions. For instance, Carlson and Repman (1999) noted that an e-learning interaction may be as simple as a learner accessing a page of text via a web interface and reading some content. Others, such as Schone (2007a, para. 2) defined an e-learning interaction as, "an exercise or activity that allows the learner to become more involved with the material, as opposed to simply reading text on the screen."

Taxonomies for classifying e-learning interactions also abound (Hirumi, 2002a, 2002b, 2006, 2009). Moore (1989), for example, published what may be the most well-known, communication-based taxonomy that specifies student-student, student-teacher, and student-content as the primary classes of distance learning interactions. Other taxonomies include what I refer to as purpose-based (e.g., Northrup, 2001; Harris, 1994a, 1994b, 1994c; Hannafin, 1989); activity-based (Department of Defense, 2001); and tool-based taxonomies (e.g., Bonk & King, 1998). Entire books have also been written about e-learning interactions, such as *75 E-Learning Activities: Making Online Learning Interactive* (Watkins, 2005) and *Engaging Interactions for E-Learning: 25 Ways to Keep Learners Awake and Intrigued* (Schone, 2007b), and companies, such as Raptivity (www.raptivity.com) have produced templates and shells that make it relatively easy for educators to create games and simulations to help make online coursework interactive.

Apparently, interactivity is fundamental to e-learning. The problem is current e-learning tools, taxonomies, and templates neither illustrate the relationship between classes of e-learning interactions, nor between key interactions and the technology that may be used to facilitate each interaction. When should you facilitate student-student versus student-teacher versus student-content interactions? When should you use email, a blog, or a wiki? Existing research and literature characterize the nature and range of e-learning interactions that may be used to facilitate e-learning, but they do not provide systematic guidelines for designing and sequencing meaningful interactions that are essential for e-learning (Hirumi, 2002a, 2002b, 2006, 2009).

Planned Interactions: A Three-Level Framework

How do you design and sequence e-learning interactions to engage learners and facilitate student achievement? One potential answer to this question came to me when I distinguished three levels of planned e-learning interactions: Level I—Internal Learner Interactions, Level II—Human and Nonhuman Interactions, and Level III—Learner-Instruction Interactions (also called Instructional Strategies or e-Learning Strategies), as depicted in Figure 2.1.

Level I interactions occur within the minds of individual learners. Level II interactions occur between the learner and human and nonhuman resources. Level III represents a set of interactions associated with an instructional unit or lesson. In other words, Level III interactions define an e-learning strategy that guides the design and sequencing of Level II interactions that, in turn, stimulate Level I interactions. Accordingly, your values and beliefs about how and why people learn (Level I interactions) drive your selection and application of Level III interactions. It is the specification and alignment of Levels I, II, and III that drive the design and sequencing of meaningful e-learning interactions and the development of effective e-learning environments.

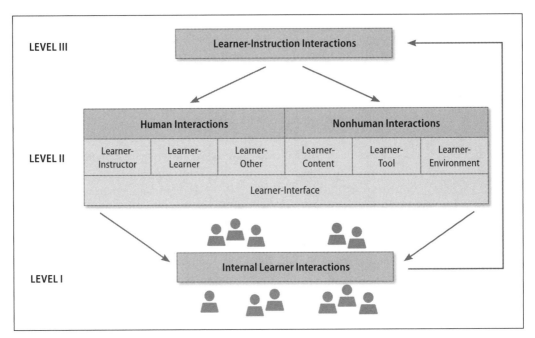

FIGURE 2.1 ▶ Three levels of planned e-learning interactions

Level I. Internal Learner Interactions

Your understanding of the mental processes that constitute learning and the metacognitive processes that help individuals monitor and regulate their learning (see Zimmerman & Martinez-Pons, 1988; Zimmerman & Paulsen, 1995; Corno, 1994) dictate your definition of Level I Internal Learner Interactions. Internal interactions may also consist of individual assessments of self-worth (e.g., Bonk, Wisher, & Nigrelli, 2004) and online presence (e.g., Christophel, 1990). Such internal interactions occur as individuals work by themselves, with others in pairs, and in small or large groups.

Whether explicit or implicit, what you believe about the specific processes that occur within learners depends on your educational philosophy and epistemological beliefs. If you are a behaviorist with a positivist epistemology, you may recognize that something is going on within a learner's mind, but you may choose not to attend to those interactions, concentrating solely on Level II and Level III interactions and how they reinforce or weaken measurable, overt behaviors. If you believe in cognitive information-processing theories of learning, you may think that people learn through a series of internal processes; thus, you may design specific instructional events to promote each process, including sensory memory, selective attention, pattern recognition, encoding into short-term memory, rehearsal and chunking, and consolidation into long-term memory. Alternatively, a developmental constructivist with an interpretivist epistemology may key on internal learner interactions that result from adaptations to the environment as the learner develops mentally and physiologically over time, forming increasingly sophisticated methods of representing and organizing information. A social constructivist who also believes that reality is subjective and that we construct meaning by interacting with the world around us may focus on internal learner interactions that occur when individuals interrelate with others in social and cultural environments.

To organize and apply knowledge of learning, I distinguish four basic categories of theories and related lines of research: behavioral, cognitive information processing, cognitive constructivist, and neurobiological explanations of how and why people learn (Hirumi, 2013). An important attribute of my three-level framework is that it does not adhere to any particular theory, ontology, or epistemology. It espouses a pragmatist view of the world where meaning is constructed by individuals, based on their interpretations and understandings of an objective reality. How you apply this framework is based on how you see the world and your values and beliefs about how and why people learn, as well as the context and the desired learning outcomes. Level I Internal Learner Interactions depicts your beliefs about learning, self-regulation, self-image, and presence, all of which will drive your selection of Level III Learner-Instruction Interactions, that is, the e-learning strategy that will guide your subsequent design and sequencing of Level II Human and Nonhuman Interactions. I'll give examples of how to apply each level of interactions and explain how they can affect each other in this chapter.

Level II. Human and Nonhuman Interactions

Level II interactions occur between the learner and human or nonhuman resources. Seven classes of Level II interactions are defined in this section, based on refinements I've made to a framework originally posited by Reigeluth and Moore (1999) for comparing instructional strategies, including the repositioning of learner-interface interactions and the distinction between learner-tool interactions and learner-environment interactions (Hirumi, 2006).

Learner-Interface Interactions. A graphical user interface (GUI) typically mediates interactions between learners and human and nonhuman resources during e-learning. Students may use a GUI to send and receive email from their instructor, post messages to bulletin boards, and otherwise share information and documents with their peers. Students may also use a GUI to access lessons and content information made available through a learning management system. The extent to which a learner is proficient with a specific medium is thought to be positively correlated with the success the learner has in extracting information from the medium (Hillman, Willis, & Gunawardena, 1994). Poor interface design can place high cognitive demands upon learners that may take their attention away from the subject matter (Metros & Hedberg, 2002). As you define or evaluate the effectiveness of Level II interactions, you should consider how human-interface interactions enable learners to manipulate electronic tools, view and access content, and interact with others.

Learner-Instructor Interactions. The student or the instructor may initiate learner-instructor interactions before, during, and after instruction. Such interactions serve different purposes. Instructors may interact with learners to (1) establish learning outcomes or objectives; (2) provide timely and appropriate feedback; (3) facilitate information presentation; (4) monitor and evaluate student performance; (5) provide (facilitate) learning activities; (6) initiate, maintain, and facilitate discussions; and (7) determine learning needs and preferences (Thach & Murphy, 1995). These seven interactions underscore the importance of and serve to delineate the instructor's role in the learning process. From the learners' perspectives, similar interactions may be seen. The learner may interact with the instructor(s) to clarify and confirm learning outcomes or objectives, facilitate information presentation, monitor and evaluate teachers' performance, and so forth.

The push toward learner-centered instruction also highlights the significance of the students' role during the learning process, and publications, such as Chapter 5 in this book by Watkins and Corry, help remind us of the importance of preparing students for e-learning.

Learner-Learner Interactions. Learner-learner interactions occur "between one learner and another learner, alone or in group settings, with or without the real-time presence of an instructor" (Moore, 1989, p. 4). Learner-learner interactions are designed to help individuals and groups interpret information, construct knowledge, apply skills, and solve problems. Often, learner-learner interactions ask students to discuss important topics by using an online discussion forum to share information, opinions, and insights. Other learner-learner interactions may ask students to work in teams to analyze and interpret data and solve problems.

Assigning individuals to teams, however, does not mean that they will work collaboratively (Johnson & Johnson, 1993). For the most part, considerations for effective learner-learner interactions are similar in traditional classrooms and e-learning environments (e.g., group size, composition, goals, roles and responsibilities, tools, contact information, and grading). The challenge lies in planning and managing such interactions in a meaningful manner at a distance through the use of telecommunication technologies. The good news is that many applications are now available for facilitating teamwork and the sharing of information and resources among groups, including blogs, wikis, and popular programs, such as Google Docs, Facebook, and Twitter. Learning management systems, such as Blackboard, Canvas, and Moodle also feature options to help teachers form and facilitate teamwork. (See Chapter 4 by Willis, "Web 2.0 Technologies for Facilitating Learning and Assessment," for an analysis of technology capabilities and features. Also refer to Chapters 1, 2, and 3 in the third book in this series, *Online and Hybrid Learning Trends and Technologies,* for discussions of how emerging technologies are being used to facilitate e-learning).

Learner-Other Human Interactions. Learners may obtain help in interpreting and applying information from a variety of resources through learner-other human interactions. You may task learners with communicating with individuals outside of class to gain insights and to promote knowledge construction and social discourse (e.g., Bonk & King, 1998). In education, such interactions may include exchanges with teaching assistants, electronic pen pals, mentors, subject matter experts, and academic support staff. In industry, learners may interact with others, such as workplace managers, supervisors, colleagues, and subject matter experts. Learner-other human interactions may occur both online and face-to-face depending on the location and configuration of the learners and the other human resources.

Accrediting agencies remind us that distance learners must be afforded the same services provided to local students. If you are teaching the same course in conventional classroom mode as well as online or as a hybrid class, and you plan some type of field trip or experience for students attending face-to-face sessions, you must provide similar experiences for online students (e.g., virtual tours and field trips, such as those posted at www.theteachersguide.com/virtualtours. html). During the design of e-learning programs, you must also consider how online learners can contact and elicit support and services from other staff, such as librarians, advisors, and counselors; the pervasive use of computer technology also makes fast, if not immediate, access to technical support staff essential.

Learner-Content Interactions. Learner-content interactions occur when learners access audio, video, text, and graphic representations of the subject matter under study. Applications may also be programmed to push content information to learners. For example, YouTube videos and podcasts may be sent to learners' cell phones or other mobile devices to facilitate e-learning. Each multimedia element may present learners with content information or other instructional events. The key distinction between Level II learner-content interactions and Level III learner-instruction interactions is that Level III presents a comprehensive sequence of instructional events (also referred to as an instructional or e-learning strategy) necessary to achieve a specified set of unit or lesson objectives, whereas Level II interactions focus on the design of individual events and the specific interactions that occur between the learner and human and/or nonhuman resources.

Learner-Tool Interactions. Both within and outside the virtual computer environment, learners may be tasked with, or otherwise given access to tools to complete, various learning tasks. Electronic mail, discussion forums, chat, wikis, blogs, and desktop conferencing are common telecommunication tools integrated within learning management systems to facilitate learner-human interactions. Productivity tools, such as word processors, databases, spreadsheets, and graphic applications may also be used to facilitate e-learning. Outside the virtual environment, the use of cell phones, microscopes, building blocks, and other hand-held manipulatives may be integrated with lessons to complete assignments and facilitate e-learning. Of particular interest now are tools, such as video cameras and other recording devices, that allow learners to generate their own content information. The popularity of today's social media clearly illustrates learners' interests in sharing their own stories. Whatever courses you are teaching, the use of telecommunication tools during e-learning warrants consideration. You must ensure that learners have access to required tools during and after instruction (as a learner, it can very frustrating to be educated on a software application that is not available outside class). Furthermore, you must take into account the prerequisite skills and knowledge necessary to use specified tools.

Learner-Environment Interactions. Learner-environment interactions occur when learners visit locations and work with resources outside the virtual computer environment. Just because your course is to be offered online does not mean all interactions must occur online. Learners may be asked to seek or travel to specific locations (e.g., nearby zoos, museums, schools, hospitals, daycare and community centers that learners may readily locate and visit) to gather, observe, and otherwise use external resources to complete assignments and activities and to participate in planned educational events. In many cases, learner-environment interactions may be essential for promoting experiential learning (if that's your pedagogical preference). Learner-environment interactions truly break down the barriers of classroom walls.

Learner-environment interactions may be difficult to manage at a distance, but when necessary, they can be arranged. Like planning complex learner-other human interactions, the keys are to (a) clearly delineate the desired learning outcomes and identify when learner-environment interactions are essential for the achievement of those outcomes, (b) plan and coordinate the interactions so that learners readily understand what is expected of them and why it is important for them to interact with their environment, and (c) integrate the event with other interactions and embed them within a sound instructional strategy to optimize the experience and ensure learners reach the specified objectives.

Level III. Learner-Instruction Interactions

Learner-instruction interactions involve a deliberate arrangement of events to promote learning and facilitate goal achievement (Driscoll, 2005). Consider Level III a meta-level that transcends and is used to guide the design and sequencing of Level II interactions. Learner-instruction interactions illustrate how key design decisions may be grounded in research and theory to facilitate e-learning. Specifically, you use an instructional strategy, grounded in research and theory, to design and sequence e-learning interactions as well as to select and integrate technology that facilitates each interaction.

Educators and instructional designers often fail to ground their coursework and the design of related lessons and instructional modules in research and theory (Bonk & King, 1998; Bednar, Cunningham, Duffy, & Perry, 1995). While there is no substitute for practical experience, relying solely on past practices, fads, and political agendas to create online courses and generate e-learning strategies may prove somewhat problematic. With limited time, training, or support, educators and designers may have little recourse but to rely on what they know best (i.e., teacher-directed methods and materials). At times, such methods and materials may be satisfactory; however, they may be inadequate for facilitating e-learning and the achievement of certain types of learning outcomes.

So, how do grounded instructional strategies help guide the design and sequencing of Level II interactions? Hannifin, Hannifin, Land, and Oliver (1997) define "grounded design" as "the systematic implementation of processes and procedures that are rooted in established theory and research in human learning" (p. 102). A grounded approach uses theory and research to make design decisions. It neither subscribes to nor advocates any particular epistemology, but it promotes alignment between theory and practice.

A cursory review of the literature reveals a number of instructional strategies grounded in research and theory that may be classified, in general, as learner-centered or teacher-directed pedagogical approaches (Supplement 2.A). Table 2.1 shows the outlines of nine of the 21 strategies included in Supplement 2.A's Table 2.A.1.

Each event associated with a strategy represents an interaction or transaction that occurs between the learner and other human or nonhuman resources. The application of a grounded strategy gives you a foundation for planning and sequencing a comprehensive set of e-learning interactions as well as for selecting and integrating technology for an instructional unit or lesson based on a combination of research, theory, and practical experience. Supplement 2.A contains these and several more strategies. All of the chapters in the second book of this series, *Online and Hybrid Learning Designs in Action,* are dedicated to illustrating how you may apply specific strategies to ground the designs of your own totally online and hybrid learning environments.

TABLE 2.1 ▶ Outlines of Nine Grounded Instructional Strategies

LEARNING-CENTERED INSTRUCTIONAL STRATEGIES		
Experiential Learning (Kolb, 1984) 1. Concrete Experience 2. Reflective Observation 3. Abstract Conceptualization 4. Active Experimentation	**Guided Experiential Learning** (Clark, 2004) 1. Goals 2. Reasons and Activation 3. Demonstration 4. Application 5. Integration 6. Assessment	**Learning by Doing** (Schank, Berman, & Macpherson, 1999) 1. Define Goals 2. Set Mission 3. Present Cover Story 4. Establish Roles 5. Operate Scenarios 6. Provide Resources 7. Provide Feedback
Problem-Based Learning (Barrows, 1985) 1. Start New Class 2. Start a New Problem 3. Problem Follow-Up 4. Performance Presentation(s) 5. After Conclusion of Problem	**InterPLAY Strategy** (Stapleton & Hirumi, 2011) 1. Expose 2. Inquire 3. Discover 4. Create 5. Experiment 6. Share	**BSCS 5E Model** (Bybee et al., 2006) 1. Engage 2. Explore 3. Explain 4. Elaborate 5. Evaluate
TEACHER-DIRECTED INSTRUCTIONAL STRATEGIES		
Nine Events of Instruction (Gagné, 1977) 1. Gain Attention 2. Inform Learner of Objective(s) 3. Stimulate Recall of Prior Knowledge 4. Present Stimulus Materials 5. Provide Learning Guidance 6. Elicit Performance 7. Provide Feedback 8. Assess Performance 9. Enhance Retention and Transfer	**Elements of Lesson Design** (Hunter, 1990) 1. Anticipatory Set 2. Objective and Purpose 3. Input 4. Modeling 5. Check for Understanding 6. Guided Practice 7. Independent Practice	**5-Component Lesson Model** (Dick, Carey, & Carey, 2009) 1. Pre-Instructional Activities 2. Content Presentation and Learning Guidance 3. Learner Participation 4. Assessment 5. Follow-Through Activities

Applying the Framework

The first time you apply the framework, I recommend following the five-step process listed in Figure 2.2. Over time, you will find it relatively easy to combine steps or even to complete all the steps at once to generate a plan for your instructional unit. Eventually, you may even find it unnecessary to generate a plan before you prototype or otherwise generate your online or hybrid lessons and instructional materials. You may also find it unnecessary to complete Step 5 as you gain experience and expertise in designing e-learning materials.

Step 1.	Select a Level III grounded instructional strategy based on specified objectives, lesson content, and your values and beliefs about teaching and learning.
Step 2.	Operationalize each event, embedding essential experiences and describing how the selected strategy will be applied during instruction.
Step 3.	Determine the type of Level II interaction(s) that will be used to facilitate each event.
Step 4.	Select the tool(s) (e.g., chat, email, bulletin board system) that will be used to facilitate each event, based on the nature of the interaction.
Step 5.	Analyze materials to determine frequency and quality of planned e-learning interactions and revise as necessary.

FIGURE 2.2 ▶ Five-step process for designing and sequencing e-learning interactions

Completion of Steps 1–4 results in an instructional treatment plan (ITP) that is best illustrated through an example. Table 2.2 depicts an ITP I recently created for a unit of a new hybrid course on cognitive neuroscience, learning, and instructional design. The specific instructional unit represented in the example covers cognitive neuroscience research on rewards and human emotions with the terminal objective of students applying what they learned to redesign an existing instructional unit. I began with a defined set of objectives and learner assessments (as discussed in Chapter 1). The course was designated for hybrid delivery with a face-to-face class session scheduled each week for six weeks.

To show you how to apply the three-level framework (Figure 2.1), I will refer back to Table 2.2 and explain how I used the five-step process to generate the sample ITP. The resulting instructional unit on Human Rewards and Emotions is presented in Supplement 2.B.

TABLE 2.2 ▶ Sample Instructional Treatment Plan Based on the 5E Instructional Model

EVENT	DESCRIPTION	INTERACTION(S)	TOOLS
Engage	Present students with a picture that evokes emotion, maybe something particularly shocking or inspiring. Note how emotions play a major role in learning and behavior. Consider posting an exciting video talking about the potential applications of affective neuroscience research. Ask learners to post a short description of a particularly emotional event in their past and discuss how people tend to remember emotional experiences.	Learner-Content Learner-Instructor Learner-Learner Learner-Interface	WWW (text, videos) Online Discussion
Explore	Present learners with different levels of content information based on required prior knowledge of biology, anatomy, and/or physiology. Basic level should not require any prior biology, anatomy, and/or physiology coursework to comprehend. Highest level may require college biology, anatomy, and/or physiology. Distinguish the degree of technical difficulty associated with each set/level of resources.	Learner-Content Learner-Interface	WWW (text, videos) Textbook
Explain	Ask learners to explain what they learned from their exploration, meeting standards for critical thinking to earn credit for their work. Encourage but do not require students to read and respond to each other's explanations. Class discussion of what individuals learned will be facilitated during the face-to-face class sessions. Test use of Paul and Elder's *Miniature Guide to Critical Thinking Concepts and Tools* to evaluate team elaborations.	Learner-Content Learner-Learner Learner-Instructor Learner-Interface	Face-to-Face WWW Online Discussion
Elaborate	Ask learners to elaborate on their individual explanations by working with team members to redesign an existing instructional unit based on what they've learned about the neuroscience of human rewards and emotions. Ask learners to discuss their individual explorations and explanations of what they've learned about rewards and emotions. Encourage learners to post questions regarding any discrepancies in findings. Evaluate team elaborations using Paul and Elder's *Using Intellectual Standards to Assess Student Reasoning*.	Learner-Content Learner-Learner Learner-Environment	Face-to-Face WWW Email, phone
Evaluate	Evaluate both individual learner explanations and team elaborations. Use criteria for evaluating critical thinking (Paul & Elder, 2010) to assess critical thinking. Use criteria for evaluating reasoning (Paul & Elder, 2006) to evaluate team elaborations. Gather data from learners about the design of unit and appropriateness/ value of using published criteria.	Learner-Content Learner-Instructor	WWW Email (feedback templates)

Sources: The first column is based on the BSCS (Biological Sciences Curriculum Study) 5E (five event) Model from Bybee et al., 2006. Columns two through four are the author's examples with references to Paul & Elder, 2010, *Miniature Guide to Critical Thinking Concepts and Tools* and Paul & Elder, 2006, *Using Intellectual Standards to Assess Student Reasoning.*

Step 1. Select a Grounded Instructional Strategy

It is probably good to begin by selecting an appropriate (Level III) instructional strategy to guide the design and sequencing of (Level II) e-learning interactions. The strategy determines the nature of the e-learning environment and requires you to consider the desired learning outcomes, as well as your personal values and beliefs about teaching and learning, that is, your educational philosophy and epistemological beliefs (Level I). Following this process may also be enjoyable if you're willing to step out of your comfort zone to apply a strategy that may not be familiar to you.

A fundamental principle of instructional design is that how you design and deliver instruction should be based on the nature of the desired learning outcomes. The specific technique used to analyze an instructional situation should be based on targeted learning outcomes (Jonassen, Tessmer, & Hannum, 1999). Similarly, as I noted in the previous chapter, learner assessment methods should be determined by the nature of specified objectives. The same idea applies to the selection of a grounded instructional strategy.

Years of educational research indicate that the methods used to design and deliver instruction should differ based on the desired learning outcome (see Smith & Ragan, 1993, 1999). In other words, the methods used to teach problem solving should differ from the methods used to teach a procedure, which should differ from methods used to teach concepts, and so on. For example, if I were training someone to use a new photocopying machine, I would use a direct instructional strategy (e.g., Joyce, Weil, & Showers, 1992) because it is an effective and efficient method for teaching someone a simple procedure. In cases where there is basically one correct answer and/or one correct method for deriving the answer, learners may not have to interact with others to derive meaning and construct knowledge through social discourse. In contrast, if I wanted to teach someone how to solve a complex, real-world problem with more than one correct answer or more than one method for deriving the correct answer, then I would use a more learner-centered approach that encourages learners to interact with each other to help interpret and apply targeted skills and knowledge.

In selecting an appropriate strategy, it is also important to take into account your educational philosophy and epistemological beliefs. If you believe that people derive meaning and construct knowledge through social interactions, then constructivist, learner-centered, and collaborative instructional strategies are more aligned with your values than teacher-directed methods. If you believe people learn best by "doing" and from addressing relevant real-world problems or challenges, then an experiential approach may resonate with your educational philosophy. If you believe in drill and practice and that it's the role of the teacher to organize and present content information, teacher-directed strategies may be more in line with your values and beliefs.

Selecting an appropriate instructional strategy is neither simple nor straightforward. Much depends on the desired learning goals and objectives, but concerns for the learner, the context, and fundamental beliefs about teaching and learning also mediate the selection process. Perhaps an even stronger influence is time and expertise. With insufficient time or training, educators often revert to what they know best, that is, teacher-directed methods and materials. To select an appropriate instructional strategy, you must have the time and skills necessary to analyze several important variables and develop a good understanding of alternative strategies. You must also have the confidence, desire, and the opportunity to apply alternative instructional strategies within the context of your job.

Throughout the Human Rewards and Emotions course, I wanted to give learners the opportunity to examine key lines of cognitive neuroscience research related to learning and instructional design, based on their individual needs, interests, and backgrounds. I wanted students to work hard and demonstrate critical thinking and reasoning skills but did not have any specific, predefined learning or performance goals and objectives in mind other than to apply what they learned to instructional design. So, I selected the 5E instructional model (Bybee et al., 2006) as the Level III interaction (instructional strategy) because (a) it is based on a pattern of natural inquiry and problem-solving (i.e., initial engagement, exploration of alternatives, formation of explanations, use of the explanations, and evaluation of the explanations based on efficacy), and (b) the five events encourage conceptual change and a progressive reforming of ideas. The 5E model is also consistent with my basic belief (and instructional design principle) that a learner-centered approach should be used when targeting learning outcomes and/or when methods used to derive the outcomes may differ by student. To complete Step 1, I listed the key events associated with the 5E Model in Column 1 of the ITP, as depicted in Table 2.2.

Step 2. Operationalize Each Event

To operationalize your selected strategy (Step 2), provide a short description of how you plan to design and deliver each event. Your narrative may include a summary of how you would facilitate the event and/or may include a copy of the actual text information to be presented to learners. How much detail you include about each event at this point is up to you. If you are an instructional designer, you must provide sufficient detail to clearly communicate your intentions so that team members and/or clients can react in an informed manner. You want to concentrate on areas of improvement rather than spending time answering questions, such as, what do you mean by this or that? Also keep in mind the truism: you can do the work now, or you can do the work later. Eventually, someone will have to write the actual words to be read or heard by learners. If you provide a just summary of how you will implement each event at this point, you will need to spend significant time writing later, as you or your team develop the instructional materials. If you take the time now to detail each event, less time will be required during development. In cases when different people may be tasked with developing the instructional materials, the more detail you put into the treatment plan, the less time it will take to generate your instructional materials or to explain your designs to writers, programmers, and other course developers. Of course, the flip side is if you put a lot of time into fleshing out details in your treatment plan and then find out your client, manager, team members, and target learners want to make significant changes to the design, you may have to redo a significant amount of work.

Column 2 of Table 2.2 illustrates how I operationalized each instructional event associated with the 5E model. The first event (Engage) is meant to gain and focus learners' attention, spark their interest, and elicit prior knowledge (Bybee et al., 2006). So, to engage learners in the unit topic (cognitive neuroscience of rewards and emotions), I thought it would be effective to present learners with either an inspiring or shocking picture that evokes emotions. I also thought snippets of information on how emotions affect learning and behavior would spark their curiosity and that asking them to describe a particularly emotional event in their lives would stimulate recall of prior knowledge.

The second event (Explore) presents learners with current knowledge, skills, and processes that are related to the learning objective (Bybee et al., 2006). I wanted to give students the opportunity to explore the topic at different levels of technical (physiological, anatomical, and neurobiological) detail. Based on the results of a learner analysis, I knew that students taking the course differed greatly in terms of their interests, experience, and prior knowledge of anatomy, physiology, and cognitive neuroscience. So, I looked for, compiled, and organized content-related resources, and encouraged students to explore the resources at their levels of interest (with the understanding that they would then explain what they had learned from their explorations to earn credit).

As students explored the topic, I wanted them to think critically about what they were learning. I also wanted them to demonstrate critical thinking when they explained what they had learned from their explanation. So, to operationalize the third instructional event (Explain), I posted published intellectual standards for evaluating critical thinking (Paul & Elder, 2010) to communicate my expectations, provide guidance, and evaluate student explanations. I found that the 5E model really distinguished itself when I taught this event. Rather than the teacher explaining the content to students, the students are tasked with explaining what they learned to the teacher and other students. I could then fill in any gaps as well as correct any misconceptions during the following instructional event.

The fourth event (Elaborate) is meant to give learners the opportunity to "elaborate on, correct mistakes or misconceptions, and otherwise extend their understanding of concepts" (Bybee et al., 2006, p. 2). To elaborate, I first asked students to review each other's explanations of what they learned about human rewards and emotions. I then asked them to discuss their individual explorations and explanations together and to identify areas of common as well as discrepant findings. I also encouraged students to post questions to clarify any points or misconceptions. To complete their elaboration, teams applied what they'd learned to redesign an existing instructional lesson. Specifically, I tasked students to work in teams to consider what aspects of this lesson they would and would not change, based on what they learned about the neuroscience of rewards and emotions.

For the final instructional event (Evaluate), students are to assess their mastery of specified skills and knowledge, and instructors are to evaluate learners' progress toward and achievement of learning objectives. As noted earlier, I used Paul and Elder's (2010) guide to critical thinking to evaluate learners' explanations. To evaluate learners' elaborations, I used published intellectual standards for evaluating reasoning (Paul & Elder, 2006) because I felt that students had to use reasoning skills to properly redesign their instructional lessons and elaborate on what they had learned.

Before advancing to Step 3, it is important to note that the sample instructional unit was designated for hybrid delivery. I'd already decided to teach parts of the course online and parts of it face-to-face. The course was being taught over the summer, so I had six weeks to teach the course and six scheduled face-to-face sessions (one per week). So, as with most hybrid designs, I had to answer the fundamental question, "Which aspects of the course and lessons should I put online, and which aspects should I facilitate face-to-face?" Although the answer to this question is not necessarily documented until Step 4, I mention it here because as you begin to imagine how the lesson will flow and operationalize each instructional event in Step 2, you should start asking yourself, are face-to-face interactions necessary to facilitate the event? Would the event be more effective, efficient, or engaging if it were completed online or face-to-face? By using my instructional strategy to help figure out what to do online and what to facilitate face-to-face, I am grounding key design decisions in a defensible framework as I move on to Step 3.

Step 3. Determine Type(s) of Level II Interactions

To complete Step 3, identify the type(s) of interactions that will be used to facilitate each event based on the classes of Level II interactions posited in the planned interaction framework. Does the event require learner-instructor interactions, learner-learner interactions, or interactions with other human resources? What nonhuman interactions are necessary to facilitate each event? Identifying the types of Level II interactions that will be used to facilitate each event will help you select the appropriate media and tools necessary to develop and deliver your instruction (Step 4), as well as help you ensure you are not designing a lesson that involves too many interactions to manage or too few interactions to promote active learning (see Step 5 for further details).

As you identify Level II interactions, keep in mind that a single event may require multiple interactions. For example, to engage learners at the beginning of an online lesson, you may want to post a thought-provoking image or video on a website (learner-content and learner-interface interactions), as well as ask learners to discuss their initial reactions to the image in an online discussion forum (learner-learner and learner-tool interaction). Table 2.2 depicts the Level II interactions I identified to facilitate each event associated with the 5E model. As you can see, I identified multiple Level II interactions for several events. It is important to identify the primary Level II interactions at this point to help you complete the design of your instructional unit.

Step 4. Select Tools

For Step 4, select the communication tools and/or media that are to be used to facilitate each event and interaction. Although your primary delivery method (e.g., totally online or hybrid) may have already been determined, you still have several options and decisions to make. Your task is to determine the appropriate tool(s) for facilitating each interaction (defined in Column 3, Table 2.2) that also fall within the confines of available resources. Consider these relevant questions: Who are the primary senders and receivers of the communications? Do learners need audio, video, text, and/or graphics? Are synchronous or asynchronous communications necessary? Are the communications one-to-one, one-to-some, or one-to-many? What kind of budget do you have? What kind of technologies and human resources are available? How much time do you have to prepare course materials?

For the sample lesson depicted in Table 2.2, the course and unit were already designated for hybrid delivery. Knowing I was designing a hybrid course, I used my instructional strategy to help me determine which aspects of the course and instructional unit to put online and which aspects to facilitate face-to-face. For each instructional event, I asked myself, "Are real-time, synchronous interactions necessary or desired?" and "Would it be better or necessary to interact with students (or have students interact with each other) face-to-face to facilitate this event or key aspects of this event?" Some instructional events, such as hands-on and role-playing activities or providing extensive, immediate feedback, may be easier or necessary to facilitate in real-time with face-to-face interactions. For example, in Table 2.2, you can see that I decided to facilitate some aspects of the Explanation and Elaboration events in class because real-time, face-to-face interactions would be more effective and efficient. Specifically, I felt that it would be useful to discuss individual explanations in class in order to go over key points that may have been missed and to clarify any misconceptions, as well as to facilitate teamwork on group elaborations. These important tasks would have taken considerably more time online than they did in class. The web and other telecommunication tools were prescribed to *Engage* learners, facilitate student *Explorations*, share individual *Explanations* and team *Elaborations*, and *Evaluate* students' work. In addition to helping identify the primary tools that must be accessible to both the teacher and students, completing Column 4 of the ITP also helps educators and instructional designers keep track of and plan for the use of additional tools necessary to deliver the instruction.

Your instructional strategy provides the means for determining which aspects of a hybrid course or lesson to put online and which aspects to facilitate face-to-face, based on pedagogy rather than fads or uninformed opinions. Examples of how grounded strategies may be used to design hybrid lessons are provided throughout the second book of this series, *Online and Hybrid Learning Designs in Action,* and are further detailed by Hirumi, Bradford, and Rutherford (2011). Operationalizing your instructional strategy for either totally online or hybrid instruction enables you to determine the specific types of Level II interactions to plan as well as the media and tools that are necessary to facilitate each event.

After filling in the four columns of your instructional treatment plan (ITP), you can then use the resulting plan to generate flowcharts, storyboards, and/or prototypes of your instruction (as discussed in the next section of this chapter under Next Steps). At this stage, I recommend that rather than taking the time to generate an ITP for all the instructional units or lessons you may include in a course or training program, you may want to generate a detailed treatment plan for one instructional unit, create flowcharts and storyboards (if necessary), and then generate and test a prototype of the unit. After testing and revising your initial instructional unit, you can use it to create a template and establish standards for designing and developing the remaining instructional units or lessons in your course or training program to facilitate the overall development process.

Step 5. Analyze Planned e-Learning Interactions

Analyzing planned interactions during the design process, before developing and delivering your instruction, may help you improve the quality of e-learning materials and, subsequently, the quality of the students' e-learning experiences. Completed early, an analysis of planned interactions may reduce the need for costly, time-consuming revisions during program development or implementation. This is a good time to reflect on the quantity and quality of your planned interactions to determine whether you have included an appropriate combination of experiences for your students. How many learner-instructor and learning-learner interactions are planned? Do students have sufficient opportunities to interact with one another and with the instructor? Do learners require access to others? Are there too many learner-instructor interactions, making it difficult or impossible for the instructor to manage all of the communications? You may find that you need to go back to revise your description of one or more events; this built-in flexibility illustrates the iterative nature of the five-step process.

Web-based courses with greater interactions can be more complicated to use (Gilbert & Moore, 1998). Berge (1999), for example, found that the overuse or misuse of interactions can lead to frustration, boredom, and overload. For students, too many online interactions may cause confusion and eventual dropouts. Students may also quickly become dissatisfied if they perceive online interactions as meaningless busy work. Too many interactions may also overwhelm the instructor; a common concern expressed by educators who take far more time and effort to manage an online versus a traditional class.

Table 2.3 represents an analysis of completed planned interactions from the sample ITP depicted in Table 2.2.

TABLE 2.3 ▶ Analysis of Planned Interactions from the Sample ITP

INTERACTION	QUANTITY (frequency)	QUALITY (nature of the interaction)	DESIGN CONSIDERATIONS
Learner–Instructor	8	Learners are to post a message about an emotional experience. Learners are to post explanations of what they learned, requiring evaluation and response by instructor. Learners are to post elaborations of what they learned, requiring evaluation and response by instructor. Instructor is to provide guidance for explorations. Instructor is to provide guidance for and evaluate explanations. Instructor is to provide guidance for and to evaluate elaborations.	There may be too many learner-instructor interactions to manage. Consider eliminating request for students to post descriptions of an emotional experience. Group students for elaborations. Use bulletin board to facilitate guidance.
Learner–Learner	3	Share an emotional experience. Share and review explanations. Extensive amount of teamwork and communication necessary to complete elaborations.	May be too much considering requirement for all instructional units. Consider eliminating requirement to share emotional experience and requiring teamwork for some rather than all units.
Learner–Other Human	0	None planned.	Consider encouraging students to seek input from neuroscience and/or design experts.
Learner–Content	5	Thought-provoking image, video, and text. Two levels of content information on the study of human rewards and emotions (text and videos) plus additional resources. Instructions and recommendations for explorations, explanations, and elaborations. Evaluation criteria for explanations and elaborations.	Considerable amount of content made available online. Be sure to check links.

(Continued)

TABLE 2.3 ▶ *(Continued)*

INTERACTION	QUANTITY (frequency)	QUALITY (nature of the interaction)	DESIGN CONSIDERATIONS
Learner–Environment	3	Acquire and read textbook. Acquire and read journal articles.	Need to ensure ready access to textbook and journal articles.
Learner–Tools	2	Learners to use bulletin board to share emotional experience, explanations, and elaborations. Assumed that learners will use word processor to prepare explanations and elaborations report. Learners may use document-sharing application to facilitate teamwork.	Need to ensure learners have access to and can use word processor and document-sharing applications.
Learner–Interface	30+	All Learner-Instructor, Learner-Learner, and Learner-Content interactions are mediated through computer interface.	Important to assess students' ability to use interface early and to provide supplemental resources on use of interface if required.

Column 1 lists each type of interaction specified in the ITP. Column 2 denotes the frequency of each type of interaction. Column 3 provides a brief description of the nature of the interactions, and Column 4 specifies potential revisions or factors to consider during development, implementation, and evaluation.

As you can see, by analyzing each class of planned interactions, several critical issues become apparent. To start, the analysis reveals far too many planned learner-instructor interactions (8) for one lesson or unit. For each interaction, the instructor may have to: acknowledge receipt of the initial message; save, organize, and track relevant documents; review learners' work; generate and send timely feedback; and ensure that learners receive and understand the feedback. If you multiply the time required to manage each interaction by the number of students in class, as well as consider that the ITP represents just one of several units contained in the course, it's evident that the instructor as well as the students may quickly become overwhelmed. In such cases, you may want to group or eliminate interactions to reduce the total number of required communications, group learners to reduce the number of assignments, or automate one or more interactions so that preprogrammed responses are provided prompted by student input.

The analysis also reveals three learner-learner interactions. At first, three interactions may not appear to be too many, but one in particular (teamwork on elaborations) may require extensive communication between learners. As such, the planned learner-learner interactions may be too much for learners, especially if you consider the number of planned learner-instructor interactions. In conventional classrooms, such learner-learner interactions occur through speaking and listening, two modes of synchronous classroom communications that take less time and effort than reading and writing in an online course. To reduce the number of planned learner-learner interactions, I considered and eventually eliminated the requirement to share emotional experiences for the initial instructional event labeled Engage. I also made sure that required teamwork for the Elaborate event (discussing how an existing course or lesson should be revised, based on what students learned about human rewards and emotions) was facilitated, at least in part, in class.

The specification of learner-other human interactions highlights an important consideration; although no interactions with others outside of class were planned for the lesson, they could be and should be considered. Interactions with other experts and/or students outside of the class may bring important insights about content and related applications. Learner-other human interactions are also important to address prior to implementation. The instructor must inform experts with enough lead time to allocate resources so that they can respond in a timely fashion. Outside participants must also be solicited far enough in advance to ensure sufficient numbers and adequate plans for addressing learner inquiries effectively.

Examination of learner-content and learner-interface interactions pinpoints the pervasive use of the computer to facilitate learner-instructor, learner-learner, and learner-content interactions. Such reliance on technology emphasizes the importance of the user interface, suggesting that it may be worthwhile to conduct heuristic (i.e., hands-on) and scenario-based usability tests (see Neilson, 1993), especially if you do not use a commercially available learning management system to deliver your courses.

Analysis of the learner-environment and learner-tool interactions contained in the ITP identifies several resources that must be readily accessible to learners. In this case, I had to make sure that all learners could obtain the course textbook and related journal articles in a timely fashion (e.g., through a bookstore, library and/or online). Such considerations are also required in traditional on-campus classes. However, ensuring access to required resources for students who may live at a distance may take additional time. In addition, I had to make sure that learners have access to a word processor and a document-sharing application (e.g., Google Docs), plus the skills and knowledge to use the two applications in an effective and efficient manner.

Too few, too many, or poorly designed interactions can lead to learner and instructor dissatisfaction and discontent as well as to insufficient learning and poor performance. Failure to consider planned interactions may also require additional time, effort, and expertise to revise your instructional materials, resources that could be spent on other projects. Advances in interface design and improved web course authoring and delivery tools can help make the technical aspects of online interactions more transparent to you and your students. However, you should also keep in mind that quantity does not equal quality. By analyzing planned e-learning interactions, specified in initial drafts of your instructional treatment plan, you can avoid potential problems prior to development and identify key factors to consider during course delivery.

Next Steps

After designing and analyzing the interactions for your instructional unit or lesson, you should consider a number of steps before you begin to design other units or start putting together your entire course, including (a) searching for existing resources (as discussed by Regan in Chapter 3 of this book), (b) possibly flowcharting and storyboarding resources that need to be developed, (c) developing your unit, and (d) formatively evaluating your unit. Entire books may be written to detail each step, which goes far beyond the scope of this chapter, so I'll give you a brief summary of each step along with references to related literature to guide your efforts.

Searching for Existing Materials

After designing your unit, your next step may be to search for existing instructional resources that you may use to develop your unit and bring your design to life. Why reinvent the wheel? You may discover that other educators have spent significant time and money to generate high-quality simulations, videos, and multimedia elements that would complement your unit. Chapter 3, "Reusing Educational Resources," in this book, details digital repositories and national efforts to gather instructional resources; it also describes strategies for searching for and locating relevant resources, so I won't go into much detail here. In short, review the purpose and description of each of your instructional events and then go online to see if materials exist that could be used to enhance your events; then reconstruct or revise those lessons or modules. As you do so, be sure to check for and adhere to fair use and copyright policies.

Generating Flowcharts and Storyboards

After you search for relevant resources, you will know what materials you have access to and what else you need to develop for your unit or lesson. You can then use your ITP to generate flowcharts, storyboards, and/or prototypes of your instruction. If you are designing a relatively complex instructional unit or lesson that may require help from others (e.g., graphic artists or programmers) to develop and includes multiple branching opportunities and/or elaborate video clips and animations, you should consider flowcharting the sequence of frames and storyboarding each frame to be presented to learners. If you are designing a relatively simple instructional unit that includes a series of web pages and existing graphics or videos, you may not need to flowchart and storyboard your lesson. Go straight into developing and testing your unit or lesson.

Developing Your Unit

You may use an array of software programs and multimedia applications to develop your instructional unit. While some tools may cost a significant amount to acquire and may take some training to use, other free or inexpensive applications may be used to generate instructional materials that will make your online or hybrid course easier to teach and more appealing to students.

You may need software to create the media elements that support and enhance instruction; look for web pages and sites that package the instruction and the scripting elements that add interactions to the instructional process. Additional tools may also be needed to deliver and manage your course. Increasing interest in modern telecommunications technologies has resulted in a plethora of tools. Making sense of the tool market and determining when to use which tools may be more difficult than learning how to use the tools. e-Learning development and delivery tools can be organized into five basic categories: (1) media creation tools (e.g., Adobe Photoshop, Audacity, Flash); (2) web page and site creation tools (e.g., Dreamweaver); (3) scripting and database tools (e.g., AJAX, JavaScript); (4) web course delivery and management tools (e.g., Blackboard, Moodle); and (5) analysis, design, and evaluation tools (e.g., Articulate Studio, Raptivity).

It is possible to create effective e-learning environments by simply using a web delivery and management tool. One advantage is that these tools typically bundle features, such as email, chat, bulletin boards, class rosters, and test-item banks, in one application. The disadvantage is that they often impose a particular interface or design for both teachers and students. In contrast, web page and website development tools can support innovative designs, but their downside is that they typically require considerable resources, including, but not limited to, scripting and database access tools. Variation within each tool set may further complicate matters, and new releases continue to increase power, flexibility, and cost but also often add complexity.

So, how do you select the most appropriate tool set for developing your instruction? The simple answer: use whatever is available. However, much depends on the nature and degree of available personnel support. Are you the only one creating the course? If so, how much time and what skills do you have in using various development and delivery tools? Is the course already created, and can you make any modifications? Do you have access to web and database programmers? How about instructional designers, graphic artists, and multimedia specialists? What are their particular areas of expertise, and what programs do they prefer? Time and money will also weigh heavily on your decisions. Ideally, instructional and learner requirements will drive the selection of development or delivery tools. The reality is that often you must continually balance various stakeholders' conflicting interests.

For further discussion of instructional development and delivery tools, I refer you to Chapter 4 in this book, "Web 2.0 Technologies for Facilitating Learning and Assessment," as well as another chapter titled "Contemporary Issues Facing Distance Educators: An e-Learning Perspective" in a book I wrote with Gary Kidney (Hirumi & Kidney, 2010). I also recommend consulting other works, such as Mayer's (2009) *Multimedia Learning* and Williams' (2008) *The Non-Designer's Design Book,* to develop high-quality instructional multimedia resources for your lesson or unit.

Testing Your Unit

After developing a working prototype of your instructional unit, you should test it with some of your students or other representative members of your target learners. Educators will often use new instructional materials with their entire class before they test it, and if things don't go well, they typically blame the students for not studying or not trying hard enough. Students, on the other hand, typically blame the teacher for being boring or confusing. However, it may be that the instructional materials are not designed well. I always try to get at least a few students (and often asked my kids when they were younger) to test out new materials before going "live" with my instruction.

Given time and resources, I may include one-to-one, small group, and field tests to formatively evaluate and improve my materials. If the unit covers new content, I may also ask a subject matter expert to review it for accuracy and timeliness. Whether you use prescribed or more informal methods, you should test your unit for (a) clarity (Is the message or what is being presented clear to individual learners?); (b) usability (Can learners readily navigate to and from desired resources?); (c) impact (What is the impact of the instruction on an individual learner's attitudes, motivation, and achievement of the objectives and goals?); and (d) feasibility (How feasible is the instruction, given the available time and context?) (Dick, Carey, & Carey, 2009).

After testing and, if necessary, revising your instructional unit, you may then use it to set programming and formatting standards and as a template for creating your other instructional units. For instance, you may decide all text information should be presented in 12 pt. regular Verdana font and that to distinguish subheadings you want to use 14 pt. font size for level one subheadings, 12 pt. boldface for level two subheadings, and 12 pt. underlined boldface for level three subheadings. You may also decide that you want to use a light blue background for every page and include a banner identifying the unit number at the top of each web page. All such details, along with methods for addressing ADA (Americans with Disabilities Act) requirements for accessibility and means for navigating through your instruction, must eventually be worked out. Doing so with the testing of an initial unit will enable you to set high standards and create effective templates for developing the remaining units of your course.

Concluding Thoughts

In this chapter, I argued that the development of modern online and hybrid learning environments requires research and the application of grounded instructional strategies to fully utilize the capabilities of telecommunication technologies and the potential they afford collaborative and independent learning (Hirumi, 2002a, 2002b, 2006, 2009). To help educators and instructional designers analyze, design, and sequence planned e-learning interactions, I posited a three-level framework based on instructional strategies grounded in research and theory: Level III (learner-instruction) interactions provide educators and designers with a grounded approach for designing and sequencing Level II (human and nonhuman) interactions that, in turn, stimulate Level I interactions, which occur within the learners' minds.

After describing the classes of interactions associated with each level, I posited a five-step process for applying the framework and presented two examples illustrating how the framework may be used to design both totally online and hybrid coursework. First, the frequency and quality of planned interactions were inspected during design to reduce the need for costly revisions and to optimize both the learners' and the instructor's time online. Second, the design and sequencing of planned interactions in an instructional unit were recorded and analyzed to illustrate how the framework may be used to optimize e-learning within an existing course. The eight chapters contained in the second book of this series, *Online and Hybrid Learning Designs in Action,* further illustrate how grounded instructional strategies may be used to analyze e-learning interactions and to design online and hybrid coursework.

References

Aamodt, A. & Plaza, E. (1994). Case-based reasoning: Foundational issues, methodological variations, and system approaches. *Artificial Intelligence Communications, 7*(1), 39–59. Retrieved from www.idi.ntnu.no/emner/it3704/lectures/papers/Aamodt_1994_Case.pdf

Barrows, H. S. (1985). *How to design a problem-based curriculum for the preclinical years.* New York, NY: Springer Publishing.

Bednar, A., Cunningham, D. J., Duffy, T., & Perry, D. (1995). Theory in practice: How do we link? In G. Anglin (Ed.), *Instructional technology: Past, present, and future* (2nd ed., pp. 100–112). Englewood, CO: Libraries Unlimited.

Berge, Z. (1999). Interaction in post-secondary web-based learning. *Educational Technology, 39*(1), 5–11.

Bonk, C. J., & King, K. (1998). Computer conferencing and collaborative writing tools: Starting a dialogue about student dialogue. In C. J. Bonk & K. King (Eds.), *Electronic collaborators: Learner-centered technologies for literacy, apprenticeship, and discourse* (pp. 3–23). Mahwah, NJ: Lawrence Erlbaum.

Bonk, C. J., Wisher, R. A., & Nigrelli, M. L. (2004). Learning communities, communities of practices: Principles, technologies and examples. In K. Littleton, D. Faulkner, & D. Miell (Eds.), *Learning to collaborate, collaborating to learn* (pp. 199–219). New York, NY: Nova Science.

Bybee, R. W., Taylor, J. A., Gardner, A., Van Scotter, P., Powell, J. C., Westbrook, A., & Landes, N. (2006). *The BSCS 5E instructional model: Origins and effectiveness.* Colorado Springs, CO: BSCS.

Carlson, R. D., & Repman, J. (1999). Web-based interactivity. *WebNet Journal, 1*(2), 11–13.

Christophel, D. (1990). The relationship among teacher immediacy behaviors, student motivation, and learning. *Communication Education, 39,* 323–340.

Clark, R. E. (2004). *Design document for a guided experiential learning course.* Submitted to satisfy contract DAAD 19-99-D-0046-0004 from TRADOC to the Institute for Creative Technologies and the Rossier School of Education, University of Southern California.

Corno, L. (1994). Student volition and education: Outcomes, influences, and practices. In D. H. Schunk & B. J. Zimmerman (Eds.), *Self-regulation of learning and performance: Issues and educational applications* (pp. 229-254). Hillsdale, NJ: Lawrence Erlbaum.

Damasio, A. (1994). *Descartes' error: Emotion, reason, and the human brain.* New York, NY: Penguin Putnam.

Department of Defense (DOD). (2001). Development of interactive multimedia (Part 3 of 5 Parts). MIL-HDBK-29612–3. p. 45.

Dick, W., Carey, L., & Carey, J. O. (2009). *The systematic design of instruction* (7th ed.). Upper Saddle River, NJ: Pearson.

Dodge, B. (2007). WebQuest.org. Retrieved from http://webquest.org.

Driscoll, M. P. (2005). *Psychology of learning for instruction.* Boston, MA: Allyn and Bacon.

Gagné, R. M. (1977). *The conditions of learning* (3rd ed.). New York, NY: Holt, Rinehart, and Winston.

Gilbert, L., & Moore, D. R. (1998). Building interactivity into web courses: Tools for social and instructional interactions. *Educational Technology, 38*(3), 29–35.

Hannafin, M. J. (1989). Interaction strategies and emerging instructional technologies: Psychological perspectives. *Canadian Journal of Educational Communication, 18*(3), 167–179.

Hannafin, M. J., Hannafin, K. M., Land, S. M., & Oliver, K. (1997). Grounded practice and the design of learning systems. *Educational Technology Research and Development, 45*(3), 101–117.

Harris, J. (1994a). People-to-people projects on the Internet. *The Computing Teacher.* (February), 48–52.

Harris, J. (1994b). Information collection activities. *The Computing Teacher.* (March), 32–36.

Harris, J. (1994c). Opportunities in work clothes: Online problem-solving project structures. *The Computing Teacher.* (April), 52–55.

Hillman, D. C., Willis, D. J., & Gunawardena, C. N. (1994). Learner-interface interaction in distance education: An extension of contemporary models and strategies for practitioners. *The American Journal of Distance Education, 8*(2), 30–42.

Hirumi, A. (2002a). A framework for analyzing, designing, and sequencing planned e-learning interactions. *Quarterly Review of Distance Education, 3*(2), 141–160.

Hirumi, A. (2002b). The design and sequencing of e-learning interactions: A grounded approach. *International Journal on E-learning, 1*(1), 19–27.

Hirumi, A. (2002c). Student-centered, technology-rich, learning environments (SCenTRLE): Operationalizing constructivist approaches to teaching and learning. *Journal for Technology and Teacher Education, 10*(4), 497–537.

Hirumi, A. (2006). A framework for analyzing and designing e-learning interactions. In C. Juwah (Ed.), *Interactivity and interactions in distance and online education* (pp. 46–72). London, UK: Kogan Page.

Hirumi, A. (2009). A framework for analyzing, designing, and sequencing planned e-learning interactions. In A. Orellana, T. L. Hodgins, & M. Simonson (Eds.), *The perfect online course: Best practices for designing and teaching* (pp. 201–228). Charlotte, NC: Information Age.

Hirumi, A. (2013). Three levels of planned elearning interactions: A framework for grounding research and the design of elearning programs. *Quarterly Review of Distance Education, 14*(1).

Hirumi, A., Bradford, G., & Rutherford, L. (2011). Selecting delivery systems and media to facilitate blended learning: A systematic process based on skill level, content stability, cost, and instructional strategy. *Journal for Online Learning and Teaching, 7*(4), 489–501.

Hirumi, A., & Kidney, G. (2010). Contemporary issues facing distance educators: An eLearning perspective. In G. Anglin (Ed.), *Instructional technology: Past, present and future* (3rd ed., pp. 145–160). Santa Barbara, CA: ABC-CLIO.

Hunter, M. (1990). Lesson design helps achieve the goals of science instruction. *Educational Leadership, 48*(4), 79–81.

Johnson, D. W., & Johnson, R. T. (1993). Simulation and gaming: Fidelity, feedback and motivation. In J. V. Dempsey & G. C. Sales (Eds.), *Interactive instruction and feedback* (pp. 197–227). Englewood Cliffs, NJ: Educational Technology.

Jonassen, D. H. (1999). Designing constructivist learning environments. In C. M. Reigeluth (Ed.), *Instructional-design theories and models: A new paradigm of instructional theory* (Vol. II, pp. 215–239). Mahwah, NJ: Lawrence Erlbaum.

Jonassen, D. H., Tessmer, M., & Hannum, W. H. (1999). *Task analysis methods for instructional design,* Mahwah, NJ: Lawrence Erlbaum.

Joyce, B., Weil, M., & Showers, B. (1992). *Models of teaching* (4th ed.). Needham Heights, MA: Allyn and Bacon.

Kolb, D. A. (1984). *Experiential learning: Experience as the source of learning and development.* Englewood Cliffs, NJ: Prentice-Hall.

Mayer, R. E. (2009). *Multimedia learning* (2nd ed.). New York, NY: Cambridge University Press.

Metros, S., & Hedberg, J. (2002). More than just a pretty (inter)face: The role of the graphical user interface in engaging online learners. *Quarterly Review of Distance Education, 3*(2), 141–60.

Moore, M. G. (1989). Three types of interaction [Editorial]. *The American Journal of Distance Education, 3*(2), 1–6.

Neilson, J. (1993). *Usability engineering.* Boston, MA: AP Professional.

Nelson, L. (1999). Collaborative problem-solving. In C. M. Reigeluth (Ed.), *Instructional design theories and models: A new paradigm of instructional theory* (Vol. 2, pp. 241–267). Hillsdale, NJ: Lawrence Erlbaum.

Northrup, P. (2001). A framework for designing interactivity in web-based instruction. *Educational Technology, 41*(2), 31–39.

Oliver, D., & Shaver, J. (1971). *Cases and controversy: A guide to teaching the public issues series.* Middletown, CT: American Education.

Paul, R., & Elder, L. (2006). *Using intellectual standards to assess student reasoning.* Retrieved from www.criticalthinking.org/pages/using-intellectual-standards-to-assess-student-reasoning/469

Paul, R., & Elder, L. (2010). *The miniature guide to critical thinking concepts and tools.* Dillon Beach, CA: Foundation for Critical Thinking Press.

Pfeiffer, J. W., & Jones, J. E. (1975). Introduction to the structured experiences section. In J. E. Jones & J. W. Pfeiffer (Eds.), *The 1975 annual handbook for group facilitators.* La Jolla, CA: University Associates.

Reigeluth, C. M., & Moore, J. (1999). Cognitive education and the cognitive domain. In C. M. Reigeluth (Ed.), *Instructional-design theories and models: A new paradigm of instructional theory* (Vol. II, pp. 51–68). Mahwah, NJ: Lawrence Erlbaum.

Schank, R. C., Berman, T. R., & Macpherson, K. A. (1999). Learning by doing. In C. M. Reigeluth (Ed.), *Instructional-design theories and models: A new paradigm of instructional theory* (Vol. II, pp. 161–179). Hillsdale, NJ: Lawrence Erlbaum.

Schone, B. J. (2007a). Designing e-learning interactions. *e-Learning Weekly.* Retrieved from http://e-learningweekly.wordpress.com/2007/05/29/designing-e-learning-interactions

Schone, B. J. (2007b). Engaging interactions for e-learning: 25 ways to keep learners awake and intrigued. Retrieved from http://management-class.co.uk/education_sub/EngagingInteractionsForELearning.pdf

Schwartz, D., Lin, X., Brophy, S., & Bransford, J. D. (1999). Toward the development of flexibly adaptive instructional designs. In C. M. Reigeluth (Ed.), *Instructional-design theories and models: A new paradigm of instructional theory* (Vol. II, pp. 183–213). Hillsdale, NJ: Lawrence Erlbaum.

Smith, P. L. & Ragan, T. J. (1993). Designing instructional feedback for different learning outcomes. In J. V. Dempsey & G. C. Seles (Eds.), *Interactive instruction and feedback* (pp. 75–103). Englewood Cliffs, NJ: Educational Technology.

Smith, P. L., & Ragan, T. J. (1999). *Instructional design* (2nd ed.). Upper Saddle River, NJ: Prentice-Hall.

Stapleton, C., & Hirumi, A. (2011). Interplay instructional strategy: Learning by engaging interactive entertainment conventions. In M. Shaughnessy & S. Fulgham (Eds.), *Pedagogical models: The discipline of online teaching* (pp. 183–211). Hauppauge, NY: Nova Science.

Taba, H. (1967). *Teacher's handbook for elementary school social studies.* Reading, MA: Addison-Wesley.

Thach, E. C., & Murphy, K. L. (1995). Competencies for distance education professionals. *Educational Technology Research and Development, 43*(1), 57–79.

Watkins, R. (2005). *75 e-learning activities: Making online learning interactive.* San Francisco, CA: John Wiley & Sons.

Williams, R. (2008). *The non-designer's design book* (3rd ed.). Berkeley, CA: Peachpit Press.

Zimmerman, B. J., & Martinez-Pons, M. (1988). Construct validation of a strategy model of student self-regulated learning. *Journal of Educational Psychology, 80*(3), 284–90.

Zimmerman, B. J., & Paulsen, A. S. (1995). Self-monitoring during collegiate studying: An invaluable tool for academic self-regulation. In P. R. Pintrich (Ed.), *Understanding self-regulated learning* (pp. 13–27). San Francisco, CA: Jossey Bass.

Supplement 2.A

Supplement 2.A
Grounded Instructional Strategies

Grounded instructional strategies are rooted in established theories and research in human learning, and form the basis for designing and sequencing learning interactions and creating alternative e-learning environments. Table 2.A.1 outlines the primary instructional events associated with published grounded instructional strategies. Each strategy is grouped according to general approaches.

TABLE 2.A.1 ▶ Primary Events Associated with Grounded Instructional Strategies

INQUIRY, EXPERIENTIAL AND PROBLEM-BASED (LEARNER-CENTERED) APPROACHES		
Experiential Learning (Pfeiffer & Jones, 1975)	**Experiential Learning Model** (Kolb, 1984)	**Guided Experiential Learning** (Clark, 2004)
1. Experience	1. Concrete Experience	1. Goals
2. Publish	2. Reflective Observation	2. Reasons and Activation
3. Process	3. Abstract Conceptualization	3. Demonstration
4. Internalize	4. Active Experimentation	4. Application
5. Generalize		5. Integration
6. Apply		6. Assessment
Learning by Doing (Schank, Berman, & Macpherson, 1999)	**Problem-Based Learning** (Barrows, 1985)	**Collaborative Problem-Solving** (Nelson, 1999)
1. Define Goals	1. Start New Class	1. Build Readiness
2. Set Mission	2. Start a New Problem	2. Form and Norm Groups
3. Present Cover Story	3. Problem Follow-Up	3. Determine Preliminary Problem
4. Establish Roles	4. Performance Presentation(s)	4. Define and Assign Roles
5. Operate Scenarios	5. After Conclusion of Problem	5. Engage in Problem-Solving
6. Provide Resources		6. Finalize Solution
7. Provide Feedback		7. Synthesize and Reflect
		8. Assess Products and Processes
		9. Provide Closure
BSCS 5E Model (Bybee et al., 2006)	**WebQuest** (Dodge, 2007)	**InterPLAY Strategy** (Stapleton & Hirumi, 2011)
1. Engage	1. Introduction	1. Expose
2. Explore	2. Task	2. Inquire
3. Explain	3. Process	3. Discover
4. Elaborate	4. Resources	4. Create
5. Evaluate	5. Evaluation	5. Experiment
	6. Conclusion	6. Share

(Continued)

TABLE 2.A.1 ▶ *(Continued)*

Simulation Model (Joyce, Weil, & Showers, 1992)	**Inquiry Training** (Joyce, Weil, & Showers, 1992)	**Inductive Thinking** (Taba, 1967)
1. Orientation 2. Participant Training 3. Simulation Operations 4. Participant Debriefing 5. Appraise and redesign the simulation	1. Confrontation with the Problem 2. Data Verification 3. Data Experimentation 4. Organizing, Formulating and Explanation 5. Analysis of inquiry process	1. Concept Formation 2. Interpretation of Data 3. Application of Principles
Jurisprudential Inquiry (Oliver & Shaver, 1971)	**Case-Based Reasoning** (Aamodt & Plaza, 1994)	**Constructivist Learning** (Jonassen, 1999)
1. Orientation to the Case 2. Identifying the Issues 3. Taking Positions 4. Exploring the Stance(s) 5. Refining and Qualifying the Positions 6. Testing Factual Assumptions Behind Qualified Positions	1. Present New Case 2. Retrieve Similar Cases 3. Reuse Information 4. Revise Proposed Solution 5. Retain Useful Experiences	1. Select Problem 2. Provide Related Case 3. Provide Information 4. Provide Cognitive Tools 5. Provide Conversation Tools 6. Provide Social Support
Eight Events of Student-Centered Learning (Hirumi, 2002c)	**Adaptive Instructional Design** (Schwartz, Lin, Brophy & Bransford, 1999)	
1. Set Learning Challenge 2. Negotiate Goals and Objectives 3. Negotiate Learning Strategy 4. Construct Knowledge 5. Negotiate Performance Criteria 6. Assess Learning 7. Provide Feedback (Steps 1–6) 8. Communicate Results	1. Look Ahead & Reflect Back 2. Present Initial Challenge 3. Generate Ideas 4. Present Multiple Perspectives 5. Research and Revise 6. Test Your Mettle 7. Go Public 8. Progressive Deepening 9. General Reflection and Decisions 10. Assessment	

TABLE 2.A.1 ▶ *(Continued)*

TEACHER-DIRECTED APPROACHES		
Nine Events of Instruction (Gagné, 1977) 1. Gain Attention 2. Inform Learner of Objective(s) 3. Recall Prior Knowledge 4. Present Stimulus Materials 5. Provide Learning Guidance 6. Elicit Performance 7. Provide Feedback 8. Assess Performance 9. Enhance Retention and Transfer	**5-Component Lesson Model** (Dick, Carey, & Carey, 2009) 1. Pre-Instructional Activities 2. Content Presentation and Learning Guidance 3. Learner Participation 4. Assessment 5. Follow-Through Activities	**Elements of Lesson Design** (Hunter, 1990) 1. Anticipatory Set 2. Objective and Purpose 3. Input 4. Modeling 5. Check for Understanding 6. Guided Practice 7. Independent Practice
Direct Instruction (Joyce, Weil, & Showers, 1992) 1. Orientation 2. Presentation 3. Structured Practice 4. Guided Practice 5. Independent Practice		

Supplement 2.B
Sample Instructional Unit

Human Rewards and Emotions

Engage

Most recognize that our emotions have a great impact on how we think, feel and act, but due to difficulties in defining and measuring emotions, we have failed to systematically address their role in human learning and performance. Cognitive neuroscience research is now leading to great insights into how our brains process emotions and how emotions affect our memories, learning, and behavior. Begin your study of the role of emotions in human learning and performance by watching a short (4 min. and 30 sec.), introductory video on the exciting and emerging field of affective neuroscience.

Explore

Explore cognitive neuroscience research on human rewards and emotions at different levels based on your interests and experiences. As in prior units, Level I resources are more challenging to comprehend and may require prior biology, anatomy, or physiology knowledge because they represent internal learner interactions that occur within the minds of individuals.

Level I Textbook and Video

Go to the course textbook and review the diagrams and inserts included in the following chapters. If you have time and interest, we also encourage you to read the text included in each chapter as well.

1. Read Chapter 15: Chemical Control of the Brain and Behavior

2. Read Chapter 16: Motivation

3. Read Chapter 18: Brain Mechanisms of Emotion

Level II Neuroscience Online

Click on the underlined links to access the material.

1. Read about The Relevance of Affective and Social Neuroscience to Education.

2. Read about how neuroscientists are elucidating the psychological and neural mechanisms underlying human emotions and memory.

3. Read about how scientists are trying to measure human emotions.

4. Read about how neuroscientists are distinguishing neural processes associated with emotional valence and arousal.

Additional Resources

If you have time and interest, we encourage you to watch the following YouTube videos. Click on the underlined links to access the videos.

1. Watch the recipients of the Ninth Annual Oscar Sternbach Award for (Neuro) Psychoanalysis, Drs. Jaak Panksepp and Mark Solms, talk about "Theories of Human and Animal Communications" (1 hr. 49 min. YouTube video).

2. Watch Joseph LeDoux talk about "Our Emotional Brain" (2011 Copernicus Center Lecture) (1 hr. 36 min. YouTube video).

3. Watch Phillip Goldin discuss the "Neuroscience of Emotions" (1 hr. 2 min. YouTube video).

4. Watch Antonio Damasio, author of *Descartes' Error: Emotion, Reason, and the Human Brain,* talk about "Emotions and Evolution: What Would Genes Do?" (2 min. 24 sec. YouTube video). Another link features his discussion on "When Emotions Make Better Decisions."

Explain

Post an explanation of what you learned from your exploration of human rewards and emotions under the discussion topic labeled "Neuroscience of Emotions." You are also encouraged to read and respond to each other's explanations. Meet standards for critical thinking (as listed below) to earn credit for your explanation. The standards are listed in Box 2.B.1.

BOX 2.B.1 ▶ Intellectual Standards for Critical Thinking

Clarity	Explanation is clear and concise. Key points, thoughts, and ideas can be readily identified.
Accuracy	Explanation is accurate. Supported by references to credible sources. References are also appropriate and accurate.
Precision	Explanation is precise. Provides more than adequate details to explain key points.
Relevance	Explanation is relevant to topic. Statements are all clearly connected to topic.
Depth	Explanation demonstrates significant effort and depth of thought. Deals with the complexities of the issue and recognizes multiple perspectives.
Breadth	Explanation demonstrates significant effort and breadth of ideas. Addresses a variety of key points directly related to topic from multiple perspectives.
Logic	Explanation is logical. Ideas presented in rational and coherent order. Combinations of thoughts support rather than contradict or appear unrelated to each other.
Fairness	Explanation is fair. Statements consider rights and needs of others.

Elaborate

Work with team members to elaborate on what you learned about human rewards and emotions. Begin by reviewing team members' explanations of what they learned. Then, meet to discuss your individual explorations and explanations. Identify both common and discrepant findings and post any questions you may have about the topic to the specified discussion forum.

As in prior units, discuss how you would revise your instructional unit based on what you and your team members learned about rewards and human emotions. Then, demonstrate what you learned by illustrating and describing:

1. What specific aspects of your instruction you would keep as they are and why, based on what you learned about human rewards and emotions?

2. List specific aspects of your instruction you would change, how would you change them, and why, based on what you learned about human rewards and emotions.

Submit your team's elaboration using the Assignments feature of Webcourses2 by the specified due date.

Evaluate

The assessment rubric for evaluating your elaboration in presented in Table 2.B.1. Be sure to review the assessment rubric before you start working on your elaboration project.

TABLE 2.B.1 ▶ Assessment Rubric for Elaborating on What You Learned

	DEVELOPING (<79 points)	PROFICIENT (80–89 points)	EXEMPLARY (90–100 points)
Purpose	Purpose of elaboration is unclear, insignificant, and/or unrealistic.	Purpose of elaboration is clear.	Purpose of elaboration is clear, significant (yet achievable and realistic), and consistent throughout.
Problem, Question, or Opportunity	Problem, question, or opportunity is unclear and/or irrelevant.	Specifies the problem to be solved, question to be answered, or opportunity to be realized.	Formulates the problem to be solved, question to be answered, or opportunity to be realized in a clear and relevant manner.
Point of View	Point of view or frame of reference is unfair, unclear, and/or inconsistent.	Articulates point of view or frame of reference in a fair and consistent manner.	Articulates point of view or frame of reference in fair, clear, and consistent manner.
Empirical Foundation	Elaboration gives little to no evidence or support for statements.	Gives fair and accurate evidence and/or support for most statements.	Gives clear, fair, and accurate evidence and/or support for all statements.

TABLE 2.B.1 ▶ *(Continued)*

	DEVELOPING (<79 points)	PROFICIENT (80–89 points)	EXEMPLARY (90–100 points)
Conceptual/Theoretical Foundation	Ideas fail to demonstrate understanding and application of relevant facts, findings, principles, and/or theories.	Ideas demonstrate understanding and application of relevant research findings, facts, concepts, principles, rules, and theories.	Ideas demonstrate deep understanding and skilled application of relevant research findings, facts, concepts, principles, rules, and theories.
Assumptions	Neither recognizes nor articulates relevant assumptions about teaching, or assumptions are unclear, unjustifiable, and/or inconsistent.	Recognizes and articulates assumptions about teaching and learning relevant to context in a consistent manner.	Recognizes and clearly articulates assumptions about teaching and learning relevant to context in a justifiable and consistent manner.
Implications	Implications are insignificant, unrealistic, invalid, unclear, or imprecise.	Enunciates valid implications and consequences of the elaboration.	Clearly enunciates significant, realistic, and valid implications and consequences of the elaboration in a precise manner.
Inferences	Inferences in reasoning are unclear, unjustifiable, and/or inconsistent.	Makes sound inferences in reasoning in a consistent manner.	Makes clear, sound, and significant inferences in reasoning in a justifiable and consistent manner.

CHAPTER 3

Reusing Educational Resources

Damon Regan

THE PURPOSE OF THIS CHAPTER is to help educators and instructional designers find relevant educational materials that can be reused to create online and hybrid learning environments. Increasing numbers of high-quality educational resources are available online from federal, state, nonprofit, and for-profit websites. In this chapter, I describe the nature of these educational resources by clarifying terms used to describe them, identifying how they are licensed and used, and classifying the types of sites that make them available. I then review global, national, and state portals, as well as media and university websites that make these resources available. To help make effective use of these sites, I also describe different ways you can search, filter, and browse for resources, based on conditions of use, grade level, age range, subject matter, standards, type of material, and quality. Finally, I discuss how to optimize the use of available resources by aligning their use with grounded instructional strategies in a systematic design process.

We all like to create new things, but sometimes it just makes more sense to use or adapt something someone else created. This is especially true if you have limited time, tools, or funds to produce high-quality educational materials. The good news is that excellent educational resources are available from U.S. federal and state governments and from nonprofit and for-profit organizations. The challenge is finding resources that are relevant to you and your students. In this chapter, I will review the nature of educational resources along with the sites that make them available and tools you can use to find them. I will also provide practical guidelines to make the best use of these sites and resources.

Nature of Educational Resources

The term *educational resources* describes various materials (e.g., assessments, games, lesson plans) and media (e.g., video, audio, text, graphics) you might use to teach a lesson. The term *educational resources* is closely aligned with the term *open educational resources* (OER); the latter are defined as teaching and learning materials that you may freely use and reuse without charge (OER Commons, 2011). The term *learning objects* (LO) described such materials before the term *open educational resources* was introduced in 2002. The learning objects term is still used in various places (see Wiley, 2007), but historically, it lacked the clear licensing statement outlining their use and reuse that is core to the concept of an OER. Generally speaking, learning objects is a term more applicable to software engineers designing educational systems than teachers attempting to use them in a course. However, in this chapter, when I refer to educational resources or resources, I'm including learning objects as well as open educational resources, as I am focusing on reusing all relevant resources.

When we talk about reusing our grocery bags, we simply mean to use them multiple times. However, when we talk about reusing educational resources, we might reuse them in several different ways. On one end of the spectrum, we might simply want to view the resource on its website multiple times, or, on the other end of the spectrum, we may want to download the resource, edit it, and then share the result with others. Sites that make educational resources available will generally offer guidance on how their resources may be used. I'll highlight such site-specific guidelines as I review various sites. Knowing the conditions or terms of use is an important aspect of reusing educational resources. The good news is that sites are beginning to make it easier to understand conditions of use and are generally permitting greater degrees of use.

Many sites, including the White House website, are now using Creative Commons (CC) licenses to describe how their resources may be used. Creative Commons is a nonprofit organization that offers free, easy-to-use copyright licenses that provide a simple, standardized way to give the public permission to share and use creative work based on the conditions the creator chooses. These available conditions are described along with their icons in Table 3.1.

TABLE 3.1 ▶ Creative Commons Conditions

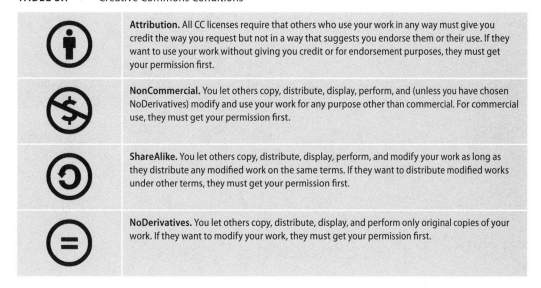

	Attribution. All CC licenses require that others who use your work in any way must give you credit the way you request but not in a way that suggests you endorse them or their use. If they want to use your work without giving you credit or for endorsement purposes, they must get your permission first.
	NonCommercial. You let others copy, distribute, display, perform, and (unless you have chosen NoDerivatives) modify and use your work for any purpose other than commercial. For commercial use, they must get your permission first.
	ShareAlike. You let others copy, distribute, display, perform, and modify your work as long as they distribute any modified work on the same terms. If they want to distribute modified works under other terms, they must get your permission first.
	NoDerivatives. You let others copy, distribute, display, and perform only original copies of your work. If they want to modify your work, they must get your permission first.

It is important to be familiar with these icons and the terms they symbolize because many sites now use them as a way to communicate conditions or terms of use for a given educational resource. The Creative Commons licenses bundle these conditions together in a combination of the owner's choosing. For more information, see http://creativecommons.org/licenses.

Educational resources are made available from many different sites. These sites are described by various names, such as website, repository, digital library, portal, database, or collection. While these names are used in rather loose ways by various sites, there are some distinctions among these types of sites. Websites generally provide only their own resources. Digital libraries or portals tend to be websites that link to resources on other websites. Repositories tend to describe sites that make it possible to download resources.

There is a relationship among the type of educational resources, the type of site that makes educational resources available, and the types of use permitted. Some sites make resources available for download, and others make resources available to interact with only on the website. Generally, if the website is providing OERs using Creative Commons licenses, it is more likely to offer resources for download. Table 3.2 describes my general observations on the relationships among the various types of resources, sites, and uses on a spectrum from permissive to protective.

TABLE 3.2 ▶ Generalized Spectrum of Licenses, Resources, Uses, and Sites

	PERMISSIVE	PRACTICAL	PROTECTIVE
Types of Licenses	Creative Commons Attribution	Creative Commons NoDerivatives	Copyright
Types of Resources	Open Educational Resource (OER)	Educational Resource	Learning Object (LO)
Types of Uses Permitted	Download and remix	Download and share	View only
Types of Sites	Repository	Digital Library or Portal	Website Property

Sites for Finding Educational Resources

The first challenge to finding educational resources is finding the sites that make relevant resources available. The way you probably find most things on the Internet is through a single search engine such as Google. If you're like me, you probably wish there were a similar, single clearinghouse to find educational resources. Unfortunately, no single clearinghouse for educational resources exists. The reality is that an increasingly complex network of sites makes the supply of educational resources available.

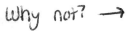 *Why not? →*

Finding resources requires checking some sites out, evaluating the strengths and weaknesses of each site, and ultimately choosing sites you want to use. Just as we may live in different cities at different times, we may use different sites at different times. To help you on this journey of finding the right site to use, I'll share with you what I've found so far on my journey. It's not an exhaustive list, but it is intended to be representative of the types of sites that are available.

Global Educational Resource Portals

While there isn't a single clearinghouse for finding educational resources, some global educational portals provide a single point of access to large collections of diverse educational resources. These portals have forged alliances with major content providers, making them a logical starting point for searching. Three of the global aggregate portals that I'm aware of are Open Educational Resources (OER) Commons, European Schoolnet's Learning Resource Exchange (LRE), and Curriki.

OER Commons. OER Commons (www.oercommons.org) is my recommended starting point. It provides an excellent interface to search and browse over 31,000 resources aggregated from more than 120 major content partners. The site provides contemporary website features, such as social bookmarking, tagging, ratings, and reviews. More than half of the resources available through OER Commons are focused on K–12. The rest are focused on higher education. I really like how many of the links used to filter content provide helpful counts that give you a sense for the data.

All the resources available through OER Commons are given one of four conditions of use labels that make it easy to see how any given resource may be used with respect to copyright licenses (see Table 3.3).

TABLE 3.3 ▶ OER Commons Conditions-of-Use Labels

LABEL	MEANING
No Strings Attached	No restrictions on your remixing, redistributing, or making derivative works. Give credit to the author as required.
Remix and Share	Your remixing, redistributing, or making derivative works comes with some restrictions including how it is shared.
Share Only	Your redistributing comes with some restrictions. Do not remix or make derivative works.
Read the Fine Print	Everything else. All rights reserved. U.S.-based educators have certain permissions under Fair Use and the TEACH Act.

OER Commons does the hard work of looking at the license associated with a given resource and categorizing it into one of these four labels so that you can quickly see and understand how you may use a given object.

Learning Resource Exchange. A similar portal to OER Commons in Europe is the Learning Resource Exchange (LRE, http://lreforschools.eun.org). The LRE portal provides a streamlined interface to search for content from 45 content providers in many different countries. A unique aspect of the LRE website is the international mix of resources it provides. To help find resources in familiar languages, the search interface provides a language filter. Some resources on the LRE website are marked as "travel well," meaning they are useful for different cultural and linguistic contexts. Criteria for these resources include (a) presence of transnational topics, (b) knowledge of a specific language is not needed, (c) stored as a file type that is usable with generally available software, and (d) clarity of alignment in curriculum. The search interface provides the ability to limit search results only to resources that travel well. Figure 3.1 shows the results of a search for "mitosis" with the options to filter results by language, subject, resource type, age, international provider, or travel well designation.

While the conditions of use for each resource are described on the resource's detail page, using the Creative Commons conditions icons, it is not clear from looking at a given resource's details page whether or not it is marked as travel well. However, under the "Find resources" link, you can check the box for "Search only travel well resources."

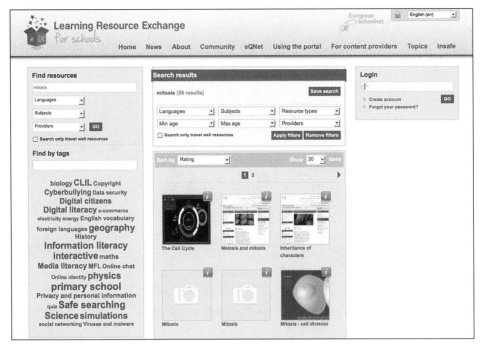

FIGURE 3.1 ▶ LRE portal search results for "mitosis" with filter options

Curriki. The last site I want to highlight in this category of global aggregate portals is Curriki (www.curriki.org). The name Curriki is a portmanteau of the words curriculum and wiki. In fact, Curriki is based on an open-source wiki platform, which makes it easy for users to post materials online. Curriki is completely focused on making it easy for K–12 teachers, students, and parents to create, share, and find open learning resources. It provides access to more than 45,000 resources and provides search and browse interfaces for grade levels and subjects. A distinguishing aspect of this nonprofit site is the community of more than 230,000 teachers and learners. All of Curriki's editorial content is shared under a Creative Commons Attribution license, and most of the resources on Curriki fall under one of the Creative Commons licenses.

National Educational Resource Portals

National portals are similar in nature to the global portals but are provided by national entities and focused more narrowly on a particular group of resources. These are excellent sources of K–12 resources. Similar to global sites, these sites have relationships with major content providers that enable you to have a single point of access, which saves you time. Three excellent national portals are the Federal Resource for Educational Excellence (FREE), the National Science Digital Library (NSDL), and Gateway to 21st Century Skills. Be sure to check all resources you want to use from any of these sites for their terms of use.

Federal Resource for Educational Excellence. The Federal Resource for Educational Excellence (FREE, http://free.ed.gov) portal makes it easy to find over 1,600 teaching and learning resources from dozens of federal agencies. Some of the most valuable media sites are provided by the federal government. For example, one of my favorite federal sites is Docs Teach (http://docsteach.org) from the National Archives (see Figure 3.2).

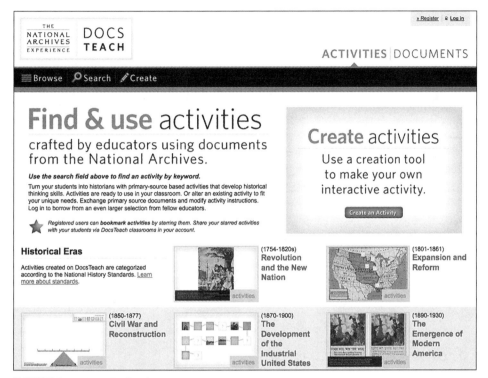

FIGURE 3.2 ▶ Docs Teach website

What better way to learn social studies than with learning activities based on the National Archives? The FREE portal also allows you to find educational resources from the Smithsonian Institute, the National Aeronautics and Space Administration (NASA), the National Gallery of Art, the National Science Foundation, and other federal sites. A nice feature of the portal is the subject map, which lists on one page a breakdown of all the subjects with the number of resources on each one. Clicking on a topic will allow you to explore all the federal educational resources available for the given topic. Unfortunately, the FREE website does not offer services to determine conditions/terms of use for resources. Terms of use will vary based on the resources accessed, and many of the linked sites are website properties with very protective conditions of use.

National Science Digital Library. The National Science Digital Library (NSDL, www.nsdl.org) is the National Science Foundation's online library of over 132,000 resources for K–16 science, technology, engineering, and mathematics (STEM) education. The NSDL offers a wealth of information, searchable by education level (e.g., elementary, middle school, higher education); resource type (e.g., audio/visual, dataset, reference material); and subject (e.g., geoscience, social sciences, technology). Under the main tab "About," resources available through the library are listed under Network Partners, each with its respective URL, such as TeachingWithData. org: Pathway to Quantitative Literacy in the Social Sciences (http://nsdl.org/partners/detail/PATH-000-000-000-014).

You can find resources of interest directly from the NSDL network or from specific network partner websites. Exploring the rich collection of resources available through the NSDL network will likely require you to jump into a particular network partner website where the resources exist. It also requires some diligence to review license information. The NSDL states that the majority of resources available through the library are completely free although some of the resource providers who make their materials accessible through the library require a login, a fee-based membership, or purchase of the complete version of a resource.

Gateway to 21st Century Skills. The Gateway to 21st Century Skills (www.thegateway.org) provides access to 30,000+ quality teaching and learning resources. Because of support from the National Education Association, access to the Gateway to 21st Century Skills is free to all users, that is, no membership fee is required to use the site. The Gateway was developed with funds from the U.S. Department of Education (DOE) to provide teachers with learning resources created by over 750 publicly funded organizations. In 2005 the Gateway's DOE funding ceased, and the National Education Association stepped in to preserve this national education asset. Searches can be done based on keyword, subject, provider, or grade. Then the search results can be filtered by these criteria: subject; type; education level; price code (free, partially free, and fee-based); medium; teaching method; language; mediator; beneficiary; and assessment method. The Gateway provides counts for each filter category similar to OER Commons, which I find helpful. While the Gateway doesn't offer conditions of use information, it does provide the ability to filter based on price code.

State Educational Resource Portals

Many of the state-provided educational resource portals are similar in nature to the global and national portals. The key difference is that state portals tend to focus on users within that state. This allows state portals to potentially get focused participation from smaller, more homogeneous groups of users. Four state portals are highlighted: the Florida CPALMS (collaborate, plan, align, learn, motivate, and share) portal; the California Brokers of Expertise (BOE) portal; the California Career Technical Education (CTE) Online portal; and the Wisconsin Wisc-Online website.

Florida CPALMS. The Florida Department of Education provides the CPALMS portal (www.cpalms.org/standards/flstandardsearch.aspx) to collaborate, plan, align, learn, motivate, and share (CPALMS) educational resources. The CPALMS portal provides access to Florida standards or benchmarks, course descriptions, and instructional resources all in an integrated system. Figure 3.3 depicts links to resources and courses related to a seventh grade mathematics standard in the CPALMS portal.

Because of the tight integration of the CPALMS system, resources can be found through benchmarks, courses, or direct browsing and keyword searching. This infrastructure is focused on math and science subjects but is designed to accommodate additional subjects when funding becomes available. Over 3,600 resources are available for math and science standards. Each resource is reviewed by trained volunteer peer reviewers and staff members with research and subject matter expertise. Unfortunately, the portal does not provide conditions or terms of use information for all resources, so users must review the conditions of use on the actual resources.

FIGURE 3.3 ▶ Integrated resources available in the CPALMS portal

California Brokers of Expertise. The State of California Department of Education provides a digital library that is similar to CPALMS called the Brokers of Expertise (BOE, www.myboe.org). The BOE environment provides access to more than 64,000 educational resources and a community of California educators. You can find resources easily through an impressive interface that allows you to search by keywords and filter by subject breakdown, grade level, and resource type, as well as some fine-grained filters for license type and presence of alignment information to standards. Alternatively, you can find resources by browsing standards. Helpful resource counts are shown for each standard in the standard breakdown, which help provide a sense for the data. The BOE has at least 10 content partners whose resources help populate the library. Some of these partners are unique to BOE, and some are partners that have already been reviewed (e.g., NSDL, FREE, and the National Archives). An appealing aspect of the BOE site is its usage data (i.e., views, access, favorites) to help describe resources. Each resource page also shows the grade level and subjects aligned with the resource. While conditions of use information is provided on the resource description page within the portal, the value is frequently left unspecified, so you have to find the conditions of use information on the actual resource site.

CTE Online. The state of California provides a digital library of technical education resources called CTE (Connecting Career Technical Education Programs & Professionals) Online (www.cteonline.org). This site uses a similar interface to the BOE library. While the CTE Online library requires checking the conditions of use on the resource's website, the home page includes this line: "Except otherwise noted, content created on this site is licensed under a Creative Commons Attribution-NonCommercial-ShareAlike 3.0 license."

Wisconsin Wisc-Online. The Wisc-Online website (www.wisc-online.com) contains a useful collection of "learning objects" developed primarily by faculty from the Wisconsin Technical College System (WTCS) and produced by multimedia designers. The learning objects available through Wisc-Online are grouped by quite a number of different subjects and are available for viewing free to educators. The learning objects may be purchased in order to download them and play them without an Internet connection. However, there are no provisions for sharing or remixing content.

Media Websites

There are many for-profit and nonprofit media websites offering educational resources. Many of the portals reviewed earlier in this chapter link to such media websites. In this section, some of the media websites I find most relevant are highlighted: PBS LearningMedia (Figure 3.4), Khan Academy, and YouTube sites and channels.

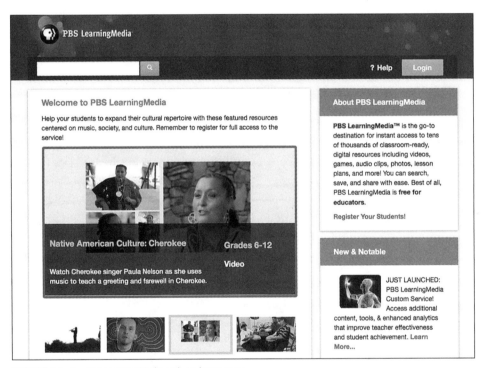

FIGURE 3.4 ▶ PBS LearningMedia website home page

PBS LearningMedia. The PBS (Public Broadcasting Service) LearningMedia website (www.pbslearningmedia.org) provides educators free access to more than 16,000 resources from the best of public media. I frequently visit this site with my own children. These resources offer good coverage across K–12 grade levels, primarily in the form of videos, interactive animations, and lesson plans. The PBS LearningMedia resources are made available through four levels of noncommercial, educational, permitted uses (1) stream only, (2) download to view, (3) download for verbatim use, and (4) download to re-edit and distribute. Ancillary materials, such as lesson plans, may be modified, altered, or revised if correct attribution is given with the understanding that the copyright holder will continue to own the materials.

Khan Academy. While the PBS Learning Media resources tend to be full-featured video productions, a new form of videos (which I call personal learning videos) are available from the nonprofit Khan Academy website (www.khanacademy.org). The Khan Academy offers over 2,700 videos in conversational, digestible 10- to 20-minute chunks covering a variety of K–12 subjects. While the Khan videos are now available through many of the global, national, and state portals previously reviewed, the Khan Academy website itself provides some unique features worth checking out, including knowledge maps, practice exercises, badges, and detailed reports. All materials and resources are available free of charge. The Khan Academy makes resources available through the Creative Commons Attribution-NonCommercial-ShareAlike 3.0 United States License.

YouTube sites and channels. YouTube for Schools (www.youtube.com/schools) offers access to videos from YouTube Education, the Khan Academy, PBS, Stanford University, TED, Steve Spangler Science, and Numberphile. While many schools block access to YouTube videos, Google's YouTube for Schools allows a school network administrator to create a custom YouTube portal and direct YouTube requests to a school's custom portal. Educationally filtered videos can then be added to the school's YouTube portal. YouTube Education (www.youtube.com/education) allows you to access thousands of K–12 educational videos. What I find most helpful for identifying K–12 educational videos is YouTube Teachers (www.youtube.com/user/teachers), which provides filtered playlists of educational videos organized by teachers into subjects, grade levels, and topics.

University Websites

University websites provide a significant source of open educational resources. A number of OpenCourseWare (OCW) websites freely share university course materials online. While these websites may have content that is relevant to K–12 education, they tend to be focused on higher education, making finding resources for elementary and middle school students somewhat difficult. Two higher education sites that may be relevant to you and your students are the Connexions repository and content management system (Figure 3.5) and the Multimedia Educational Resource for Learning and Online Teaching (MERLOT).

Connexions. The large Connexions repository (www.cnx.org) offers perhaps the best chance of finding relevant K–12 resources, and it provides a useful platform for creating new learning objects you may want to try out. According to the site's home page, "Connexions is a place to view and share educational material made of small knowledge chunks called modules that can be organized as courses, books, reports, etc. Anyone may view or contribute …" including teachers, students, and writers.

MERLOT. The Multimedia Educational Resource for Learning and Online Teaching (MERLOT, www.merlot.org) is a free, open community of more than 100,000 faculty, staff, and students of higher education who share a collection of over 32,000 peer-reviewed online learning materials catalogued by its registered members and faculty development support services. Some of the MERLOT resources, such as textbooks, courses, learning materials, and learning exercises can be used by teachers of various K–12 subjects. The site's content is licensed under Creative Commons license conditions.

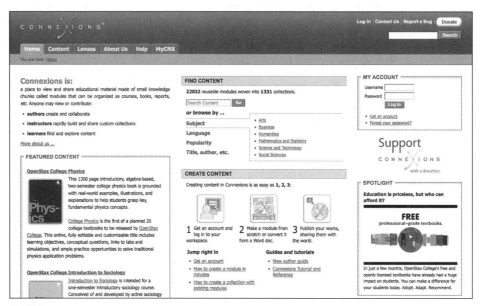

FIGURE 3.5 ▶ Connexions repository home page

How to Use the Sites

Once you've checked out some sites that seem to have relevant educational resources and provide an enjoyable user experience, the next challenge is using that site effectively to find relevant resources. There are many common aspects of using sites like those reviewed above. I want to focus on some common techniques for searching, using standards alignment, and evaluating quality.

"Search" is by far the most common feature provided by each site to help users find relevant resources. The search capabilities of educational resources sites tend to be slightly different from a traditional Google search in at least one key way. Most educational resources portals offer advanced search functionality to filter results based on educational facets such as subjects, grade levels, and standards.

Different sites, however, use different educational facets to help users conduct advanced searches. For example, some sites allow users to include conditions of use in their search while others do not. Different sites also use common educational elements but in different ways to facilitate advanced searches. For example, California's Brokers of Expertise allows users to search for resources by specific grade levels (e.g., Pre–K, K, 1, 2, etc.); whereas the European Schoolnet's Learning Resource Exchange filters resources according to minimum and maximum ages (e.g., 8 years old); and OER Commons uses general academic levels (i.e., primary, secondary, post-secondary).

In addition to advanced search features, many educational resource sites offer an ability to browse resources or resource collections. Browsing features are very helpful for sites that tend to function like libraries that you might want to stroll through, especially if you are checking out a new site. I've mentioned previously how some browse capabilities include resource counts and a detailed breakdown of browse topics, such as standards or subject areas. Figure 3.6, for example, illustrates the browsing capabilities supported by the OER Commons website. You can browse by subject area, grade level, or material type. I recommend using browsing mechanisms that provide this great functionality.

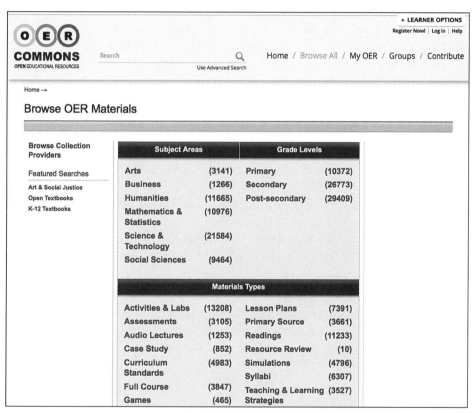

FIGURE 3.6 ▶ Example of the browsing capabilities of OER Commons

One of the increasingly valuable ways to browse or search for resources is based on standards or curricular alignment data. Many sites already provide the ability to browse or search by standards, and I expect this capability to get even better and more prevalent in educational resources sites in the future. The Common Core State Standards have now been adopted by the majority of U.S. states. These clear, understandable standards will pave the way for even better educational resource site interfaces that make finding relevant content easy. For example, on Florida's CPALMS portal, you can browse to a standard and then click to find all the related resources.

Another helpful facet for browsing or filtering results is resource type. Resource types are categorized in various ways by different organizations. For example, OER Commons defines 18 different material types (assessments, games, lesson plans, video lectures, etc.). In contrast, BOE defines just five resource types (i.e., video, photo/graphic/image, website/hyperlink, document, and Flash). These resource type filtering abilities are similar to using the Google query operator of "filetype:" and a common file extension (e.g., .docx or .swf). On educational resources sites, you can search for specific types of documents, such as lesson plans or SWF (originally "Shockwave Flash," now Adobe Flash) animations that are educational games.

All the search, browse, and filtering mechanisms described so far are very technical in nature and don't address instructional quality. The quality of an educational resource is a key determinant of its relevance in many cases. Sites provide tools to assist in making quality evaluations in various ways. For example, the Learning Resource Exchange (LRE) provides a set of quality criteria related to its "travel well" designation. LRE measures quality based on the resource being intuitive and easy to use, interactive, and containing a clear license. Other sites use both informal quality evaluations based on user ratings and comments, and formal quality evaluations derived from peer and expert evaluations. Table 3.4 shows how Curriki defines levels of its review system (CRS), through which content-area experts and teachers rate resources on a scale from 1 to 3.

TABLE 3.4 ▶ Curriki Review System (CRS) Definitions

1. Basic	A resource that requires a significant amount of cleanup or expansion to be used for teaching and learning.
2. Good	A resource that will be immediately useful to teachers and learners, but has gaps or lacks polish.
3. Exemplary	A complete and highly polished resource of publishable quality that uses best practices in instructional design.

Up to this point, I've defined the nature of educational resources, characterized sites for finding resources, and described different ways you can search, filter, and browse for resources based on conditions of use, grade level, age range, subject matter, standards, type of material, and quality (among other facets). Now, let's discuss how to optimize the use of available resources.

Effective Use and Reuse of Educational Resources

Once you're able to find relevant educational resources, the next challenge lies in using them in an effective manner. Given the topic and basic structure of your course, you can search for existing resources that are related to specified units and/or lessons. With some more details (e.g., unit and lesson objectives and assessments), you can refine your search to locate resources that are congruent with the desired learning outcomes. Finding resources that are aligned to your desired outcomes is certainly fundamental to effective use, but if you formalize your e-learning materials at this stage, you may be allowing the nature and availability of existing resources to dictate the design of your instruction, rather than your instruction driving the selection and use of resources.

For example, let's say you are teaching a freshman biology course, and one of your lessons is to cover cell division. You browse a few repositories and locate a great video clip that illustrates the process of cell mitosis, using terms and concepts at just the right level for your students. Applying some advanced search strategies, you also find a handout with relevant pictures and fill-in-the blank questions that students can use for practice, as well as a multiple-choice quiz to check their understanding. Happy that you don't have to create a lot of materials for your lesson, you prepare a web page that orients and presents lesson objectives to the students, provides a link to the video clip, directs students to download and complete the handout, and then asks them to take the quiz. Sounds pretty good—right? If you want to continue promoting the use of teacher-directed instructional methods online, I would agree. However, if you want to create a student-centered learning environment, you may want to ground the design of your course in an experiential, problem-, or inquiry-based instructional strategy before you search for, acquire, or reuse existing educational resources.

I believe the key to the effective use of existing educational resources is to follow a systematic design process. In Chapter 2 of this book, Hirumi recommended defining and aligning learning objectives and assessments first, and then he posited a systematic, five-step process for designing e-learning environments. Hirumi's five steps for grounding the design of e-learning environments are reproduced here as Figure 3.7:

Step 1.	Select a Level III grounded instructional strategy based on specified objectives, lesson content, and your values and beliefs about teaching and learning.
Step 2.	Operationalize each event, embedding essential experiences and describing how the selected strategy will be applied during instruction.
Step 3.	Determine the type of Level II interaction(s) that will be used to facilitate each event.
Step 4.	Select the tool(s) (e.g., chat, email, bulletin board system) that will be used to facilitate each event, based on the nature of the interaction.
Step 5.	Analyze materials to determine frequency and quality of planned e-learning interactions and revise as necessary.

FIGURE 3.7 ▶ Five-step process for designing and sequencing e-learning interactions

Your instructional strategy delineates the intent of the instructional events to be included in your lesson or unit (e.g., to gain learners' attention, to stimulate recall of prior knowledge, to help learners explore relevant content information, to provide learning guidance, to assess learner achievement, and so on). So, after you operationalize your instructional strategy, you can search for relevant resources to develop and facilitate the delivery of your lesson. By grounding your lesson first, you may base the selection and use of educational tools and resources on your instructional strategy. In other words, you are using a systematic approach—grounded in research, theory, and best practices—to drive your decision-making process, rather than allowing the availability of tools and resources to dictate the way you teach and facilitate learning.

Now, let's go back to the cell division example to illustrate how the lesson may differ by initially grounding the design of your unit or lesson. With lesson objectives and assessments in hand, let's say you decide to apply the 5E (five event) instructional model (Bybee, 2002) because you want to promote student-centered learning by having students follow a natural inquiry process. In other words, by applying the 5E model, you want your students to follow a pattern of initial engagement, exploration of alternatives, formation of explanations, elaboration of learned skills and knowledge, and an evaluation of the explanations. Considering each of the 5Es in turn, as you work with students, you:

1. *Engage* them by presenting pictures of different organisms and asking whether they differ in how they grow over time and, if so, how?

2. Facilitate *exploration* by presenting online examples of mitosis, meiosis, and binary fission in eukaryotes and prokaryotes.

3. Ask them to *explain* what they have learned from their explorations by identifying and distinguishing alternative ways organisms grow at a cellular level.

4. Ask them to *elaborate* on what they have learned by discussing why they think organisms may have developed different processes for cell division.

5. Engage them through *evaluation* of their explanations.

Now that you've operationalized your instructional strategy, you can search for resources that may address the intent of each event to (a) engage students; (b) facilitate students' exploration of relevant concepts, principles, rules, problems, etc.; (c) help students explain what they've learned; (d) help students elaborate on what they've learned; and (e) evaluate students' learning. So, rather than using video clips to explain the process of cell division and transmit related information to students as mentioned earlier, you can search for and use video clips that allow learners to explore alternative cell division processes and construct their own explanations of how and why the processes may differ. In other words, you are using your instructional approach to drive the selection and use of educational resources rather than allowing the availability of resources to control the way you design and deliver your instruction. After students have given their own explanations of how and why processes differ, as the fifth step, you can engage them with feedback through the evaluation process.

Searching or browsing for existing educational resources can help answer the critical question, "What multimedia content will be used to facilitate my lesson?" You may find that there are no existing resources that support your design, and you'll know what material you have to produce to complete the development of your lesson(s). However, in some cases, you may find an existing resource that can be reused in its current form, and in other cases, you may have to adapt the resource by adding some information or integrating activities before, during, or after use. Assuming the resource has permissive conditions of use that support derivative works, you can use it as a base for creating the specific resource you need, saving time for you or your multimedia developer. In the past, the reuse of existing resources was difficult because there wasn't a large collection of high-quality content available and conditions of use weren't clarified or supportive of adaption. However, an increasingly large supply of high-quality content is now available along with permissive conditions of use.

Concluding Thoughts

Instructors always need to decide between creating something new and reusing or adapting something that already exists. The nature of creativity demands that this decision be made and balanced against our time and capabilities. New tools will be increasingly available that allow us to create educational resources. Simultaneously, large supplies of existing high-quality resources are and will be available to help us design and deliver totally online, hybrid, and conventional classroom instruction.

Portals and websites are available to help find and evaluate available educational resources. Increasingly, these portals, websites, and resources themselves contain clear information about the conditions for how the resources may be used. I've shared with you some of the portals and websites I'm aware of that offer high-quality content. Surely many more sites fit into these general categories, and you may discover, as I have, that checking out, evaluating, and choosing the ones that best fit the needs of you and your students is a productive use of your time. I wish you the best of luck on your journey as you locate, reuse, and adapt existing educational resources and hope you'll find that your courses will be significantly enhanced.

References

Bybee, R. W. (2002). Scientific inquiry, student learning, and the science curriculum. In R. W. Bybee (Ed.), *Learning science and the science of learning: Science educator's essay collection* (pp. 25–35). Arlington, VA: National Science Teachers Association. Retrieved from http://books.google.com/books?id=txpoHzAb6qEC

OER Commons. (2011). What are open educational resources (OER)? Retrieved from www.oercommons.org/about

Wiley, D. A. (2007). The learning objects literature. In J. M. Spector, M. D. Merrill, J. van Merrienboer, & M. P. Driscoll (Eds.), *Handbook of research on educational communications and technology* (pp. 345–353). New York, NY: Lawrence Erlbaum.

CHAPTER 4

The Promise of Web 2.0 Technologies

Jana Willis

THE EFFECTIVE USE OF WEB 2.0 TOOLS to facilitate fully online and hybrid learning requires changes in how we integrate technology into teaching. In this chapter, I discuss the promise of Web 2.0 technologies in the areas of learner efficacy, self-confidence, motivation, and collaboration. The focus of this chapter is the need for educators to employ strategies to integrate Web 2.0 technologies as tools for engaging students in learning, in fully online and hybrid environments. To use these strategic tools, educators need to become familiar with foundational Web 2.0 technologies.

E ducators are charged with ensuring that learners obtain the skills and knowledge necessary to be successful in this constantly changing digital world. Technology integration must move beyond using software packages and online, read-only resources to using the vast array of Web 2.0 tools that are available online. Web 2.0 technologies empower educators to create online and hybrid learning environments that (a) are learner-centered, (b) encourage collaboration, (c) promote discovery, (d) develop critical thinking skills, and (e) provide activities that are engaging to learners and relevant to their individual needs. To build these 21st-century learning environments, educators must explore and gain confidence in the use of online, interactive technology tools; be prepared to integrate those tools effectively into the curriculum; and be able to implement new teaching methods enabled by the new technologies.

Fully online or hybrid courses that provide instruction mainly through large amounts of online text are no more effective at increasing learners' motivation and engagement than the lecture-based classrooms of the past—and possibly less successful. Effectively using Web 2.0 tools to promote and support online and hybrid class environments requires changes in traditional teaching and learning practices (Greenhow, Robelia, & Hughes, 2009; Hicks & Graber, 2010; Mishra & Koehler, 2006). In this chapter, we'll examine some of the opportunities offered by Web 2.0 technologies to expand online and hybrid learning environments.

Defining Web 2.0

Web 2.0 technologies set themselves apart from Web 1.0 in their facilities for interaction and publication. Web 2.0 technologies allow visitors to a website to interact—with the website, its content, its authors, and each other—and to publish content easily to a broad audience. Web 2.0 is referred to as the read/write web, the social web, and the collaborative web. Wikipedia (2013) says, "A Web 2.0 site may allow users to interact and collaborate with each other in a social media dialogue as creators of user-generated content in a virtual community, in contrast to websites where people are limited to the passive viewing of content. Examples of Web 2.0 include social networking sites, blogs, wikis, folksonomies, video-sharing sites, hosted services, web applications, and mashups" (p. 1).

Core Web 2.0 technologies include blogs, where readers are able to comment, blog authors are able to reply, and blogging communities offer support and feedback to bloggers; wikis, where many users access a single information repository and make real-time additions and edits; social media, such as Facebook and Twitter; and media-sharing sites, such as YouTube, Instagram, and Flickr.

Table 4.1 lists common learning activities, comparing strategies and tools used in traditional, face-to-face learning environments versus strategies, tools, and applications (apps) used in fully online and hybrid learning environments. Column 1 lists common educational activities. Column 2 identifies strategies and tools used to facilitate the activities in a traditional, face-to-face classroom. Column 3 introduces Web 2.0 strategies to show how we can address the same activities through e-learning with the support of interactive Web 2.0 tools. Columns 4 and 5 provide specific examples of tools and apps that can be implemented.

TABLE 4.1   ▶   Face-to-Face versus Web 2.0 Strategies and Tools

ACTIVITY	FACE-TO-FACE STRATEGIES/TOOLS	WEB 2.0		
		STRATEGIES	TOOLS	APPS
Discussing	Traditional, face-to-face classroom discussion	Online chat, web conferencing, discussion forums, blogs, and wikis	Chatzy EtherPad Clackpoint TokBox Phonevite Nicenet Yugma	Club Penguin Fantage
Collaborating	Learning communities within the classroom population or outside the school day	Online documents, blogs, wikis, and web conferencing	Google Drive Wikispaces Blogger TitanPad Edmodo Kidblog DimDim Web Meeting	Google Drive Blogger WebEx
Brainstorming	Paper/pencil, word processor, or concept-mapping software	Online concept mapping	bubbl.us MindMeister Mindomo Webspiration	MindMeister SimpleMind
Publishing	Brochures, flyers, word processing documents, and paper-based materials	Online publication generators	Scribd Letterpop Formatpixel Openzine	PosterMyWall Cool Flyers
Journaling	Paper-based journals, logs, and word-processing documents	Online writing tools, journals, wikis, and blogs	Google Docs Wikispaces Classroom ClassChatter Wordpress Blogger	VJournal for Evernote iDiary for Kids Wonderful Days—Diary with Style
Presenting	Oral, written, performances, and digital presentations	Online audio, video, and multimedia options	podcasting tools vodcasting tools Prezi Animoto Voicethread ComicMaster CoSketch	AnimationExpress Comic Creator

(Continued)

TABLE 4.1 ▶ *(Continued)*

| ACTIVITY | FACE-TO-FACE | WEB 2.0 | | |
	STRATEGIES/TOOLS	STRATEGIES	TOOLS	APPS
Creating	Poster board and paper-based presentations of information	Online posters, collages, and mashups	Glogster ScrapBlog Artskills PosterMyWall Photovisi Shape Collage Squidoo MashUpPhotos	Photo Mosaica Photo Collage Creator
3-D Modeling	Solar models, molecular models, geometric models, and architectural models	2-D/3-D creators, simulations, and animations	GoogleSketchUp for Education Scratch Lego Digital Designer Sculptris Pivot StickFigure Animator	Animation Studio Toontastic Verto Studio 3D

Comparing traditional instructional tools to Web 2.0 tools across a sample of educational activities allows us to see how the newer tools may enhance instruction, learner engagement, motivation, and collaboration. For example, if you look at the "Discussing" row in Table 4.1 and contrast conventional, face-to-face strategies with online strategies for facilitating discussions, you can see that Web 2.0 dramatically expands the number of options. Educators often find it difficult to get all students in their classes to participate, just as some students find participation intimidating, but interactive Web 2.0 tools, such as online chats, web conferencing, discussion forums, blogs, and wikis, offer differentiated ways for students to participate.

Reflect on your own educational experience: Do you remember class discussions that were limited to a select number of students, while most others appeared to be uninterested or found it hard to join in? Students' unwillingness to participate in discussions or express themselves verbally can be caused by lack of preparation, low levels of self-confidence, and a variety of social and personal factors. Most face-to-face discussions require instant responses, leaving little or no time for reflection. Web 2.0 tools allow for synchronous and asynchronous exchanges that offer participants opportunities to consider their responses more thoroughly before posting, which affords some learners a less stressful setting for expressing their ideas than traditional, face-to-face discussions. Blogs and wikis are especially helpful for students who prefer to communicate in writing.

Not all learners are comfortable speaking up in class. Confidence levels, shyness, and fear of failure or humiliation in front of peers are just a few examples of individual barriers that can negatively impact students' levels of engagement in traditional discussions. The anonymity of the online environment often increases learner participation. Web 2.0-supported interactions offer a safe place for learners to share and exchange ideas. These tools can allow for fully anonymous or pseudonymous interchanges, which protect participants' identities. Over time, as their ideas are validated by instructors and peers, learners' confidence levels and sense of belonging can increase.

Furthermore, traditional discussions are too often just moments in time with few options for archiving the information for later reflection and review. Assessment measures are limited to observable indicators of contribution, which can be complicated during periods of rapid interchange. Group interactions in the classroom also allow for only limited moments of observation by teachers as they move from group to group. Educators can manage and access individual discussions and group projects more easily by using archival logs and date/time stamps generated by the Web 2.0 tools and then retrieved and stored in a digital format. Chat rooms and collaborative areas can also supply a space for alternative assessment opportunities, such as one-on-one or small-group evaluations, where instructors can talk with learners to gain a better understanding of their knowledge mastery. Chat rooms can also double as office hours to allow instructors and students to meet for guidance, instruction, and evaluation.

Web 2.0 online collaboration tools that enable students to generate collaborative documents, share drawing spaces, and develop interactive concept maps can replace the static software of the past, allowing for two-way exchanges of ideas in the learning environment and beyond. Traditionally, group projects have resulted in learners taking a "divide and conquer" approach with minimal collaborative efforts. (Most of us recall feeling as if we were the only ones in a group who did the work for everyone.) Engaging learners socially in Web 2.0 collaborative workspaces provides a foundation for an active exchange of ideas. The archival logs and date/time stamps also provide a mechanism for accountability during the collaborative process. Students' participation is observable and, except for anonymous interchanges, more accurately measured. In Table 4.1, you can see how paper-based work products, such as essays, journals, and desktop publishing, can be replaced with read/write digital elements that can be created individually or collaboratively and shared globally.

Potential Impact on Efficacy, Confidence, and Motivation

A shift to learner-centered, project/problem-based instruction gives students more control over their learning and often improves their motivation. With the appropriate integration of Web 2.0 technologies, online and hybrid learning experiences can further increase self-efficacy by offering the learners mechanisms for two-way communication and receipt of timely feedback during their quest for content mastery. Wikis, blogs, and social media tools offer learners collaborative venues to extend and share their knowledge and observations. Sharing and collaborating during knowledge discovery and exploration can promote advances in efficacy and confidence. Then, as students' self-efficacy and confidence grow, so do their motivation and desire to return to the same or similar learning activities or content.

One-way transmissions of content from teacher to students can be replaced with exchanges of information that encourage a sense of involvement and ownership by learners. Web 2.0 technologies, such as wikis and blogs, are unique in their ability to facilitate social interaction and the development of collaborative content in hybrid and online communities. Wikis and blogs offer venues for the exchange, extension, and exploration of ideas among learner populations.

Blogs, while usually generated by a single or limited number of authors, permit the distribution of information from one to many and also allow many students as well as the instructor to give timely feedback to the one in the form of comments. Numerous informative blogs become primary sources of regularly updated information about given topics. For example, the George Lucas Foundation's Edutopia hosts blogs on a variety of topics that include brain-based learning, education trends, game-based learning, and technology integration (www.edutopia.org/blogs). Another example is Richard Byrne's blog, Free Technology for Teachers, which focuses on technology resources for classroom use (www.freetech4teachers.com).

Wikis, on the other hand, are usually the result of multiple authors and provide for communication from many to many. The intricate web of information created in wikis can extend a topic in both breadth and depth. The interactive nature of this Web 2.0 technology helps learners move from extrinsic motivation to intrinsic motivation. For instance, K–12 Tech Tools is a kid-friendly wiki that provides resources by subject, grade level, and standard to support student learning (http://edutechdatabase.wikispaces.com).

As noted in Table 4.1, via Web 2.0, students may create a 2-D/3-D model of a concept, using an online interactive tool that allows them to work in an environment free from glue disasters, material malfunctions, and bus-ride catastrophes. For example, an assignment that requires students to create a multidimensional representation of a molecule could find you with a classroom full of molecules made from Styrofoam balls, candy, pipe wire, or even marshmallows. While the representations may be accurate, much of the science learning was probably lost during the cumbersome assembly process. Working with a tool like Molinspiration's WebME Molecule Editor (www.molinspiration.com/docu/webme) allows users to manipulate the objects on the screen, exploring the intricacies of a molecule's makeup instead of building the model from a diagram. Individualized connections through interactions and experience can facilitate learners' attention, cognitive processing, effort, and subsequent interest. If students maintain these connections over time, their sustained interest and motivation can lead to well-developed knowledge bases and experience in using scientific methodology. Individuals' interests can then directly promote continued use of the new task or activity (Hidi, 1990; Hidi & Harackiewicz, 2000), as well as the motivation to work with others.

Impact on Collaboration

In support of the findings that link increases in motivation, confidence, and self-efficacy to interactive learning experiences, today's online and hybrid learning environments are also being recognized as knowledge-building collaborative communities. While Web 1.0 technologies increased access to information, Web 2.0 technologies increase opportunities for collaboration. Educators, now more secure in their roles as learning facilitators, are forming collaborative, knowledge-building communities in various learning environments. Educators are creating stimulating experiences with blogs, wikis, and a variety of social media that can involve their students in continuous dialogues about their learning experiences both in and outside school.

Such exchanges of knowledge can now move beyond simple dissemination of static information to more complex interactions, where knowledge can be shared, analyzed, expanded, and applied by the learner population. Far beyond e-pal projects that were limited to text interchanges, new technologies include digital and multimedia elements. Global projects, such as *Journey North* by the Annenberg Foundation (www.learner.org), allow students to collect information from sources far beyond their classrooms and to build learning communities that share a common focus.

In online and hybrid settings, the synchronous exchange of ideas allows for idea development as well as validation for the contributor. In a traditional classroom, opening a discussion with a brainstorming activity often results in only a handful of learners orally contributing their thoughts on the topic. As noted in Table 4.1, in a learning environment supported with Web 2.0 technology, brainstorming can be accomplished synchronously or asynchronously by all members of the classroom, allowing for equal levels of contribution and reward. Web 2.0 concept mapping tools, such as bubbl.us, Webspiration, and MindMeister, allow for multi-user contributions where the results can be shared externally. For example, students may share information they currently possess on any given topic with their classmates. The teacher can collect and store the information on a concept map and then work with students as they make collaborative connections and begin to understand relationships among pieces of information. At the conclusion of the lesson, revisiting the concept map allows for clarification of misconceptions, reconciliations of errors in relational connections, and modifications to the concept map.

Today's Web 2.0 options for facilitating publications allow learners in online and hybrid settings to make concurrent contributions to the content and design of products. An increased number of interactions during the publication process supports growth in technology and social skills for each of the learners involved in the activity. Book reports, essays, oral presentations, and PowerPoint presentations can now become collaborative productions fully supported by multimedia. Multi-user tools, like CoSketch, can provide learners with an open forum that accepts a variety of multimedia elements. For example, imagine a cultural collaboration with two classrooms in two different countries or regions that offers students a synchronous drawing tool for sharing ideas and events about their diverse cultures. The drawing occurs in real time, affording all the students opportunities to engage with their classmates from a different culture just as they would in their own classrooms. Through the use of socially oriented online tools, learners enrolled in online and hybrid courses can now collectively create posters, collages, and even multimedia mashups as evidence of subject matter and skills mastery (See Table 4.1).

Concluding Thoughts

Today's students already exist in a digital world, where the use of technology is a seamless, integral part of their daily lives. Smart phones and mobile devices afford access to information and offer collaborative spaces where information is shared, evaluated, and extended anytime, anywhere. As growing numbers of students are avid users of new technologies outside school, it is essential for teachers to learn to use these technologies in their online and hybrid classes. With facilities to share and generate information, Web 2.0 technologies provide the tools to meet the needs of today's learners.

When educators use Web 2.0 tools in online and hybrid class settings, students become engaged in learning, improve their technology skills, and perform with increased confidence.

When educators employ Web 2.0 technology tools in their classes, learners shift from simply memorizing information that appears to have little relevance to their lives to acquiring knowledge as they become engaged learners. These technology tools are not a substitute for content; rather, they help us to design learning environments that support students as they construct and collaborate on projects they understand are relevant to them now and will help them in their future careers. All learning environments are defined by teachers, experts in their subject matter. Those of us who use Web 2.0 technologies are convinced that these tools have transformed our students into enthusiastic, engaged learners. Students can use Web 2.0 tools to create, publish, and share a wealth of multimedia resources to demonstrate what they've learned as well as contribute to the learning of others (Hendron, 2008).

Meeting the individual learning needs of students with the support of Web 2.0 technologies enables them to develop skills that are supported by but not limited to the instructional environment. Instructional settings including Web 2.0 encourage students to extend their learning beyond the walls of the classroom and the timeframes of the traditional school day. Mobile technologies are already enabling our students to communicate, collaborate, and share information in a variety of settings with diverse communities. By adopting Web 2.0 technologies as tools in our classrooms, we have the satisfaction of fostering our students' learning as an integral part of everyday life, leading them to internalize the positive values of lifelong learning. Navigating the ever-changing world of e-learning through Web 2.0 technologies makes for exciting journeys—for our students and our own professional growth.

Bibliography

An, Y. J., & Williams, K. (2010). Teaching with web 2.0 technologies: Benefits, barriers and lessons learned. *International Journal of Instructional Technology and Distance Learning, 7*(3). Retrieved from http://itdl.org/Journal/Mar_10/article04.htm

Brewster, C., & Fager, J. (2000, October). *Increasing learner engagement and motivation: From time-on-task to homework.* Portland, OR: Northwest Regional Educational Laboratory. Retrieved from http://educationnorthwest.org/webfm_send/452

Brown, J. S., & Adler, R. P. (2008). Minds on fire: Open education, the long tail, and learning 2.0. *Educause Review, 43*(1), 16–32. Retrieved from http://net.educause.edu/ir/library/pdf/erm0811.pdf

Dodge, B. (1995, 1997). Some thoughts about WebQuests. (February 1995 draft updated May 5, 1997.) Retrieved from http://webquest.sdsu.edu/about_webquests.html

Dodge, B. (2008). What is a WebQuest? Retrieved from http://webquest.org

Greenhow, C., Robelia, B., & Hughes, J. E. (2009). Learning, teaching, and scholarship in a digital age. Web 2.0 and classroom research: What path should we take now? *Educational Researcher, 38*(4), 246–59. Retrieved from http://engage.doit.wisc.edu/dma/research/docs/Greenhow-LearningTeachingScholarship.pdf

Hendron, J. G. (2008). *RSS for educators.* Eugene, OR: International Society for Technology in Education.

Hicks, A. & Graber, A. (2010). Shifting paradigms: Teaching, learning and web 2.0. *Reference Services Review 38*(4), 621–633.

Hidi, S. (1990). Interest and its contribution as a mental resource for learning. *Review of Educational Research, 60*(4), 549–571.

Hidi, S., & Harackiewicz, J. M. (2000). Motivating the academically unmotivated: A critical issue for the 21st century. *Review of Educational Research, 70*(2), 151–179.

Himowitz, M. (2007, September 27). 3 challenges raised to Microsoft Office. *Baltimore Sun.* Retrieved from http://articles.baltimoresun.com/2007-09-27/business/0709270063_1_microsoft-corp-microsoft-office-microsoft-word

Interactive Educational Systems Design (IESD). (2011, March). *Digital districts: Web 2.0 and collaborative technologies in U.S. schools.* New York, NY: IESD. Retrieved from http://edulab.wikispaces.com/file/view/web+2.0+brug+i+skolen+Digital+District+Survey+-+2011+Full+Report.pdf

Kruger-Ross, M., & Holcomb, L. B. (2011). Toward a theoretical best practices for Web 2.0 and web-based technologies. *Meridian: A Kindergarten through High School Communication Technologies Journal, 13*(2), 1–6. Retrieved from www.ncsu.edu/meridian/winter2011/krugerross

Linn, A. (2005, December 20). Free, web-based alternatives challenge Microsoft Office. *Seattlepi.com.* Retrieved from www.seattlepi.com/business/article/Free-Web-based-alternatives-challenge-Microsoft-1190515.php

March, T. (1998, September 10). Why WebQuests? [Blog post]. Retrieved from http://tommarch.com/writings/why-webquests

March, T. (2003–2004). The learning power of WebQuests. *Educational Leadership, 61*(4, December/January), 42–47.

Mishra, P., & Koehler, M. J. (2006). Technological pedagogical content knowledge: A new framework for teacher knowledge. *Teachers College Record, 108*(6), 1017–1054.

Nagel, D. (2009, April). Teachers lead adoption of Web 2.0, but perceptions stifle social networking. *THE Journal.* Retrieved from http://thejournal.com/articles/2009/04/07/teachers-lead-adoption-of-web-20-but-perceptions-stifle-social-networking.aspx

Odom, L. (2010, January–February). Mapping web 2.0 benefits to known best practices in distance education. [Archived Webinar]. Retrieved from http://deoracle.org/de-oracle-live/archived-webinars/mapping-newly-identified-web-20.html?PHPSESSID=b7a9748dc75dfc42eeaec754fc9c91f0

Singh, B. (2010, February 2). Difference between web 1.0, web 2.0, & web 3.0—with examples. Retrieved from http://ezinearticles.com/?Difference-Between-Web-1.0,-Web-2.0,-and-Web-3.0---With-Examples&id=3683790

Strickland, J. (2005). Using WebQuests to teach content: Comparing instructional strategies. *Contemporary Issues in Technology and Teacher Education, 5*(2), 138–148.

Vassileva, J. (2008). Toward social learning environments. *IEEE Transactions on Learning Technologies, 1*(4), 199–214.

Web 2.0. (2005; 2013, July 23). In *Wikipedia, the free encyclopedia.* Retrieved from http://en.wikipedia.org/wiki/Web_2.0

CHAPTER 5

Preparing Students for e-Learning Success

Ryan Watkins and Michael Corry

EVEN FOR STUDENTS WHO have grown up with the Internet and who spend more time online than on the playground, building appropriate and effective study skills for the e-learning classroom is a challenge. While students often feel comfortable with many new technologies, they rarely have the study strategies in place to maximize their learning through e-learning. From taking notes while watching online video lectures to analyzing the quality of webpage content, numerous study strategies can help students become successful e-learners. In this chapter we examine what it takes to prepare your students for e-learning success and how you can integrate the development of e-learning study skills into your learning design.

Developing effective study strategies for e-learning can be essential to improving learner retention and performance. Some e-learning study skills can be adaptations of strategies developed in the traditional classroom, such as time management and preparing for exams. Others can be unique to e-learning, such as participating in online discussions or collaborating on a wiki. In all cases, the wider the range of strategies that your students can apply when learning, the greater their odds of success. Therefore, this chapter is filled with tips and resources for you and your students, offering practical guidance for how all students can become successful e-learners.

n its many forms, e-learning has become an integral part of education in the United States and around the world. Whether e-learning in your school includes the use of online resources to supplement conventional face-to-face courses, a limited number of hybrid or blended courses that are delivered partially online and partially face-to-face, or courses that are delivered totally online, including MOOCs (massive open online courses), the use of e-learning is an expanding component of education for most schools. As a consequence, you and your students must be prepared to successfully meet the new educational challenges; that is, to teach and learn effectively in today's high-tech—and often demanding—e-learning classrooms.

Learning how to use the technology, while important, is not the only essential aspect of e-learning success. From adapting note-taking skills to adopting new online communication skills, students need to master many study skills to thrive in this new learning environment. The strategies that have led students to be successful in traditional classrooms with chalkboards and encyclopedias must now be updated to ensure equivalent success in e-learning classrooms with interactive whiteboards and Internet access. By helping your students to build on the techniques that they have used in the past, such as note taking, time management, and critical reading skills, you can help them improve their performances in courses as well as their abilities to apply those techniques and skills in other areas of their lives. Likewise, by building on the skills that have made you a successful teacher in the past, you can also adapt to this environment and help your students become successful e-learners.

Prepared to Learn

Academic success in the traditional classroom doesn't always translate into success in the e-learning classroom. Often there are barriers that prevent normally high-achieving students in the traditional classroom from achieving the same levels of success when e-learning technologies replace the traditional lecture hall or teacher-centric classroom. Many students who are adept at taking notes during class lectures, for example, can struggle when they are required to employ online library search engines independently to find appropriate materials for a term paper. Likewise, students who are accustomed to being engaged in classroom discussions may struggle to participate in interactive online chats—regardless of how often they check Facebook or play online video games.

In response, preparing students for success in the traditional classroom, the blended classroom, and the e-learning classroom is a growing requirement for teachers, schools, colleges, and universities. Two sets of essential skills for student success in online courses are (1) adapting old skills and habits from the traditional classroom for use in the online classroom and (2) developing and applying new e-learning skills and habits for the online classroom (Figure 5.1). From building a robust vocabulary of technology-related terminology to adequately preparing for online discussion board debates, essential skills for success in the online classroom build on many of the skills necessary for success in the traditional classroom, while students learn to apply them in new ways (Watkins & Corry, 2013). In addition, some technologies have dramatically changed how students interact with their instructors, peers, and course materials, requiring the development of new learning strategies as well.

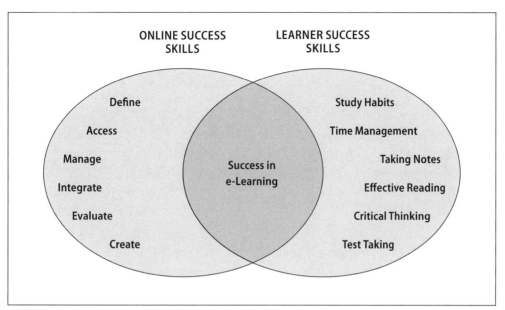

FIGURE 5.1 ▶ Building e-learning success (Watkins & Corry, 2013)

As we discuss in our book (Watkins & Corry, 2013), instructors need to guide students to learn basic online success skills as part of their e-learning courses:

Define what you hope to achieve in each of your online courses, as well as each time you go online.

Access sometimes requires planning ahead so that you have the available resources (for instance, internet connectivity, specific software) when you want it.

Manage your time, your computer, and your online relationships in a manner that leads to success.

Integrate e-learning success strategies into your routine study skills, even for courses that meet on-campus.

Evaluate how well your study skills are helping you accomplish your goals, at least once a month throughout any course.

Create new ideas and relationships that allow your education to expand beyond the boundaries of the classroom.

Successful e-learners take advantage of new e-learning technologies rather than letting them present obstacles to their learning and success. Likewise, rather than trying to build an entirely new set of study habits, they adapt what has worked well for them in the past (such as using flash cards, consulting an instructor during office hours, or developing study groups) to meet the challenges of an online course. For example, while online journal articles provide your students with easy and flexible access to quality information, new study skills are required to replace highlighting, taking notes in the margins, or creating index cards with critical information. With online content, students must develop the skills to capture citation information—author, date, title, publication details, and so forth—in a format that will be useful to them when writing their term papers. Likewise, students must adapt conventional note-taking techniques to identify and record essential information from the article and prepare for upcoming exams.

Since students can send text messages all day and play online games with friends all night, educators too often assume that students can also seamlessly translate these skills into e-learning success. David Baird, director of Innovative Technology Solutions for Learning at Colgate University, contends, "There is an assumption that all students grow up with technology and know how to use it, [when] in fact our students display a great spectrum of abilities and comfort levels with technology" (as quoted in Arabasz, Pirani, & Fawcett, 2003, p. 42). These assumptions are what typically lead instructors to overlook the real challenges that students face when trying to learn in high-tech classrooms.

Every day, people around the world are learning in high-tech, online classrooms. But if you rely on the assumption that your students are already prepared for learning in this new environment, then you could be setting many of them up for failure. However, by giving them just a little purposeful practice, combined with many useful tips and tricks, you can help your students build the study skills and learning strategies that will prepare them for success.

Student Success Skills

From developing time-management skills to learning how to take effective notes, students who develop foundational study skills and learning strategies are more likely to have a successful [college] learning experience (Cuseo, 2004a). According to Cuseo, professor of psychology and director of the first-year seminar at Marymount College, "It is reasonably safe say to say that there has been more well-conducted research on, and more compelling empirical evidence gathered in support of the first-year seminar than any other course offered in the history of higher education" (2004a, p. 1). As a result, more than 700 college campuses in the United States have developed "first-year experience" (also called "student success") courses to teach practical study skills to today's college students (National Resource Center, 2000). Many of these classes combine study skills lessons with campus orientations or other college-life skills (e.g., money management, decision making, reading comprehension) to create holistic first-year programs for students. Yet, the basic function of preparing students with the knowledge and skills to become academically successful students is consistent across the curriculum (Watkins, 2009).

However, there is little evidence of study-skills preparation being systematically and pervasively integrated into middle school or high school curriculums. Likewise, e-learning programs at the secondary and post-secondary levels—though growing at unprecedented rates in the past decade—have done relatively little to ensure the academic success of their students.

Although no definitive figures are available on retention rates in online college courses (see Phipps & Merisotis, 1999), it has been suggested that distance education courses retain from 10 to 20% fewer students than traditional classroom courses (Carr, 2000). Even if the estimated retention rates are off by a magnitude of three or four times the actual rates, the impact of dropouts on the success of an online course is considerable, both in terms of the academic achievement and persistence of students. College students, for instance, drop out or underperform for a variety of reasons, including personal, institutional, and circumstantial variables (Berge & Huang, 2004). For online students, the factors influencing student achievement and retention are most often quite similar to those of on-campus students. Yet, the online classroom typically creates unique variations of the problems, such as poor online technical support, inferior course design, social isolation, strained time management, and/or deficiencies in e-learning study skills (see Hughes, 2004). Adding to this is the potential for differences in students' commitment to persist with their educations when courses are available right in their living rooms.

For most online students, the development of effective study habits and learning skills is also critical to their engagement, academic achievement, and eventual graduation (i.e., their success and our success as educators). After all, "Students enrolling in an e-learning class must not only master the course's subject matter but also possess the technical skills to participate in the course and study effectively" (Arabasz, et al., 2003, p. 42). And while students can adapt many traditional study habits for use in online courses, they must develop new, high-tech learning skills for e-learning success (Watkins & Corry, 2013).

e-Learning Study Skills

While it is probable that the number of students entering e-learning courses with minimal Internet experience will diminish in the coming years, instructors will continue to be concerned that their students of all ages have effective online study habits and learning skills (Watkins, 2004). For example, can students apply critical thinking skills when watching lectures online or listening via podcast? Can online students utilize effective substitutes for nonverbal cues when class discussions take place in an online chat room rather than a traditional classroom? Are e-learners able to maintain consistent levels of academic motivation in courses that do not meet on campus? Do e-learners create appropriate study environments to maximize prolonged concentration on their studies?

While many students arrive at school with remarkable skills to search for and download music from the Internet, most have little experience or knowledge of how to use technologies effectively to advance their studies. In a report prepared for Educause, Morgan (2003) affirms that despite the popular myth that students are technologically savvy and converse mainly through phone texting, instant messaging, and, to a lesser extent, e-mail, the study illustrated that many students are not proficient with technology. "[Faculty members] consistently report that their students seem to have inadequate technology proficiency and that this inhibits their CMS [course management system] use" (Morgan, 2003, p. 76). As a result, building skills for communicating effectively when using email, synchronous chat rooms, or asynchronous discussion boards, are among the basic study skills that many students must develop to be successful e-learners (see iNACOL Standards, Chapter 7; www.inacol.org/research/nationalstandards). Additional skills, such as creating a positive study environment, managing their time, building constructive online relationships with peers, and contending with plagiarism, are also essential to the academic success of e-learners.

The good news is that preparing your student for e-learning success does not require a great amount of time and effort (Watkins, 2005a–d). Study skills activities, resources, and materials can typically be built into current course materials, providing students with information on how to be successful e-learners as well as opportunities to practice those skills. For example, early in a course instructors may want to include an exercise where students examine issues related to the ethical use and proper citation of reference materials they retrieve from an online library database. Likewise, introductory activities related to note taking, critical thinking skills, time management, email communication skills, and other e-learning success topics can also introduce important skills without distracting from the course's subject matter (see iNACOL standards, Chapter 7).

You can often successfully introduce valuable study habits, for both traditional classes and e-learning classes, by blending lessons, tips, and resources regarding effective study strategies into course materials. At an Arizona K–12 school, for example, a "rookie camp" is the first module of a student's online course (Niemczyk, Dwyer, & Savenye, 2000). In this module, students prepare for success by gaining competencies in using the navigational and discussion tools that are part of the course. The rookie camp includes, for instance, a reminder card for note taking and a mnemonic device representing the names of the web-environment icons (Watkins, 2009).

Online tutorials, online scavenger hunts, and online video (or audio) lectures are also useful techniques for introducing effective study skills. From tutorials on using the online library search engines to quick tips on applying critical thinking skills to online readings, you can reference existing online lessons as resources to introduce important e-learning success skills to your students. Many of these resources may have been developed by others in your school district, thus making it easier for you. You can simply link to or reference these resources in course materials, offering students access to useful information 24 hours a day and giving them the tools and resources they require to be successful e-learners.

Ways to Prepare Your Students for Success

While your students can address many study skills to become successful e-learners, you can also make many valuable changes in how you teach your e-learning courses to help you and your students do better.

Don't Try to Simulate the Traditional Classroom without Modifications

You can, and often should, have similar learning objectives for your e-learning courses as you have for your traditional face-to-face courses. However, the means to achieve the learning objectives may be different. These can include different learning strategies and techniques from those you have used in the past. For example, applying grounded strategies (such as problem-based or experiential learning strategies) can be effective in many online situations. Likewise, small group techniques that use online tools (such as Google Docs or Facebook) can be effective. Many learner-centered strategies for e-learning are discussed in further detail in the second book in this series, *Online and Hybrid Learning Designs in Action.*

Some of these new techniques will be challenging at first, and others will come easily. Some techniques will be successful the first time you apply them, and others may require some refinements the next time you offer the course. But once you come to terms with the fact that what you did in the classroom may not work online, then you can move forward to designing successful online courses.

To get started in the right direction, spend time evaluating the technological resources you have available to achieve your learning objectives. For example, is a course management system (such as Blackboard) available to you? If so, will it improve the structure and consistency of your online courses? Next, consider what types of activities are necessary to achieve your objectives. Should you use discussion boards, chat rooms, wikis, blogs, or other online tools? Each of these technologies has pros and cons; evaluate them carefully and use them not just to add bells and whistles to your course, but because they can help your students achieve the learning objectives.

Preparing students for success in technology-rich courses is consistent with iNACOL standards (see Chapter 7). For example, iNACOL standard A4 recommends, "Information literacy and communication skills are incorporated and taught as an integral part of the curriculum." And standard A5: "Multiple learning resources and materials to increase student success are available to students before the course begins" (iNACOL, 2011, p. 8). By focusing on student success at all stages of your design and development processes, you can enrich your materials and courses with experiences that will promote valuable skills students can apply in your courses, in other classes (regardless of delivery formats), and in life outside the classroom, such as e-learning in the workplace.

Focus on Learner Performance

As with any course, online courses should also include a well-defined set of measurable objectives. They should be in writing, used to guide your course design, and available to students so they know what to expect. These objectives form the basis upon which learner performance not only is focused but also assessed. All course activities should then be geared toward the achievement of the stated objectives by learners. As you construct objectives, make sure they are clearly written and can be measured within the course. For example, "By the end of the module, learners will be able to accurately identify, measure key characteristics, and log at least 10 insects into their science journal."

Online courses often benefit from both content-related objectives and e-learning study skills objectives. It is important to remember that if your students do not possess valuable e-learning success skills, then these barriers to learning will frequently prevent them from achieving the content-related objectives. For example, you may ask new e-learners to evaluate information on three websites that you have selected, and then, based on their evaluations, you can help guide them to be more selective about the information they use in your course assignments.

Don't Be Afraid to Learn from Your Students

The plain and simple truth is that many students are living and working on the cutting edge of new technologies. They are frequently early adopters of new technologies, and many have access to technologies long before they are available in the classroom. Coupled with this is the fact that the new technologies (from smartphone apps to web-based tools) come out every day, making it nearly impossible for most people to keep up with them on their own.

So keep your mind open to the possibilities. If you read, see, or hear about a student using a technology with which you are unfamiliar, take a minute to ask about it. Not only will the student be thrilled that you asked, you will likely learn something new. What you learn may then be useful to all of your students. Don't let the fact that your students may know something you don't prevent you from opening doors that could lead to successful learning opportunities.

Help e-Learners Learn

Many of your students will not have all the skills necessary to be successful. Just because they know how to send text messages, download music, and talk on their cell phones (all at the same time), doesn't mean they'll succeed in your online course. With that in mind, design and revise your course to include tips, strategies, and skills for students on how they can be successful. These might include sharing thoughts on how to take online notes, providing outlines students can use to follow along with online videos or PowerPoint presentations, and giving them tips on how to participate in online groups successfully. Sometimes, helping students understand how to link these skills together can be beneficial. For example, while demonstrating skills related to reading online documents, you could discuss how they can transform these skills into online note taking.

Break the Ice Online

Because e-learners can be spread out around the globe and feel isolated to some degree, it is a good idea to start each course by getting students involved and giving them the opportunity to get to know each other. One way of doing this is through ice-breaking activities. As an ice-breaker, students can be asked to:

▶ Describe to the rest of the class their first time doing something memorable.

▶ Identify websites about themselves or post a biography for the rest of the class.

▶ Tell something about themselves, such as their most embarrassing moment or closest brush with fame, in an online discussion forum (see Watkins [2005c] for additional examples).

In addition to these activities, the model you set as an instructor carries a great deal of influence with your students. If you are not open and willing to participate in discussions and "getting to know you" activities, your students will be less likely to do so. In some cases, when students are having trouble overcoming feelings of isolation, additional ice-breaking activities can also be used throughout the course.

Intersperse Online Activities throughout the Course

Help students feel as if they are part of the course and overcome feelings of isolation by making the course engaging. Include, for example, online activities that bring students together. Activities such as team-building exercises, content reviews, blogs, wikis, discussion boards, and other social networking tools can be great if they are properly designed for courses. Two keys to success are (1) be creative and (2) participate along with your students. Online activities are where "the rubber meets the road" in most e-learning courses because they give students chances to learn through interactions with you and their peers. The end result is a learning community whose members share and learn from each other. If properly designed, this type of learning opportunity can be very successful.

Integrate Student-Generated Content

Many online tools now ask or allow students to generate content that can be used in your course. For example, you can have students in the class contribute to a shared wiki, giving each student the opportunity to help shape the document and edit the contributions of others. Likewise, collaborative tools, such as Google Docs, can be used by student groups to generate reports, papers, and other team assignments. Student-generated content can also offer a flexible environment to provide feedback and guidance, rather than waiting for final assignments to be submitted at the end of the course.

Provide Clear and Specific Guidelines for Participation

In any course, whether it is delivered traditionally in a face-to-face environment or as an online course, some students will be active participants, and others will hardly participate at all. As participation is so important to online courses, it is crucial that instructors communicate clearly the minimum amounts and types of participation required. For example, if you have an online discussion board as the primary means of student interaction, you need to state how often, how much, and at what quality level you want each student to post. The "how often" part is the easiest to quantify and make clear; the "how much" is often harder to explain to students. You may, for instance, require a certain number of sentences or pages. The quality levels of postings, however, can be even more complex and require some forethought before the course begins (see Box 5.1). Whatever approach you choose, it is important to communicate the requirements clearly and to provide strategies to help students be successful.

Create a Positive Learning Environment in Your Online Course

Positive learning environments are important to success in any setting. In the online learning setting, it is even more important due to the loss of physical and verbal cues. Review all communications to your students, for instance, to make sure that they are as clear and precise as possible. Some specific ways of overcoming the loss of physical and verbal cues include the use of emoticons and acronyms. However, be careful to make sure you know what you are saying when using these means of communication—you don't want to say something you might later regret.

BOX 5.1 ▶ Quality criteria for online discussions

Example Criteria for Online Discussion Quality

(Paul & Elder, 1996, 2010)

Clarity. The "gateway standard" is clarity. If a statement is unclear, we cannot determine whether it is accurate or relevant. We cannot tell anything about it because we don't yet know what it is saying. Could you elaborate further on that point? Could you express that point in another way? Could you give me an illustration or example?

Accuracy. Is that really true? How could we check that? How could we find out if that is true? A statement can be clear, but not accurate (e.g., Most dogs weigh over 300 pounds).

Precision. Could you give more details? Could you be more specific? A statement can be both clear and accurate, but not precise. For example, "Jack is overweight."

Relevance. How is that connected to the question? How does that bear on the issue? A statement can be clear, accurate, and precise, but not relevant to the question at issue. For example, students often think the amount of effort they put into a course should be used to raise their grade. However, "effort" does not measure the quality of student learning, so it is irrelevant to their grade.

Depth. How does my answer address the complexities in the question? Am I taking into account the problems in the question? Is it dealing with the most significant factors? A statement can be clear, accurate, precise, and relevant, but superficial (lacking depth). For example, the statement "Just say no!" treats an extremely complex issue superficially.

Breadth. Do we need to consider another point of view? Is there another way to look at this question? A line of reasoning lacks breadth if it only recognizes the insights on one side of the question.

Logic. Does this really make sense? Does that follow from what you said? How does that follow? Before you said this, and now you say that; how can both be true? Thinking is logical when the combined thoughts are mutually supportive, not contradictory, and generally make sense.

Fairness. Do I have a vested interest in this issue? Am I sympathetically representing the viewpoints of others? We must actively work to make sure we are applying the intellectual standard of fairness to our thinking because our natural tendency is to not consider the rights and needs of others as we do our own.

You should also model good netiquette (that is, online etiquette) and try to moderate any student differences of opinion quickly and professionally. Removal of some offending posts to bulletin boards, blogs, or chat rooms may be necessary. Make sure you understand how to do this before starting your course. Throughout your courses, provide feedback that is clear, professional, and positive. This is particularly important in online courses as most communication is done via writing. You may have to fine-tune your own written communication skills to model quality writing for your students. Remember, keeping things positive (for example, giving constructive feedback on assignments rather than just letter grades) results in happier students who are more likely to achieve success.

Take Time for Feedback

e-Learners crave feedback on assignments, postings, and other course activities; this can be due partially to their isolation from one another. The development of a positive, online learning community involves timely feedback from you and from other classmates. Design your online courses in ways that provide adequate time for you to give feedback and for students to offer peer reactions (see iNACOL standards, Chapter 7). It is also helpful to use a feedback template that you can modify for different courses and use in subsequent semesters (see Hirumi, 2003). You can cut and paste feedback, for example, from your template into most course management systems and then modify the feedback to reflect individual differences in the activity or assignment.

Don't hesitate to participate in online discussions, and don't hesitate to use students to give feedback to other students on draft assignments. It can be a lot of work and require more time than you are used to in a traditional course, but the results can be rewarding to you and your students. You might also consider online office hours that can be accomplished via email, chat rooms, or even Second Life (www.secondlife.com).

Use the Resources Available to You

You do not have to create all of your course materials from scratch. Find out what resources you have available to you and then use them. This might be course management systems (such as Blackboard), speech-to-text software, blog software, or other online resources that can provide useful labs, examples, videos, or other course content. A wide variety of online activities are available on the web for free, such as WebQuests, videos, and lesson plans. For further details on how to use available resources, see Chapter 3 in this book and the second and third books in this series, *Online and Hybrid Learning Designs in Action* and *Online and Hybrid Learning Trends and Technologies*.

A good person to get to know for help with resources is your librarian. Your school's library may have materials relevant to your courses readily available. Also ask the librarian to visit your course's bulletin board or blog and post a note to guide students on using online library materials.

Next, get to know your technology support team. They may have tutorials for e-learners on such topics as how to join discussion forums, post assignments, participate in course activities, or check grades online. Remember to talk to other instructors. Find out if they have a model or template that you can follow. They can also be sources of useful knowledge with tips and ideas on how to design and teach a successful online course. Many times you will find that you have more resources than you imagined available among colleagues and services at your institution.

Conclusion

Now you have an understanding of why it is important and what it takes to prepare students for e-learning. We have included four supplements at the end of this chapter that focus on specific ideas, activities, and tips that you can give your students to help get them on the path toward success. Use these as guides for your discussions with students, or copy them as handouts that students can use throughout your course.

e-Learning can be a valuable experience for you and your students, but online success rarely happens by chance. Take time to prepare your students for their online learning experience. Their success often requires adapting previous study habits for the e-learning classroom, as well as learning new study skills that take advantage of e-learning technologies. Likewise, when you move from the traditional classroom to the online classroom, you'll need to make some changes in how you present course materials, structure learning, engage students, assess learning, and create a community of learners. Nevertheless, by adapting what you and your students have done successfully in the past and adopting a few new skills, you can effectively guide your e-learners to success.

Bibliography

Arabasz, P., Pirani, J., & Fawcett, D. (2003). *Supporting e-learning in higher education.* Boulder, CO: Educause Center for Applied Research.

Berge, Z., & Huang, Y. (2004). A model for sustainable student retention: A holistic perspective on the student dropout problem with special attention to e-learning. *DEOSNews, 13*(5).

Carr, S. (2000, February 11). As distance education comes of age, the challenge is keeping the students. *Chronicle of Higher Education.* Retrieved July 14, 2004, from http://chronicle.com/article/As-Distance-Education-Comes-of/14334

Corry, M., & Watkins, R. (2007). A student's guide to e-learning success. In W. Brandon (Ed.), *The elearning guild's handbook on e-learning strategy.* Santa Rosa, CA: eLearning Guild Press.

Cuseo, J. (2004a). The empirical case for first-year seminars: Well-documented effects on student retention & academic achievement. Retrieved July 14, 2004, from www.geocities.ws/deheky/fyejcase.html

Cuseo, J. (2004b). The case for faculty-student contact outside the classroom. Retrieved July 14, 2004, from www.geocities.ws/deheky/fyejstufac.html

Hirumi, A. (2003). Get a life: Six tactics for reducing time spent online. *Computers in Schools, 20*(3), 73–101.

Hughes, J. (2004). Supporting the online learner. In T. Anderson & F. Elloumi (Eds.), *Theory and practice of online learning.* Athabasca, Canada: Athabasca University.

International Association for K–12 Online Learning (iNACOL). (2011). *National standards for quality online courses (Ver. 2).* Vienna, VA: Author.

Morgan, G. (2003). *Faculty use of course management systems.* Boulder, CO: Educause Center for Applied Research.

National Resource Center for First-Year Experience and Students in Transition. (2000). National survey of first-year seminar programming. Retrieved July 22, 2004, from www.sc.edu/fye/research/surveyfindings/surveys/survey00.html

Niemczyk, M., Dwyer, H., & Savenye, W. (2000, October 25–28). Rookie Camp: An introductory unit for web-supplemented instruction at the high school level. Paper presented at the national conference of the Association of Educational Communications and Technology, Denver, CO.

Paul, R., & Elder, L. (1996). Universal intellectual standards. Published by the Foundation for Critical Thinking. Reprinted in October 2010. Retrieved on March 14, 2013, from www.criticalthinking.org/pages/universal-intellectual-standards/527

Phipps, R. A., & Merisotis, J. P. (1999, April). What's the difference? A review of contemporary research on the effectiveness of distance learning in higher education. Report for the American Federation of Teachers and the National Education Association. Washington, DC: Institute for Higher Education Policy.

Ronsisvalle, T., & Watkins, R. (2005). Student success in online K–12 education. *Quarterly Review of Distance Education, 6*(2), 117–124.

Watkins, R. (2003). Determining if distance education is the right choice: Applied strategic thinking in education. *Computers in the Schools, 20*(2), 103–120.

Watkins, R. (2003). Determining if distance education is the right choice: Applied strategic thinking in education. In M. Corry & C. H. Tu (Eds.), *Distance Education: What works well* (pp. 103–120). Binghamton, NY: Haworth Press.

Watkins, R. (2003). Online readings: Gaining the most from what you read. In G. Piskurich (Ed.), *Preparing for e-learning: A learner's perspective.* San Francisco, CA: Jossey-Bass.

Watkins, R. (2003). Readiness for online learning self-assessment. In E. Biech (Ed.), *The 2003 Pfeiffer annual: Training.* San Francisco, CA: Jossey-Bass Pfeiffer.

Watkins, R. (2004). 20 essential study tips for e-learners. In E. Biech (Ed.), *The 2004 Pfeiffer annual: Training.* San Francisco, CA: Jossey-Bass Pfeiffer.

Watkins, R. (2005a). Developing interactive e-learning activities. *Performance Improvement Journal, 44*(5).

Watkins, R. (2005b). E-learning study skills for online students. In J. V. Boettcher, L. Justice, K. Shenk, G. A. Berg, & P. L. Rogers (Eds.) *The encyclopedia of distance education* (Vol. II, pp. 794–800). Hershey, PA: Idea Group Reference.

Watkins, R. (2005c). *75 e-learning activities: Making online courses more interactive.* San Francisco, CA: Jossey-Bass Pfeiffer.

Watkins, R. (2005d). Three activities for making online courses more interactive. In E. Biech (Ed.), *The 2005 Pfeiffer annual: Training.* San Francisco, CA: Jossey-Bass Pfeiffer.

Watkins, R. (2008). Creating positive e-learning experiences for online students. In P. L. Rogers, G. A. Berg, J. V. Boettcher, C. Howard, L. Justice, & K. Shenk (Eds.), *The encyclopedia of distance education* (2nd ed.), (Vol. I, pp. 517–524)). Hershey, PA: IGI Global.

Watkins, R., & Schlosser, C. (2003). Conceptualizing educational research in distance education. *Quarterly Review of Distance Education, 4*(3), 331–341.

Watkins, R., & Corry, M. (2004). E-learning: It's not just for distance education students anymore. *E-Source, 1*(6), 1–2.

Watkins, R., Leigh, D., & Triner, D. (2004). Assessing readiness for e-learning. *Performance Improvement Quarterly, 17*(4), 66–79.

Watkins, R., & Corry, M. (2013). *E-learning companion: A student's guide to online success* (4th ed.). New York, NY: Cengage.

Supplement 5.A
Ten Tips for Students for Online Success

1. **Assess Your Readiness.** Before you begin an online course, you should spend a few minutes assessing your readiness. There are many similar resources available to check your e-learning readiness, including several online surveys (see example, http://distance. uh.edu/online_learning.html). These will help ensure that you take a look not only at your study skills, but also your technical skills and the availability of the required technology. Don't get discouraged if you have to increase your readiness in some way; the barriers are often fairly easy to overcome. As you examine your readiness, be honest with yourself and take the time to prepare adequately. Your success with this course and the overall e-learning experience depends on your preparation.

2. **Choose the Right Opportunities for Success.** It is important to recognize that e-learning is not ideal for all topics and all students. The decision about when to take an e-learning course depends on the subject matter, the technology, the instructor, and you—the learner. With this in mind, take a few minutes to look at the course description, the class syllabus, or an overview of your course options before deciding which format (classroom or online) is right for you. And if you have questions, don't hesitate to ask the instructor or your academic advisor. Your success depends on finding a good match between your readiness for e-learning and the e-learning course being offered. The essential question is "Can I be successful in this class?" Consider how the course requirements match up with your study skills and habits. For example, if the e-learning course requires a lot of independent note taking from streaming videos, and note taking is not your strongest skill even in traditional classroom courses, you may want to consider a different option. Another example would be an e-learning course that is mostly self-directed learning and has few due dates. If you are a person who requires more structure and guidance to be successful, then you may want to think twice about enrolling in this course. To be successful, try to understand your strengths and take courses that give you the best opportunities for success.

3. **Update Your Study Skills.** Sometimes your study habits won't match up well with course requirements. Maybe in past courses you rarely read required chapters, or you didn't like to take notes during lectures, and yet your e-learning course will require that you apply both of these skills. Or, if your course requires participation in an online group to strengthen study skills, but study groups haven't worked for you in the past, consider getting help through the use of software like Google Docs (docs.google.com) or Yahoo Groups (groups.yahoo.com). Similarly, if your note-taking skills when watching podcast lectures are a detriment to your learning, spend some time practicing this skill. And if practicing doesn't help, you can ask your instructor for a written transcript of the videos. If your study skills will be tested, then take the time to upgrade them. Many times you will find that the skills you have learned in a traditional classroom will get you started in an e-learning class, but then you'll need to modify them to be truly successful. The good news is that once you have updated your e-learning study skills for one class, they will

usually carry over to other classes; when you learn a new study skill, you will not have to learn it again.

4. **Actively Participate in Your Learning.** E-learning is not a passive activity. Your success in the traditional classroom is usually achieved through active participation and engagement through interactions with the instructor, the content, and your peers. The same is true for e-learning and maybe even more so because many times you will be working away from your instructors and classmates. It is much easier to get lost in cyberspace, for example, if you are not actively involved with the course. Some ways to stay actively involved include:

   ▸ Take notes while reading online,

   ▸ Participate in chat or discussion board conversations,

   ▸ Respond to emails promptly,

   ▸ Create online study groups,

   ▸ Create online social groups with your classmates, and

   ▸ Learn to e-learn.

5. **Use Appropriate Netiquette and Develop Written Communication Skills.** Online communication is very important to success in all courses and particularly in e-learning courses. This is due in part to the loss of cues—both physical and verbal—that generally help guide your communications with other people. In many respects, online learners become dependent on written communication, which offers far fewer cues that you can rely on to help transmit your message. To compensate for the loss of physical and verbal cues, develop outstanding written communication skills through email, chat, and other technologies (see Supplement 5.B for an email communications checklist). It is important to understand the nature of written communication in these new learning environments. If, for example, your primary means of communication with your instructor is through emails or online discussion boards, how does that change your study strategies? Students who have not developed appropriate netiquette skills run the risk of offending others and getting into online confrontations. Another example is the use of abbreviations. What would you do, for instance, if you did not know the meanings of AAMOF (as a matter of fact), AFAIK (as far as I know), AOTA (all of the above), TTYL (talk to you later), or TU (thank you)? You may want to ask peers that use lots of abbreviations to spell out each of these the first time they use them. A great online source for looking up unfamiliar abbreviations is NetLingo (www.netlingo.com/category/acronyms.php).

6. **Join Teams and Carry Your Weight.** Participating in an online group or team is new to many e-learners. Though a valuable starting place, talking with friends in Facebook is not the same as using online tools to work with your classmates on a course project. Nevertheless, many traditional classroom and e-learning courses now require teamwork. In general, participation is valuable to most e-learners because it provides a connection to other students and helps overcome feelings of isolation. Therefore, when working in an online team, it is useful to identify and set team roles, modes and intervals of communication (such as in-person or on Skype), ways to motivate each other, collaboration

software and websites (such as Google Docs), as well as other new techniques for group success. With the advent of new and exciting technologies, it is not unthinkable that you and your group might find new ways to use technology … technologies that did not exist when we wrote this chapter. You might even identify a gap in the existing technologies and design the tool that fills that gap.

7. **Create a Good Study Environment.** When you carve out time to do your e-learning, make sure you are ready to learn. This includes your physical environment (chair, lighting, noise, etc.); your online environment (software availability, file organization, font size, email and instant messengers turned off, etc.); and your physical comfort. This last item may require some explanation. For physical comfort, you should take a break from your computer at least every 30 minutes to stretch your legs and clear your head. You should also make sure you are properly nourished. Don't sit down at the keyboard if you are starving or thirsty. Take a few minutes before you get started to make sure you are ready to learn. If you have to take a break, take it.

8. **Evaluate Online Resources.** One of the great things and one of the bad things about the web is that there is a wealth of information available at your fingertips. The web is the proverbial two-edged sword. Unfortunately, mixed in with lots of high-quality information is inaccurate information. Your job is to separate the good from the bad. This can sometimes be a tough task. One way to verify the accuracy of information that many learners use is "triangulation." In other words, if you are doing research on a topic and you find the confirming information in three different locations on the web (and not the same information linked at three different websites), the odds of it being accurate increase greatly. If you can't find the information in other locations, then you should view it with a skeptical eye. Another skill is to evaluate the source of the information. For example, if you are researching a topic in a medical field, you should trust information found on the Mayo Clinic's website more than something posted to an individual's personal website. If you can, find out what the website does to police itself and what kind of standards it has involving the validity and reliability of information (see Supplement 5.D).

   Another extremely important point is to ensure that you apply ethical standards in citing the ideas, words, images, and intellectual property of others. If you have questions regarding what is plagiarism and what is not, contact your instructor before submitting the assignment. You can also review online resources, such as Indiana University's plagiarism tutorial (www.indiana.edu/~istd). As you write a paper or turn in assignments, it is also helpful to review a quick checklist to verify that you are giving appropriate credit for the work of others (see Supplement 5.C).

9. **Manage Your Time Wisely.** As an e-learner, many times you will be asked to work independently. This independence requires you to manage your time wisely to be successful. In addition, you may not only take online courses, but also work full- or part-time and juggle family and other responsibilities. All of this puts pressure on your time. Therefore, you should plan carefully. Plan your study time and don't let other things interfere. If you study at home, for example, make sure you communicate your schedule to other family members so they know when they should leave you alone to get your work

done. Make sure that you have a quiet place where you can study—this all goes into the planning process. Also, try to identify the times of day when you can be at your best to e-learn. Just because you have free time from 11 p.m. to 1 a.m. doesn't mean that is the best time for you to e-learn. You may have to turn off the television and e-learn during primetime. Because time is a very valuable asset, manage it wisely. Overall, make your e-learning time quality time.

10. **Use Time-Saving Technologies.** Most technologies are developed to help you in your daily life. With that in mind, think about ways that technology can help your e-learning experience. It can be knowing how to use shortcut keys for common functions such as cut and paste (Cntl+X and Cntl+V) or switching between open programs (Alt+Tab). Or it can be knowing how to use speech-to-text software (such as Dragon Speech Recognition) to dictate research papers. For example, try dictating your first draft of a literature review assignment rather than typing it out. Also, to save time, learn which search engines to use to find data quickly, download the correct plug-ins and add-ons, find out how to use citation and reference software, and locate an online list of what particular subject-related acronyms mean. Most importantly, keep an open mind and a willingness to try out technologies that might save you lots of valuable time and enhance your e-learning experience.

Supplement 5.B
Email Communications Skills: A Checklist

Instructions: Use the following checklist when writing emails to ensure that you are communicating effectively.

To whom are you sending this email?

☐ Friend ☐ Professor ☐ Project team ☐ Parent ☐ Other: _____

How did you copy others who are receiving the email?

☐ Included in To line ☐ Cc (carbon/duplicate copied) ☐ Bcc (blind carbon/duplicate copied)

Did you include the names of the people copied on the message at the end of the email?

☐ Yes ☐ No

If replying to a message, did you include the old message?

☐ Yes, at the bottom ☐ Yes, with my responses inserted into the old message ☐ No, did not include it

Why are you writing this email?

☐ Fun ☐ Request information ☐ Request favor ☐ Request action ☐ Provide information
☐ Other: _____

Which best describes your subject line?

☐ Specific ☐ Short ☐ Funny ☐ Missing ☐ Informative

How did you address the recipient?

☐ Formal (name and title) ☐ Informal (first name) ☐ Did not address the recipient

Did you highlight for the recipient any of the following?

☐ Actions required based on the email message

☐ Request for a responding email message

☐ When the action is requested (for instance, a reply message)

Did you use any of the following to emphasize important points?

☐ Numbered list ☐ Bullet list ☐ Bold ☐ Italics

Did you avoid the following?

☐ Extraneous information ☐ Sarcasm ☐ Questionable jokes ☐ Idioms ☐ Slang ☐ Jargon
☐ Acronyms that are not spelled out the first time ☐ Text message acronyms (for example, LOL or IMHO)

How long is your email?

☐ Short (one paragraph) ☐ Medium (2 to 3 paragraphs) ☐ Long (requires scrolling)

Does your "signature" include the following?

☐ Full name ☐ Email address for reply messages ☐ Alternative email address ☐ Phone number

If you attached a file, did you do any of the following?

☐ Tell the recipient that a file is attached

☐ Tell the recipient the type and format of the file (for example, Microsoft Word file)

☐ Request that the recipients let you know if they have troubles with the file

Did you…

☐ review the message two times to make sure that it clearly and succinctly says what you intended?

☐ review the message two times to make sure that it is well written (grammar, spelling, punctuation, polite, etc.)?

☐ spell check the message?

☐ for important emails, ask a friend to read it over as well?

☐ double check the recipients to ensure that it is being sent to the correct people?

Based on R. Watkins & M. Corry. (2013). *E-learning companion: A student's guide to online success* (4th ed.). Boston, MA: Cengage. More information is available at www.ryanrwatkins.com.

Supplement 5.C

Can I Use This? A Plagiarism, Copyright, and Intellectual Property Worksheet

Instructions: Complete a copy of this worksheet for each online resource you use in your paper.

Title: _____

Complete Website Address: _____

Date Retrieved: _____

Author(s): _____

Website owner: _____
(If not evident, go to www.internic.net/whois.html)

Volume, Issue, Page Numbers: _____

Is the copyright holder identified?

☐ Yes ☐ No

If Yes, who owns the copyright (e.g., magazine, journal, book publisher, or website)?

_____

What did you use from this resource?

☐ Quote(s) and their page numbers

☐ Paraphrased concept(s) and their page numbers

☐ Generalized concept(s)

Did you use more than 10% of the original ideas expressed by the author(s)?

☐ Yes ☐ No

If *Yes*, did you contact the copyright holder to gain rights to use this work?

☐ Yes ☐ No

Did you use an image, graphic, or illustration from this resource?

☐ Yes ☐ No

If *Yes*, did you contact the copyright holder to gain rights to use this work?

☐ Yes ☐ No

What percentage of your work was based on this resource?

☐ Less than 10% ☐ 10–25% ☐ More than 25% (not recommended)

List the original source articles, books, reports, websites, or other resources referenced by the author you used to verify this resource: _____

_____

Based on R. Watkins & M. Corry,. (2010). *E-learning companion: A student's guide to online success* (3rd ed.). Boston, MA: Cengage. More information is available at www.ryanrwatkins.com.

Supplement 5.D
Should I Use This?
An Online Resource Evaluation Form

Instructions: Complete a copy of this form for each online resource you use in your paper. When a resource does not pass the evaluation for reliability, quality, or usefulness, do not use it in your paper

Title: _____

Complete Website Address: _____

Date Retrieved: _____

Author(s): _____

Website owner: _____
(If not evident, go to www.internic.net/whois.html)

Volume, Issue, Page Numbers: _____

TABLE 5.D.1 ▶ Evaluation of a Resource's Reliability, Quality, and Usefulness

RELIABILITY	QUALITY	USEFULNESS
☐ Contact information included	☐ Avoids broad generalizations	☐ Relates to your goals
☐ Publication data provided	☐ Up-to-date resources and references	☐ Relates to your writing or research outline
☐ Satisfactory author credentials	☐ Consistency of facts	☐ Appropriate or similar audience
☐ Publication has a respectable reputation	☐ Appropriate grammar and spelling	☐ Appropriate level of detail for your goals
☐ Sponsoring organization of the author and/or publication are identified	☐ Avoids bias or one-sided perspectives	
☐ Blind peer-review process	☐ Comprehensive review of the topic	
☐ Information is consistent with that found in at least two other resources	☐ Citations and references are accurate and complete	
☐ From an online database of journals and publications	☐ This resource is the original source of information	
☐ Contacted author for additional information	☐ Support or corroboration of facts is provided in links or documentation	

Based on R. Watkins & M. Corry. (2013). *E-learning companion: A student's guide to online success* (4th ed.). New York, NY: Cengage. More information is available at www.ryanwatkins.com.

CHAPTER 6

Designing e-Learning Environments for Students with Special Needs

Carrie Straub and Tracy McKinney

STUDENTS WITH DISABILITIES and special needs are required by law to be given access to the general curriculum. However, providing for their instruction using the principles of universal design for learning may also improve the educational experience for all students. Our goal is to help you create engaging online learning experiences for all students, including children with high- and low-incidence disabilities, such as learning disabilities, emotional and behavioral disorders, attention deficits, vision impairments, hearing impairments, autism, cognitive challenges, and physical challenges, as well as students for whom English is a second language. To achieve our goal, we interpret laws that govern education of students with special needs, introduce the principles of universally designed instruction, and provide examples of how online instruction can be universally designed using the Web Accessibility Initiative guidelines to meet the varied needs of students.

Meet Alex

Alex is an eleventh grader enrolled in a boarding school for students with special needs. Alex has attention deficit hyperactivity disorder (ADHD) and a learning disability. Alex desperately wants to take an advanced physics course, but the school, which is located in a rural area, does not offer advanced physics because it has no qualified teachers for the subject. The school director decides to explore online accredited course options for Alex. A quick Internet search leaves her optimistic after she identifies at least 10 fully online high schools with advanced physics classes. Things are looking good for Alex, so he writes home to his father, an engineer. As a team, the school and Alex's father evaluate the online courses and choose the one that looks as if it is the most engaging and rigorous. After a five-minute, online enrollment procedure, which mostly consists of entering credit card information, Alex has his username and password and is ready to jump into his new physics course.

Alex starts his online coursework with motivation and interest, but his motivational level quickly wanes when he is faced with the realities of the course's activities. The course is divided into modules, each of which contains lengthy readings interspersed with images, links to outside resources, and a multiple-choice test at the end. When Alex prints out the readings, he is faced with almost 50 pages of printed content per module that he must read, essentially on his own. Sure, his online teacher is "always available," but the phone calls cannot replace in-depth interaction with the teacher or the material, and Alex's comprehension of the content suffers. Alex plods forward to complete the course activities; he follows the hyperlinks that lead him to websites containing material written well above his reading level and even more information that he must wade through. The multiple-choice tests contain even more reading, but Alex is determined to do well. He must earn an 80% to pass on to the next module. Alex takes the test three times and finally memorizes the missed answers he needs to pass, although as Alex says, "I have no clue about physics, but I know how to take the test."

Alex proceeds in this manner for two more modules, but as the content becomes more challenging, his lack of comprehension causes problems. Alex's inability to focus on the text leaves him vulnerable to distractions, so he begins to surf the Internet rather than reading the required contents. He asks for help from his teachers on campus, but they do not know the content area and are unable to explain the concepts. His online teacher answers what questions she can over the phone and instructs him to reread the chapter to "get it." He bombs the fourth module and is unable to pass the test. His motivation level takes a nosedive. Alex begins acting out to avoid his physics class, so his dad and the boarding school director decide to withdraw him from the class. Because Alex does not have a physics credit, he does not get into the college of his choice and instead attends the local community college. When he realizes that many of his classes are online, he drops out of college because he knows he "can't learn online."

Alex's experiences with online education could have been avoided. In his case, the design of the online course materials, not the technology, was the barrier to learning. The large amount of reading without adequate comprehension support proved to be too challenging for him to tackle with a learning disability. The open-ended nature of the online activities did not provide the scaffolding Alex needed to focus on and attend to his schoolwork. In addition, the multiple-choice test format did not allow Alex to demonstrate his learning in creative, meaningful ways.

Although Vasquez and Straub's (2012) systematic review of the research literature on online instruction found that "very little attention is devoted to the use of distance education technology with K–12 special education or at-risk students…" (p. 38), there are articles that report direct measures of achievement associated with distance education for students with special needs. For example, research by Savi, Savenye, and Rowland (2008) indicated that universally designed online instruction and materials were effective in providing online access to students with special needs. Englert and colleagues (Englert, Wu, & Zhao, 2005; Englert, Yong, Dunsmore, Collings, & Wolbers, 2007) also found value in utilizing online technologies to weave supportive scaffolding into instruction. When teachers are well versed in the principles for designing online materials for students with special needs, teachers can avoid designing online and hybrid environments that create barriers to learning.

Our goal in this chapter is to help you create engaging online learning experiences and materials for students with special needs by doing the following:

▶ Interpreting U.S. laws that govern education of students with special needs (Elementary and Secondary Education Act; Individuals with Disabilities Education Improvement Act).

▶ Introducing the principles of universally designed instruction, which help to create learning environments that are accessible to all students and aligned with learning objectives.

▶ Illustrating and providing examples of how online instruction can be universally designed, using the Web Accessibility Initiative guidelines to meet the varied needs of students with high- and low-incidence disabilities, such as learning disabilities, emotional and behavioral disorders, attention deficits, vision impairments, hearing impairments, autism, cognitive challenges, and physical challenges, as well as meeting the needs of students for whom English is a second language.

Defining Categories of Special Needs

Numerous categories are used to classify students with special needs. However, these categories can be defined in various ways, and even the legal definitions can be ambiguous. We will explore the following categories: learning disabilities, emotional and behavioral disorders, attention deficits, hearing impairments, vision impairments, autism, intellectual disabilities, and physical disabilities. Many of the definitions of disabilities are taken from U.S. legislation pertaining to students with disabilities and the Individuals with Disabilities Education Improvement Act of 2004 (IDEA), which we will explore later.

Learning Disabilities

Gargiulo (2009) explains that no two individuals with learning disabilities (LDs) are identical, and professionals in different areas of specialization (e.g., speech language pathologists, teachers, psychologists) often use different terms to define the disabilities. Learning disabilities are sometimes also referred to as perceptual disabilities, minimal brain dysfunction, dyslexia, or developmental aphasia. These disabilities are thought to have the common characteristic of central nervous dysfunction. However, it is commonly agreed that children with learning disabilities have normal intelligence; they just do not perform at the level of their classmates and peers. The U.S. federal legal definition of an LD states that the student's struggles cannot be attributed to another factor, such as mental retardation or hearing impairment (IDEA, 2004). They may occur with other disabilities, but are not the result of those conditions, and they are also not the result of environmental factors such as cultural differences or deficit in skills as a result of poor instruction. A learning disability is defined in the Individuals with Disabilities Education Improvement Act (2004) as a "disorder in one or more of the basic psychological processes involved in understanding or in using written or spoken language which may manifest itself in an imperfect ability to listen, think, speak, write, spell, and do mathematical calculations."

To explain the difference between the learning challenges faced by students with LDs and those without, Kutscher (2005) describes a typically developing student as traveling rolling hills and, conversely, depicts a student with an LD as traveling a jagged, rocky mountain. The valleys can be thought of as learning differences, although if there are enough contrasts between the peaks and valleys, they may be described as a learning disability (Kutscher, 2005).

Emotional and Behavioral Disorders

Taylor, Smiley, and Richards (2009) note that finding a global definition of emotional and behavioral disorders is difficult, similar to the difficulty of finding a definition for LDs. Behavior considered "normal" can be relative to the environment (Gargiulo, 2009). As all children are unique and behave differently in varying situations, measuring emotions and behaviors is challenging. To further complicate assessment, different cultures have varied beliefs and norms about acceptable and nonacceptable behaviors (Gargiulo, 2009).

The defining feature of an emotional or behavioral disability is that these types of disabilities impair students' abilities to learn and to maintain satisfactory relationships (IDEA, 2004). Individuals with these disabilities also display inappropriate behaviors and feelings during normal circumstances, appear unhappy or depressed much of the time, and connect physical symptoms to personal or school difficulties (IDEA, 2004). The phrase "serious emotional disturbance" has fallen out of favor due to its stigmatizing terminology; now professionals are more likely to use some variation of "emotional and behavioral disorder" (Gargiulo, 2009). For our purposes, it is important to remember that students with emotional or behavioral disorders are also entitled by law to supports that help them succeed academically.

Attention Deficits

Key terms typically used when defining individuals with attention deficits include *inattention, impulsivity,* and *hyperactivity* (Smith, 2007). Attention deficits are not combined and listed as a disability in IDEA but, instead, fall under the category of "other health impaired." Kutscher (2005) explains that individuals with attention deficits can focus on videos, games, and other highly preferred activities for long spans of time. However, the attention deficits are more evident when a student is asked to participate in or complete a task that is not highly preferred or captivating. Kutscher (2005) goes on to explain that while individuals with attention deficits struggle to block out internal and external distractions, they lack the self-control to refrain from acting upon these distractions.

The prefrontal lobe, in coordination with other areas of the brain, controls impulsiveness and does not function properly in individuals with attention deficits (Kutscher, 2005). Hyperactivity is typically manifested as an inability to be still and can manifest in the areas of communication and motor skills. Inattentiveness includes poor attention span, incomplete tasks, poor short-term memory, and avoidance of tasks with sustained mental effort (Pauc, 2006).

Hearing Impairments

Hearing impairments can be simply defined as hearing that is impaired (IDEA, 2004) or disordered (Gargiulo, 2009). Szelazkiewicz (2002) states that a student with a hearing impairment can be classified as hearing impaired, deaf, or hard of hearing. Hearing impairment is used to explain any intensity of hearing loss from mild to profound. Individuals described as deaf have hearing losses so profound that hearing cannot be their sole source of verbal communication. Individuals who are classified as hard of hearing have a hearing loss but still use hearing as their foremost means of receiving verbal communication (Szelazkiewicz, 2002).

Visual Impairments

Visual impairments are characterized in IDEA as impairments in vision that have a negative impact on an individual's academic achievement. Visual impairments encompass partial sight or low vision and blindness (2004). To differentiate between individuals with partial sight or low vision and those with blindness, one must understand how visual acuity is measured. Generally speaking, visual acuity is measured at 20 feet (Taylor, Smiley, & Richards, 2009). If individuals being assessed can discriminate letters or forms perfectly at 20 feet, they can see what individuals with typical vision can see at that same distance and are said to have 20/20 vision (Taylor et al., 2009).

Autism

Autism is a disorder that involves impaired communication, limited social skills, and restricted areas of interests (American Psychiatric Association (APA), 2000; IDEA, 2004). It is one of the five disorders grouped under the Autism Spectrum Disorders category of the *Diagnostic and*

Statistical Manual of Mental Disorders (DSM). The most recent version of the DSM, often referred to as the DSM-IV-TR (the fourth edition with text revisions), lists the following as common characteristics of individuals with autism: repetitive speech, abnormal language, insistence on routines, limited interests, and onset prior to age 3 (APA, 2000). According to an autism advocacy organization, Autism Speaks (2011), 1 out of every 110 children and 1 out of every 70 boys are diagnosed with autism. While autism is defined in the DSM-IV-TR, the criteria to receive special education services vary from state to state (MacFarlane & Kanaya, 2009).

Intellectual Disabilities

Smith (2001) explains that there are variations on the definition of an intellectual disability. However, most definitions include considerations of an individual's intelligence, cognition, and/or impaired ability to learn and/or perform functional living skills. Some definitions have age of onset requirements; for example, the American Association on Intellectual and Developmental Disabilities (AAIDD, 2013) states that intellectual disability originates early in an individual's life. The AAIDD's definition says, "Intellectual disability is a disability characterized by significant limitations both in intellectual functioning and in adaptive behavior, which covers many everyday social and practical skills. The disability originates before the age of 18."

Physical Disabilities

The U.S. Department of Education (2009) reports that in the 2006–07 school year, 0.1% of all students, ages 3 to 21, enrolled in schools have physical disabilities. Cerebral palsy, spina bifida, and muscular dystrophy are some of the most common physical disabilities (Heller & Gargiulo, 2009). King, Law, Hurley, Petrenchick, and Schwellnus (2010) describe physical disabilities as physical functional limitations that are related to ongoing conditions, such as cerebral palsy. IDEA (2004) expands on this to say that physical disabilities may adversely affect the individual's educational performance. Hardman, Drew, Egan, and Wolf (1993) add that physical disability may also impact individuals' mobility and coordination in addition to affecting their communication, ability to achieve at the same academic level as their peers, and personal adjustment. However, individuals with physical disabilities whose impairments do not have a negative impact on their educational performance typically do not qualify for special education services as outlined by IDEA 2004.

High-Incidence versus Low-Incidence Disabilities

Sabornie, Cullinan, Osborne, and Brock (2005) explain that high-incidence disabilities include learning disabilities, intellectual disabilities, and emotional and behavioral disorders. Jackson (2005) places attention deficits in the category of high-incidence disabilities, indicating that teachers are more likely to provide educational services to students in high-incidence categories. Autism, severe physical disabilities, hearing impairments, and vision impairments are categorized by Grigal, Neubert, Moon, and Graham (2003) as low-incidence disabilities. Although the prevalence of autism has risen to nearly 1 in 70 among boys, it continues to reside in the low-incidence category.

Services among high-incidence and low-incidence disabilities should be based on the individuals' needs as opposed to their labels. There should not be a list of predetermined services that relate to specific disabilities. Each individualized education plan (IEP) should be explicitly tailored for a specific individual (Yell & Busch, 2012). Further, the educational placement should not be set according to a label (Yell & Drasgow, 2013). Individuals with disabilities are entitled to an education in the least restrictive environment. The continuum of placement options range from full inclusion to a complete self-contained classroom.

Legislation Governing Students with Special Needs

Congress reauthorized the Elementary and Secondary Education Act as the No Child Left Behind Act of 2001 (NCLB, 2002). This law reiterated former President George W. Bush's belief in increasing educational accountability, and included an expectation that all students would demonstrate mathematics and reading proficiency. Although the term "No Child Left Behind" has fallen out of favor, its principles remain in place. We will call the law by its original name, the Elementary and Secondary Education Act (ESEA).

While calling for proficiency in mathematics and reading, the 2001 reauthorization of ESEA also mandated that most students (including the majority of students with special needs) between Grades 3 and 8 take yearly assessments and that schools show adequate annual progress with 100% proficiency by 2012 (NCLB, 2001). The law stated that schools that consistently failed to meet adequate yearly progress would be provided more resources and parents would be provided the opportunity to transfer their children into other schools. ESEA also placed expectations on teachers by mandating that all teachers be "highly qualified," according to each state's criteria, by the school year 2005–06 (Gargiulo, 2006). ESEA was designed to raise academic achievement levels, close the achievement gap among all students, and offer more quality teachers (Darling-Hammond, 2007).

In 1975, the Education for All Handicapped Children Act was passed. It is now commonly referred to as Public Law 94-142 or the Individuals with Disabilities Education Act (IDEA) (IDEA, 2004; Wright & Wright, 2004). Before the passage of this law, one million students with special needs were excluded from public schools. IDEA was most recently revised in 2004 and is responsible for ensuring that students receive a free and appropriate education and for advocating research-based practices. As a result of IDEA, parents are expected to play a larger role in their child's education, as formalized by an IEP, customized to meet their child's needs. IDEA (2004) includes four parts. Part A is dedicated to definitions and general provisions. Part B focuses on private school services, unilateral placement changes by parents, evaluations, eligibility, and IEPs. Placement decisions and procedural safeguards are also addressed in this section of IDEA. Infants and toddlers with disabilities are covered in Part C of IDEA. Part D, titled "National Activities to Improve Education of Children with Disabilities," discusses the need for positive growth in the areas of special education programs, teacher preparation, sharing information, and supporting and applying relevant research to education.

Meeting the Needs of an Increasingly Diverse Student Population

An increasing number of students with special needs are being included in general education settings (whether online, a hybrid of online and face-to-face, or traditional classrooms) as a result of legislation and accountability measures. The trend toward inclusion is part of the larger civil rights movement, beginning with the 1954 landmark court case *Brown v. Board of Education,* which mandates equal access to opportunity.

Today's regular classroom teachers are faced not only with increasing numbers of students with special needs, but also increasingly diverse students. The U.S. Census Bureau (2008) predicts that by 2050, 62% of children will be from minority ethnic groups. One semester you may find that your class includes students with learning disabilities and students with autism, while the next semester's class comprises several students who are English language learners and others with emotional and/or behavioral disorders. As a teacher, you will be held accountable for meeting their educational needs by giving them equal access to the curriculum.

Equal Access to Facilities

The concept of equal access to opportunity is grounded in the civil rights movement, which gained momentum in the 1960s. Reforms began with equal access to physical structures, reflected in the Architectural Barriers Act of 1968 (ABA), which required that buildings financed by federal grants or loans be designed and constructed to be accessible to persons with disabilities. In 1990, section II of the Americans with Disabilities Act (ADA) further extended the reach of the law and required that all public transportation and telecommunication systems be accessible to those with disabilities.

Equal Access to Curriculum

Around the same time that the ADA was signed into law, education reformers called for equal access to educational curricula as well. Educational researchers at the Center for Applied Special Technology (CAST) envisioned a curriculum that was flexible and adaptable to the needs of varied learners, much like structures and products from the universal design movement in architecture that were designed to provide access for the broadest range of people, with and without disabilities. CAST researchers called for educators to design materials that, "from the outset consider the needs of the greatest number of possible users, eliminating the need for costly, inconvenient, and unattractive adaptations" (CAST, 2011b, para. 3). This concept is especially relevant when designing online environments, which require more upfront time for planning and design than traditional lecture-style classes. Later, we'll explore how CAST guidelines can help you design materials that are flexible and adaptable to varied learner needs.

Today, the belief that individuals deserve equal access to educational opportunities is now reflected in legislation at all levels. In 2008, universal access to curricula was codified in the federal Higher Education Opportunity Act as the "Universal Design for Learning" and described as a "scientifically valid framework" that "reduces barriers in instruction, provides appropriate accommodations, supports, and challenges, and maintains high achievement expectations for all students, including students with disabilities and students who are limited English proficient." Although this legislation is applicable to the higher education setting, it indicates a trend toward universal access, which may eventually be reflected in legislation at the K–12 level (Higher Education Opportunity Act, 2008).

Web Accessibility Initiative

The Web Accessibility Initiative (WAI) is a global project by the World Wide Web Consortium to make the Internet fully accessible to people with disabilities. The WAI disseminates information for and offers guidelines about designing online materials for the Internet. You may be overwhelmed by the thought of technical demands for web content accessibility, but the WAI offers a quick reference guide to assist designers. Following the guidelines will help you make your website flexible and accessible to individuals with many types of disabilities. If you are not sure how to achieve some of the technical requirements, the WAI provides technical help. Check out the website's guide to meeting requirements at www.w3.org/WAI/WCAG20/quickref. Under the Web Content Accessibility Guidelines (WCAG) 2.0 requirements (success criteria) and techniques, is the WCAG 2.0 Quick Reference List on the site's first page:

1.1 Text Alternatives: Provide alternatives for any non-text content so that it can be changed into other forms that people need, such as large print, braille, speech, symbols or simpler language.

1.2 Time-Based Media: Provide alternatives for time-based media (such as using text to support prerecorded audio files and vice versa).

1.3 Adaptable: Create content that can be presented in different ways (for example, simpler layout) without losing information or structure.

1.4 Distinguishable: Make it easier for users to see and hear content including separating foreground from background.

2.1 Keyboard Accessible: Make all functionality available from a keyboard.

2.2 Enough Time: Provide users enough time to read and use content.

2.3 Seizures: Do not design content in a way that is known to cause seizures. Ensure that no component of the content flashes more than three times in any 1-second period, and avoid fully saturated reds for flashes.

2.4 Navigable: Provide ways to help navigate, find content, and determine where they are.

3.1 Readable: Make text content readable and understandable.

3.2 Predictable: Make web pages appear and operate in predictable ways.

3.3 Input Assistance: Help users avoid and correct mistakes.

4.1 Compatible: Maximize compatibility with current and future user agents, including assistive technologies.

These guidelines represent the minimum design standards for accessibility. A more comprehensive list of advisory guidelines on the WCAG site enables further flexibility; when followed, the detailed instructions would allow teachers to address the needs of as many individuals as possible.

Another helpful resource for implementing these guidelines is a checklist from the program of the Disability Resource Center at the University of Arkansas at Little Rock, Project PACE (1999). This checklist provides design suggestions for accessibility and HTML code or resources to execute the suggestions. Cornell University (2012) also supplies useful information before and during course design. Cornell's Intro to Web Accessibility site contains numerous suggestions for adaptations that will make its and other sites more accessible to most people with disabilities.

Brain-Based Principles for Universal Design

Researchers in the field of neuroscience (the study of the brain and the nervous system) are slowly establishing connections between learning and brain function. The general structure of the human brain can help inform us as to what components of curricula need to be adaptable and flexible to meet the needs of the varied learners (and brains) you will have in your online environment.

The human brain is a complex, multilayered, multifunctional organ. As humans learn, face challenges, and experience life, neurons (specialized brain cells) form connections with other neurons across the entire brain, and create networks of neurons (neural networks) unique to each individual. Brain scanning technologies, such as functional magnetic resonance imaging (fMRI), provide evidence that individuals have similar overarching brain structures and functions, but degrees of performance, perception, and response time vary.

The expanding knowledge in the field of neuroscience coupled with research in education point to three overlapping neural networks in the brain—recognition, strategic, and affective—that regulate learning and emotions. The recognition network involves gathering, identifying, and categorizing information. The strategic network involves organizing and expressing ideas. The affective network involves students' interest and motivation—"how they are challenged, excited, or interested" (CAST, 2011a, p. 1). These networks correspond to the three principles of universal design for learning (UDL): provide multiple means of representation, action and expression, and engagement—explained in the numbered list on the following page (CAST, 2011a, p. 1).

Acknowledging brain-based differences allows educators to recognize and plan for students' differences when creating curricula. Providing universal access to learning materials and experiences benefits all students, not only those with disabilities and special needs. For educators who create and modify materials for online learning environments, planning flexible, adaptable curricula is a valuable way to prevent problems and save time. In fact, researchers at various universities across the United States have found that well-designed online environments decrease the amount of time that teachers spend answering routine questions about assignment procedures, leaving more time for teaching and feedback (Warren, Dondlinger, & Barab, 2008; Hirumi, 2003). Well-designed lessons will save you time in the long run, and a key component to a well-designed lesson is flexibility (CAST, 2010).

Working from the premise that "one size does *not* fit all," researchers at CAST (2011a) have explored the structure and function of the human brain and developed three simple principles for designing curricula so that they can be flexible enough to accommodate variations in students' abilities and learning styles. According to CAST, these are the principles of the universal design for learning (UDL):

1. **Provide multiple means of representation (brain's recognition network).**
   Present information and content in different ways. This includes providing multiple ways to access the content (text, audio, and visual formats) and allows learners to choose their preferred format for gaining information.

2. **Provide multiple means of action and expression (brain's strategic network).**
   Differentiate the ways that students can express what they know. This involves allowing individuals to demonstrate knowledge and skills in varied ways.

3. **Provide multiple means of engagement (brain's affective network).** Stimulate interest and motivation for learning. This means making opportunities for exploration of material in a variety of settings so that learning is individualized and meaningful, increasing learners' engagement.

Multiple Means of Representation

The first principle of universal access aims to provide learners with multiple means of representation, allowing the human brain to take in information delivered in many different formats. Brain structures housed in the cortex (the gray, wrinkly matter on the outer layer of the brain) process sensory information and send it to other parts of the brain for additional activity. This web of connections has been termed the recognition network (CAST, 2010). Visual information is processed in the occipital lobe, located in the back of the cortex, while information about touch and other sensations from the skin are processed in the parietal lobe at the top of the cortex. Hearing is processed in the temporal lobes, located at the side of the cortex, just above the ears. From a survival perspective, humans benefit from gaining information about the environment from varied sensory perspectives (sight, sound, smell), which keep us informed about potential opportunities or threats to our safety. Because the brain is wired to learn from the environment by gathering information from multiple senses simultaneously, your lessons can take advantage of this specialized feature by providing learners with rich, multimedia online materials and experiences to enhance their learning.

However, when providing multiple means of representation, you should allow for the cognitive processing of information by allocating multimedia materials so learners do not have to split their attention simultaneously across channels of information (e.g., closed captions which can be turned on or off, so students who do not need them are not distracted). Multimedia engagement should also be paced during instruction to prevent cognitive overload (Mayer, Heiser, & Lonn, 2000). Multimedia that is modifiable (e.g., sound, speed, closed captions) is especially useful for students who may need extended time to process information, such as those with learning disabilities, attention deficits, and cognitive impairments.

Multiple Means of Action and Expression

The second principle of universal access, providing multiple means of action and expression, is supported by activity that takes place in the decision-making areas of the brain. Researchers term this group of neural connections in the brain the strategic network (CAST, 2010). Activities such as planning, reasoning, and decision making are controlled in the frontal lobe of the cortex, just behind the forehead, although this portion of the brain is well connected to and reliant upon many other areas of the brain. The pre-frontal cortex, at the very front of the brain, "constitutes the highest level of cortical hierarchy" and is involved with the execution of actions (Fuster, 2001, p. 319) and oversees complex strategic competencies, such as identifying goals, selecting appropriate plans, and self-monitoring. As educators, we are concerned with our learners' abilities to select and use appropriate strategies for learning; therefore, we provide opportunities for them to activate the strategic networks of their brains, so they can plan, execute, and monitor their actions and skills (CAST, 2010).

Multiple Means of Engagement

Providing for multiple means of engagement is the final principle essential to flexible curriculum planning. Engaging learners is one of the most challenging tasks for teachers, and the online environment presents unique challenges to students, so we must plan materials and experiences that keep them coming back. The affective networks of the brain attach emotional significance to objects and actions we experience, influencing what we see and do (CAST, 2010). Awareness of and planning for the emotional components of learning will give your learners opportunities to connect their feelings and motivations with your materials, engaging them and bringing them back to your online environment for more.

The Bottom Line: Flexibility Provides Accessibility

If the concepts of neuroanatomy seem overwhelming to you, the bottom line is this: Designing materials that are flexible provides students multiple opportunities for accessing curriculum. To help, the researchers at CAST created an educator's checklist that can guide you through evaluation of materials you create or modify. Keep in mind that these principles apply to all types of curricula, not only those made for the online environment, so you can use the checklist to evaluate your online and hybrid materials. The checklist is free to use and contains items that will remind you to check for basic concepts, such as text in auditory and image format, as well as complex concepts, such as the incorporation of progress monitoring. Some of the guidelines overlap with those of the Web Accessibility Initiative. The educator's checklist is one of many resources that can be found on the CAST website (http://udlonline.cast.org); go to Module 1 and then Module 2. On the upper right side of the first pages of the modules are tabs for the UDL Checklist. CAST's site provides a wealth of excellent resources as well, such as lesson planning guides and technology resources. Cornell University also has various links that give accessibility information and suggestions (www.it.cornell.edu/policies/accessibility/primer/wa1_intro.cfm#cornelle). Additionally, Colorado State University lists several suggestions and instructions for creating accessible online content (http://accessproject.colostate.edu).

The unique needs of your learners do not have to require you to plan mountains of accommodations. Systematic planning of instructional design that includes multiple means of representation, expression, and engagement can create user-friendly, accessible learning environments for all learners, not only those with special needs. Using the principles that allow for universal access to your instruction, you will also save yourself from having to make accommodations for every type of learner. Next, we'll give you specific examples of how you can apply the principles of UDL from CAST when creating your online materials and activities to ensure optimal flexibility and accessibility.

Creating Quality Materials and Activities

Quality online materials and activities have two essential features: they are aligned to course goals and accessible to learners. Whether you are creating your own materials or adapting materials created by others, it is worth your time to evaluate everything for indicators of alignment and accessibility. Well-designed materials allow teachers to spend less time answering questions about assignment procedures and spend more time ensuring that students understand critical content (Warren et al., 2008).

Alignment

When creating or evaluating materials, it is essential to consider if they are aligned to your overall goals for your coursework. Your chosen learning objectives should be clearly stated and supported by your content (Lenz, Deshler, & Kissam, 2004). In turn, your content should clearly align with your assessment plan (Deno, Fuchs, Marston, & Shin, 2001). The alignment of objectives, content, and assessment (identified by Hirumi as fundamental to high-quality instruction in Chapter 1 of this book) reduces the cognitive load needed to read and digest the materials, allowing learners to focus on the content rather than spending mental energy figuring out what is relevant and what is not.

Identifying the critical concepts that have the "highest social impact" (Lenz et al., 2004, p. 55) and ensuring that those concepts are clearly communicated, using multiple means of representation (text, audio, visuals), will set your students up for success. It is also important to evaluate the content to determine which ideas are the most difficult to understand. For example, a teacher creating materials for a unit on photosynthesis might decide that conversion of light and carbon dioxide to create food is a critical concept. As a result, she decides to spend the majority of her efforts on making sure that the concept of conversion is communicated and supported by the materials and activities presented. Students with learning disabilities and cognitive impairments will benefit from having the most important ideas communicated and supported with activities (Lenz et al., 2004).

Along with determining critical content and big ideas, if you have the ability to meet face-to-face with your students during your course, you will also need to consider which materials and experiences are best-suited for online versus face-to-face modules. In Chapter 2, Hirumi provides guidelines for determining which aspects of a course and lesson to put online and which aspects to facilitate face-to-face. Face-to-face sessions give you the opportunity to deliver and review content that is difficult to understand but important to the learning objectives. Social learning strategies, such as peer teaching, can be used in face-to-face settings to maximize learning and engage students with disabilities (Heron, Welsch, & Goddard, 2003).

Accessibility

The principles of universal design for learning (UDL) coupled with the technical guidelines provided by the Web Accessibility Initiative can help you to evaluate and create accessible materials. Now, we'll show you specific examples of how you can create universally accessible online materials.

Multiple means of representation. Using multimedia, visuals, charts, and graphics to convey information allows all types of learners to capture meaning. Using visual aids increases comprehension and retention (Bos & Vaughn, 2006). Keep a uniform organization throughout the website to help learners become familiar with the setting. This reduces the cognitive load needed to learn a new format for each lesson, module, or page. Use contrasting colors for easy reading; black and white is the most readable, while red paired with green presents problems for people who are color-blind. Ideally, your design should give your students the option of color, font size, and font type. You should use status icons (e.g., "slide 3 of 4") to help the reader to follow along easily. This practice helps students with attention deficits and learning disabilities to pace themselves and maintain attention. Use advance organizers, which are activities or materials that orient the student to upcoming content (Slavin, 2000). Advance organizers help students organize and retain the information and can also be a great way to introduce vocabulary to students learning the English language as well as those with learning disabilities.

Harris, Graham, and Mason (2002) demonstrated positive results with the use of a writing process strategy for students with special needs in traditional face-to-face settings. The strategy employs the use of mnemonic devices, in which the first letter of each step of the strategy forms a word. The writing process strategy POW (Pick idea, Organize TREE, Write and check) can be modified for an online learning environment by making an interface that advances at each step of the strategy. Another strategy for organizing writing is embedded within POW, providing an opportunity to hyperlink to the other strategy (TREE—Topic sentence, Reasons, Examples, Ending) and demonstrating the relationship between the two processes. Further, images can be used to scaffold the text. Figure 6.1 provides an example of how multiple means of representation can be used to communicate the POW writing strategy. Although the text and image in the figure are static on paper, in the online environment, they can be modified and partitioned to show only text, letters, or images in multiple orders and configurations. This enables students to memorize and internalize the strategy. The POW strategy has been identified as a promising instructional practice for students with special needs who are learning to write in synchronous online environments (Straub, 2012).

FIGURE 6.1   ▶   POW writing process strategy in multiple representations

When including images, be sure to tag all of them with labeled names that make sense with the text and allow text-reader software to read the labels. Create captions for the images that can stand on their own in case the images they describe are not visible to the reader. If you want to check your work, use the nonvisual, desktop access, open-source software at WebAIM (www. wave.webaim.org) to evaluate your online materials for the visually impaired.

Multiple means of action and expression. Allow your students to respond in multiple formats (text, image, digital or video recording). By providing flexible means of response, over time your students will learn how to choose a format that best communicates their learning, rather than becoming reliant upon only one format. We recommend that you use flexible methods of response throughout your lessons to assess students' understanding in varying formats. We also encourage you to mix multiple-choice and short-answer assessments in with your other means of assessing student progress. The guiding idea should be that you do not evaluate students using only one test or assignment or one testing or assignment format for their overall grade. Throughout the course, have students take brief, untimed, multiple-choice quizzes, which serve to reinforce learning and provide progress monitoring for you and your students. Over time, you can analyze the results of the quizzes to determine which answers are missed on a regular basis and use this information to modify your instruction or quiz questions. If students take low-stakes, multiple-choice assessments throughout the semester, for the final project, they can demonstrate a deeper understanding of the content by creating a portfolio that incorporates digital imagery, audio recordings, and written text.

Multiple means of engagement. By using real-life examples, based on typical student interests, you can also create accessibility for students with disabilities who face academic challenges. Engaging assignments that are flexible and can accommodate many interests will benefit all students and make your classes more enjoyable. Students with emotional and behavioral disorders will especially benefit from the use of materials and experiences that allow choice and flexibility. This hard-to-reach population often lacks interest in academics, but allowing them to make personal choices can increase their interest. Research shows that building choices into your assignments not only increases interest and engagement, but also decreases off-task and disruptive behavior (Kern, Bambara, & Fogt, 2002). Create learning projects that give students opportunities to apply learning to their own lives, such as taking digital pictures of images around their neighborhood, interviewing friends and family members, or applying course content to tell a personal narrative. Projects that involve personal components provide learners opportunities to engage their emotions based on their interests, an important motivator.

Another feature important to consider when creating or reviewing materials is the use of positive behavioral momentum (PBM). This behavioral strategy has been successfully used across many disciplines to bring out compliance in all types of people. Teachers, salespeople, politicians, and other influencers capitalize on this technique to persuade others to do what they want, and you can easily incorporate PBM into your materials in online or hybrid settings. First, choose a target behavior that your students might avoid but that you would like them to complete, such as a quiz, an essay, or a tedious assignment. Then choose three simple behaviors that your students are likely to do (high-probability behaviors); these may be as simple as filling out their names on an online form, choosing a favorite color or picture, or watching a short video. Arrange all four behaviors in a sequence with the three high-probability behaviors first, followed up by the target behavior. As your students complete each task, momentum will build that should carry through to the final target behavior. Research has shown that students are more likely to complete the target behavior when three high-probability behaviors have been completed before it (Lee, Belfiore, & Bundin, 2008).

You can also capitalize on the social nature of learning. Social psychologists have long theorized that learning is a social process (see discussion of Vygotsky's theories in Bos & Vaughn, 2006). Most students enjoy working together on projects and will be motivated to complete tasks when their peers are involved. Students with emotional and behavioral disorders, attention deficits, language delays, and autism benefit from supported group work with peers. In general, students with disabilities show increases in academic outcomes when working in groups, likely because they have more opportunities to present and respond to information (Bos & Vaughn, 2006). As you may know from working with your own peers in a group, sometimes group assignments can be challenging or stressful, so save your students (and yourself) headaches by articulating clear guidelines for students to follow. Johnson and Johnson (1975) offer five guidelines to follow when placing students in cooperative groups:

1. Each group should produce one project or outcome.

2. The group members should assist one another in complementary ways, rather than working independently on their assigned tasks.

3. Members within the group should seek assistance from one another.

4. Group members should only change course when persuaded by logical ideas from other members.

5. All group members should take responsibility for the group project or outcome.

It is critical to establish clear roles when students collaborate, so that students understand their responsibilities and expectations from the outset. Providing group activities with designated roles will save you time and energy in the long run and also teach your students how to work collaboratively.

Not all social learning must take place in a group setting. Another way to capitalize on the social nature of learning is to create task-oriented opportunities to collaborate with peers on small tasks or assignments. Students can respond to their peers' statements on discussion boards and social networking platforms. It is your decision whether to use Facebook, Twitter, or MySpace to communicate with students, but know that if you do, you will not be assured of your privacy, so proceed with caution. We suggest checking out Connect Safely's website (www.connectsafely. org) for teens, parents, and educators; there you will find useful information on safe practices for communicating across social networking sites.

Because students with learning disabilities or cognitive impairments benefit in reviewing material at their own pace and level, online materials such as review games and quizzes can provide an ideal way to revisit challenging content. Websites, such as Quia (www.quia.com), offer free templates to create games online. If you don't feel like creating your own games, you can take advantage of free games already created and hosted online. For example, National Geographic Kids (http://kids.nationalgeographic.com/kids/games/geographygames) offers online games, puzzles, and quizzes for elementary and middle school students. An Internet search of "free online educational games" and a selected word from your content area should yield plenty of free options and save time unless you enjoy creating games on your own.

If you use external resources to facilitate learning, be sure to pay attention to "hot spots" that may affect specific types of students, such as open-ended web surfing, games that are not user-friendly, and quizzes that provide answers after the first attempt. If you are concerned with students not actually completing the games, have them take a screen shot from their computer screen and email you the image as evidence. This is especially helpful for students with attention deficits or emotional and behavioral disorders who may have difficulty being accountable without the extra support.

Conclusion

Creating engaging online or hybrid materials and experiences for students with disabilities can be challenging but well worth your time. Material presented in multiple formats with a consistent message allows students to grasp information from a variety of modalities. By aligning the most important concepts in your course with their learning objectives, activities, and assessments, you can focus student learning on the essential topics. Well-designed games and assessments that allow for multiple means of expression will naturally engage all your students. Although students with disabilities and special needs are required by law to have access to the general curriculum, as mandated by IDEA, providing for their instruction using the principles of the universal design for learning improves the educational experience for all students.

As you begin to gather resources and materials, ask yourself how your current instructional plans can be adapted to fit as many unique learner needs as possible. Use the WAI guidelines (www.w3.org/WAI) and the UDL checklist and other resources found on the CAST website (www.cast.org) to create learning materials and activities that are flexible, and you will save yourself valuable time in the long run.

References

American Association on Intellectual and Development Disabilities (AAIDD). (2013). Definition of intellectual disability. Retrieved from www.aaidd.org/content_100.cfm

American Psychiatric Association (APA). (2000). *Diagnostic and statistical manual of mental disorders* (Rev. 4th ed.). Washington, DC: Author.

Autism Speaks. (2011). What is autism? Retrieved from www.autismspeaks.org/what-autism

Bos, C., & Vaughn, S. (2006). *Strategies for teaching students with learning and behavior problems* (6th ed.). Boston, MA: Allyn and Bacon.

Center for Applied Special Technology (CAST). (2010). Transforming education through universal design for learning. Retrieved from www.cast.org

Center for Applied Special Technology (CAST). (2011a). About UDL. Retrieved from www.cast.org/udl

Center for Applied Special Technology (CAST). (2011b). Research and development in universal design for learning. Retrieved from www.cast.org/research

Colorado State University. (2010). Access to postsecondary education through universal design for learning. Retrieved from http://accessproject.colostate.edu

Cornell University Information Technologies. (2012, October 31). Intro to Web Accessibility. Retrieved from www.it.cornell.edu/policies/accessibility/primer/wa1_intro.cfm#check

Darling-Hammond, L. (2007). Race, inequality and educational accountability: The irony of 'No Child Left Behind.' *Race, Ethnicity and Education, 10*(3), 245–260. doi: 10.1080/13613320701503207

Deno, S. L., Fuchs, L. S., Marston, D., & Shin, J. (2001). Using curriculum-based measurement to establish growth standards for students with learning disabilities. *School Psychology Review, 30,* 507–524.

Englert, C., Wu, X., & Zhao, Y. (2005). Cognitive tools for writing: Scaffolding the performance of students through technology. *Learning Disabilities Research & Practice, 20*(3), 184–198.

Englert, C., Yong, Z., Dunsmore, K., Collings, N., & Wolbers, K. (2007). Scaffolding the writing of students with disabilities through procedural facilitation: Using an internet-based technology to improve performance. *Learning Disability Quarterly, 30*(1), 9–29.

Fuster, J. M. (2001). The prefrontal cortex—an update: Time is of the essence. *Neuron, 30*(2), 319–333.

Gargiulo, R. M. (2006). *Special education in contemporary society. An introduction to exceptionality* (2nd ed.). Belmont, CA: Thomson Wadsworth.

Gargiulo, R. M. (2009). *Special education in contemporary society. An introduction to exceptionality* (3rd ed.). Thousand Oaks, CA: Sage.

Grigal, M., Neubert, D. A., Moon, M. S., & Graham, S. (2003). Self-determination for students with disabilities: Views of parents and teachers. *Exceptional Children, 70*(1), 97–112.

Hardman, M. L., Drew, C. J., Egan, M. W., & Wolf, B. (1993). *Human exceptionality* (4th ed.). Boston, MA: Allyn & Bacon.

Harris, K. R., Graham, S., & Mason, L. H. (2002). POW plus TREE equals powerful opinion essays. *Teaching Exceptional Children, 34,* 74–77.

Heller, K. W. & Gargiulo, R. M. (2009). Individuals with physical disabilities, health disparities, and related low-incidence disabilities. In S. Wainwright, D. Saoud, J. McNall, E. Caffee, & L. A. Shea (Eds.), *Special education in contemporary society* (3rd ed., pp. 487–539). Thousand Oaks, CA: Sage.

Heron, T. E., Welsch, R. G., & Goddard, Y. L. (2003). Applications of tutoring systems in specialized subject areas. *Remedial and Special Education, 24*(5), 288–300.

Higher Education Opportunity Act of 2008, Pub. L. No. 110-315, 122 Stat. 3078. (2008, August 14). Title I, General Provisions (24) Universal Design for Learning, (B), p. 6. Retrieved from www.gpo.gov/fdsys/pkg/STATUTE-122/pdf/STATUTE-122-Pg3078.pdf

Hirumi, A. (2003). Get a life: Six tactics for reducing time spent online. *Computers in Schools, 20*(3), 73–101.

Individuals with Disabilities Education Improvement Act (IDEA), 20 U.S.C. 1400–1487. (1997, 2004). Retrieved from http://idea.ed.gov/explore/view/p/,root,statute & http://idea.ed.gov/explore/view/p/%2Croot%2Cregs%2C300%2CA%2C300%252E8%2Cc%2C10%2C

Jackson, R. (2005). Curriculum access for students with low-incidence disabilities: The promise of universal design for learning. Wakefield, MA: National Center on Accessing the General Curriculum. Retrieved from http://aim.cast.org/learn/historyarchive/backgroundpapers/promise_of_udl

Johnson, D. W., & Johnson, R. T. (1975). *Learning together and alone.* Englewood Cliffs, NJ: Prentice Hall.

Kern, L., Bambara, L., & Fogt, J. (2002). Class-wide curricular modification to improve the behavior of students with emotional or behavioral disorders. *Behavioral Disorders, 27*(4), 317–26.

King, G., Law, M., Hurley, P., Petrenchik, T., & Schwellnus, H. (2010). A developmental comparison of the out-of-school recreation and leisure activity participation of boys and girls with and without physical disabilities. *International Journal of Disability, Development and Education, 57*(1), 77–107. doi: 10.1080/10349120903537988

Kutscher, M. L. (2005). *Kids in the syndrome mix of ADHD, LD, Asperger's, Tourette's, Bipolar, and more!* Philadelphia, PA: Jessica Kingsley.

Lee., D. L., Belfiore, P. J., & Bundin, S. G. (2008). Riding the wave: Creating a momentum of school success. *Teaching Exceptional Children, 40*(3), 65–70.

Lenz, B. K., Deshler, D. D., & Kissam, B. R. (2004). *Teaching content to all: Evidence-based inclusive practices in middle and secondary schools.* Boston, MA: Pearson Education.

MacFarlane, J. R., & Kanaya, T. (2009). What does it mean to be autistic? Inter-state variation in special education criteria for autism services. *Journal of Child and Family Studies, 18*(6), 662–669. doi: 10.1007/s10826-009-9268-8

Mayer, R. E., Heiser, J., & Lonn, S. (2000). Cognitive constraints on multimedia learning: When presenting more material results in less understanding. *Journal of Educational Psychology, 93*(1), 187–198.

No Child Left Behind Act of 2001, Pub. L. No. 107–110. (2002). Available at www.gpo.gov/fdsys/pkg/PLAW-107publ110/html/PLAW-107publ110.htm

Pauc, R. (2006). *The Learning Disability Myth: Understanding and overcoming your child's diagnosis of dyspraxia, dyslexia, Tourette's syndrome of childhood, ADD, ADHD, or OCD.* London, UK: Virgin Books.

Project PACE. (1999). Accessibility checklist for web content and online courses: A self-assessment tool. Disability Resource Center at the University of Arkansas at Little Rock. Retrieved from www.pcc.edu/resources/web/documentation/contribute/documents/access-checklist.pdf

Sabornie, E. J., Cullinan, D., Osborne, S. S., & Brock, L. B. (2005). Intellectual, academic, and behavioral functioning of students with high-incidence disabilities: A cross-categorical meta-analysis. *Exceptional Children, 72*(1), 47–63.

Savi, C., Savenye, W., & Rowland, C. (2008). The effects of implementing web accessibility standards on the success of secondary adolescents. *Journal of Educational Multimedia and Hypermedia, 17*(3), 387–411.

Slavin, R. E. (2000). *Educational psychology: Theory and practice.* Boston, MA: Allyn and Bacon.

Smith, D. D. (2001). *Introduction to special education: Teaching in an age of opportunity* (4th ed.). Boston, MA: Allyn and Bacon.

Smith, D. D. (2007). *Introduction to special education: Making a difference* (6th ed.). Boston, MA: Allyn and Bacon.

Straub, C. (2012). The effects of synchronous online cognitive strategy instruction in writing for students with learning disabilities. (Unpublished doctoral dissertation). Orlando, FL: University of Central Florida.

Szelazkiewicz, S. (2002). *Mainstreaming the hearing impaired student.* Retrieved from ERIC database. No. ED467249. Publisher: Author.

Taylor, R. L., Smiley, L. R., & Richards, S. B. (2009). *Exceptional students: Preparing teachers for the 21st century.* New York, NY: McGraw-Hill.

U.S. Census Bureau. (2008). An older and more diverse nation by mid-century. Retrieved from www.census.gov/newsroom/releases/archives/population/cb08-123.html

U.S. Department of Education, National Center for Education Statistics. (2009). Digest of education statistics, 2008. (NCES 2009-020), Table 50.

Vasquez, E., & Straub, C. (2012). Online instruction for K–12 special education: A review of the empirical literature. *Journal of Special Education Technology, 27*(3), 31–40.

Warren, S. J., Dondlinger, M. J., & Barab, S. A. (2008). A MUVE towards PBL writing: Effects of a digital learning environment designed to improve elementary student writing. *Journal of Research on Technology in Education, 41*(1), 113–140.

Wright, P. W. D., & Wright, P. D. (2004). *Wrightslaw: Special Education Law.* Hartfield, VA: Harbor House Law Press.

Yell, M. L., & Busch, T. W. (2012). Using curriculum-based measurement to develop educationally meaningful and legally sound individualized educational programs (IEPs). In C. Espin, K. McMaster, S. Rose, & M. M. Wayman (Eds.), *A measure of success: The influence of curriculum-based measurement on education* (pp. 37–48). Minneapolis, MN: University of Minnesota Press.

Yell, M. L., & Drasgow, E. (2013). Less to more restrictive settings: Policy and planning considerations. In D. D. Reed, F. D. Reed, & J. K. Luiselli (Eds.), *Handbook of crisis intervention and developmental disabilities* (pp. 281–297). New York, NY: Springer.

CHAPTER 7

Alignment to ISTE's NETS for Teachers and Students and Other Standards

Rhonda Atkinson and Tom Atkinson

STANDARDS, ESPECIALLY TECHNOLOGY standards, are relatively new constructs in education. They form the instructional goals in today's K–12 classrooms. They also provide direction for the integration of technology into teaching and learning. The first half of this chapter traces the development of subject-specific standards from professional organizations to state development to the national Common Core State Standards as the background for a description of the development of the International Society for Technology in Education's National Educational Technology Standards (NETS) for teachers (NETS·T), students (NETS·S), education coaches (NETS·C), and administrators (NETS·A). As technology evolved to create virtual schools, the North American Council for Online Learning (NACOL) developed new standards for online learning, and the International Council for Online Learning (iNACOL) developed standards for online programs. The second half of this chapter describes how technology standards and Common Core or subject area standards can be successfully combined in today's K–12 classrooms with specific examples of technologies and student artifacts.

All, regardless of race or class or economic status, are entitled to a fair chance and to the tools for developing their individual powers of mind and spirit to the utmost. This promise means that all children by virtue of their own efforts, competently guided, can hope to attain the mature and informed judgment needed to secure gainful employment, and to manage their own lives, thereby serving not only their own interests but also the progress of society itself. (The National Commission on Excellence in Education, 1983, *A Nation at Risk: The Imperative for Educational Reform*)

In 1983, the National Commission on Excellence in Education published the preceding words as the introduction to its report to the nation and the Secretary of Education of the U.S. Department of Education, T. H. Bell, and as its vision for American education. The reality of U.S. education, as described in the report, was quite different from the commission's vision. The commission's report characterized the American educational system as an "act of unthinking, unilateral educational disarmament" that, if undertaken by a foreign power, would be viewed as an "act of war." These powerful words spawned a number of educational reforms that continue today: improvements in teacher education programs, more stringent high school graduation requirements for students, greater accountability for school leadership and fiscal support, increased instructional time, and—the focus of this chapter—the adoption of more rigorous, measurable standards that apply to technology as well as to content areas.

In 1989, responding to the call for educational reforms, President George H. W. Bush and the governors of all 50 states met at an historic education summit to set national educational goals to be achieved by the year 2000. Congress passed the Goals 2000: Educate America Act in 1992 to sanction the development of national educational standards as a way to encourage and evaluate student achievement in specific subject areas.

As a result, by the end of the 20th century, many professional organizations developed standards to govern teaching and learning, all citing as a rationale the importance of their subject areas' content. The National Council of Teachers of Mathematics (NCTM) led the way by developing the *Curriculum and Evaluation Standards for School Mathematics* (NCTM Commission on Standards for School Mathematics, 1989), followed by the *Professional Standards for Teaching Mathematics* (NCTM Commission on Teaching Standards for School Mathematics, 1991), and the *Assessment Standards for School Mathematics* (Assessment Standards Working Group, 1995). The NCTM released an updated *Principles and Standards for School Mathematics* (Standards 2000 Project, 2000) with each content area (number and operations, algebra, geometry, measurement, data analysis and probability) or process standard (problem-solving, reasoning and proof, communication, connections, representation) consisting of several specific goals, spanning prekindergarten through Grade 12.

In 1991, the American Association for the Advancement of Science (AAAS) published *Science for All Americans* (Rutherford & Ahlgren, 1991), outlining which "understandings and habits of mind are essential for all citizens of a scientifically literate society" to help teachers decide what to include in (or exclude from) a core curriculum, when to teach it, and why. Shortly thereafter, AAAS published *Benchmarks for Science Literacy* (AAAS, 1993) to provide teachers with tools to create K–12 curricula that would address the content standards found in *Science for All Americans*.

In 1996, the Center for Science, Mathematics, and Engineering Education (CSMEE) published *National Science Education Standards* (National Committee on Science Education Standards and Assessment &National Research Council, 1996) to set standards for all students by specifying what students need to know, understand, and be able to do to be scientifically literate at different grade levels. In 2013, a 26-state consortium released a new set of standards for science: Next Generation Science Standards (NGSS Lead States, 2013). These standards include standards for professional development for teachers of science, assessment in science education, science education programs, and science education systems as well as the more traditional science teaching standards and science content standards. Box 7.1 lists the content categories for the AAAS benchmarks, the CSMEE standards for science literacy, and the NGSS content standards.

BOX 7.1 ▶ Content Categories for Benchmarks and Standards for Science Literacy

AAAS Benchmarks for Science Literacy	**CSMEE National Science Education Standards**	**Next Generation Science Standards**
The nature of science		Physical sciences
The nature of mathematics	Unifying concepts and processes in science	Life sciences
The nature of technology	Science as inquiry	Earth and space sciences
The physical setting	Physical science	Engineering, technology, and applications of sciencee
The living environment	Life science	*(NGSS Lead States, 2013)*
Human organism	Earth and space science	
Human society	Science and technology	
The designed world	Science in personal and social perspectives	
The mathematical world	History and nature of science	
Historical perspectives	*(CSMEE, 1996)*	
Common themes		
Habits of mind		
(AAAS, 1993)		

Also in 1996, the National Council of Teachers of English (NCTE) and the International Reading Association (IRA) jointly issued *Standards for the English Language Arts* (NCTE & IRA, 1996). The two groups noted that their shared purpose was to "ensure that all students are knowledge-able and proficient users of language so they may succeed in school, participate in our democracy as informed citizens, find challenging and rewarding work, appreciate and contribute to our culture, and pursue their own goals and interests as independent learners throughout their lives" (See Box 7.2).

In 1994, The National Council for the Social Studies (NCSS) published its vision for education in *Expectations of Excellence: Curriculum Standards for Social Studies* (NCSS, 1994). These were revised in 2010 and published as the *National Curriculum Standards for Social Studies* (Adler, 2010). The NCSS defined social studies as "the integrated study of social sciences and humanities to promote civic competence … [that] provides coordinated, systematic study drawing upon such disciplines as anthropology, archaeology, economics, geography, history, law, philosophy, political science, psychology, religion, and sociology, as well as appropriate content from the humanities, mathematics, and natural sciences." According to the NCSS, the primary purpose of social studies is "to help young people develop the ability to make informed and reasoned decisions for the public good as citizens of a culturally diverse, democratic society in an interdependent world." Because of the interdisciplinary nature of social studies, the standards are expressed as themes: culture; time, continuity, and change; people, places, and environments; individual development and identity; individuals, groups, and institutions; power, authority, and governance; production, distribution, and consumption; science, technology, and society; global connections; civic ideals and practices.

BOX 7.2 ▶ NCTE/IRA Standards for the English Language Arts

NCTE/IRA Standards for the English Language Arts

1. Students read a wide range of print and non-print texts to build an understanding of texts, of themselves, and of the cultures of the United States and the world; to acquire new information; to respond to the needs and demands of society and the workplace; and for personal fulfillment.

2. Students read a wide range of literature from many periods in many genres to build an understanding of the many dimensions (e.g., philosophical, ethical, aesthetic) of human experience.

3. Students apply a wide range of strategies to comprehend, interpret, evaluate, and appreciate texts. They draw on their prior experience, their interactions with other readers and writers, their knowledge of word meaning and of other texts, their word identification strategies, and their understanding of textual features (e.g., sound-letter correspondence, sentence structure, context, graphics).

4. Students adjust their use of spoken, written, and visual language (e.g., conventions, style, vocabulary) to communicate effectively with a variety of audiences and for different purposes.

5. Students employ a wide range of strategies as they write and use different writing process elements appropriately to communicate with different audiences for a variety of purposes.

6. Students apply knowledge of language structure, language conventions (e.g., spelling and punctuation), media techniques, figurative language, and genre to create, critique, and discuss print and non-print texts.

7. Students conduct research on issues and interests by generating ideas and questions, and by posing problems. They gather, evaluate, and synthesize data from a variety of sources (e.g., print and non-print texts, artifacts, people) to communicate their discoveries in ways that suit their purpose and audience.

8. Students use a variety of technological and information resources (e.g., libraries, databases, computer networks, video) to gather and synthesize information and to create and communicate knowledge.

9. Students develop an understanding of and respect for diversity in language use, patterns, and dialects across cultures, ethnic groups, geographic regions, and social roles.

10. Students whose first language is not English make use of their first language to develop competency in the English language arts and to develop understanding of content across the curriculum.

11. Students participate as knowledgeable, reflective, creative, and critical members of a variety of literacy communities.

12. Students use spoken, written, and visual language to accomplish their own purposes (e.g., for learning, enjoyment, persuasion, and the exchange of information).

(NCTE & IRA, 1996)

By the new millennium, individual states had developed their own standards, which generally aligned with the standards developed by national organizations. During the following decade, a set of national Common Core State Standards focusing on math and language arts were developed (National Governors Association Center for Best Practices, 2012). By 2013, 90% of the states had adopted the Common Core standards.

History and Purpose of ISTE's NETS

When the National Commission on Excellence in Education published *A Nation at Risk* in 1983, computers were rare commodities in average schools and nonexistent in poorly funded schools. As computers and various forms of e-learning were gradually introduced and eventually accepted and highly valued, they were often seen as the panacea for all of education's ills. However, educators soon realized that the key to successful e-learning would be to define clearly what learners were to achieve. Educators also realized that they needed to work together and focus on professional development for optimum e-learning if they were going to use it successfully as a teaching mode.

Thus, as the role of educational technology became more prominent in America's classrooms, the International Society for Technology in Education (ISTE) formed a unique partnership with teachers, teacher educators, curriculum and education associations, government, businesses, and private foundations to define educational technology standards, guidelines, and tools. ISTE and its partners needed to ensure that the tools of technology were implemented in classrooms in compliance with national subject area standards. The resulting National Educational Technology Standards (NETS) addressed the skills and knowledge needed in the technology and information environment by students (ISTE, 1998); teachers (ISTE, 2000); and administrators (ISTE, 2001).

These national standards were widely adopted or adapted in nearly every state in the United States. The 21st century quickly came to be known as the digital age, and the classroom technologies that were in vogue in the late 1990s—audiotape, videotape, telecommunications, overhead projectors, and some computer software and Internet applications—were becoming outdated by new technologies, such as high-speed Internet access, a greater quantity and quality of online materials, podcasting, cell-phone technologies, instant messaging, blogs, wikis, social media, and virtual environments. Additionally, students entering school in the first two decades of the 21st century were becoming sophisticated and knowledgeable users of technology. For them, computers and the Internet were ubiquitous aspects of their environments that they saw more as extensions of themselves rather than tools to be used. The question was no longer, "What technological knowledge and skills do students need?" but, "What technological expertise will students need to live, learn, and succeed in a world that requires innovation and creativity?"

Consequently, the NETS for Students (NETS•S) were updated in 2007, the NETS for Teachers (NETS•T) in 2008, and the NETS for Administrators (NETS•A) in 2009. The resulting ISTE standards for students, teachers, and administrators provide ways for America's schools to assess technological expertise and set new and higher goals for the kinds of technological knowledge, skills, and attitudes needed for students to succeed in the digital age (ISTE, 2007; ISTE, 2008; ISTE, 2009).

ISTE's NETS for Teachers and Students

The refreshed NETS for teachers and students (ISTE, 2008; ISTE, 2007) focus on the use of technology to think, learn, and work more creatively and efficiently in contrast with the earlier focus on the technology itself. For example, the order of both the teacher and student NETS emphasizes the importance of creativity as the first standard (Teachers: Facilitate and Inspire Student Learning and Creativity; Students: Creativity and Innovation) instead of accentuating technology operations and concepts. The remaining standards for teachers focus on instructional actions (Design and Develop Digital-Age Learning Experiences and Assessments; Promote … Digital Citizenship and Responsibility) and teacher behavior (Model Digital-age Work and Learning; … Model Digital Citizenship and Responsibility; Engage in Professional Growth and Leadership). Student standards address communication and collaboration; research and information fluency; critical thinking, problem solving, and decision making; digital citizenship; and technology operations and concepts. As stated by former ISTE Chief Executive Officer Don Knezek, "… teachers must become comfortable as co-learners with their students and with colleagues around the world. Today it is less about *staying ahead* and more about *moving ahead* as members of dynamic learning communities. The digital-age teaching professional must demonstrate a vision of technology infusion and develop the technology skills of others. These are the hallmarks of the new education leader" (ISTE, 2008). Box 7.3 lists ISTE's NETS for teachers and students.

BOX 7.3 ▶ ISTE's NETS for Teachers and Students

ISTE's NETS for Teachers

All classroom teachers should be prepared to meet the following standards and performance indicators.

1. **Facilitate and Inspire Student Learning and Creativity**

   Teachers use their knowledge of subject matter, teaching and learning, and technology to facilitate experiences that advance student learning, creativity, and innovation in both face-to-face and virtual environments. Teachers:

   a. promote, support, and model creative and innovative thinking and inventiveness

   b. engage students in exploring real-world issues and solving authentic problems using digital tools and resources

   c. promote student reflection using collaborative tools to reveal and clarify students' conceptual understanding and thinking, planning, and creative processes

   d. model collaborative knowledge construction by engaging in learning with students, colleagues, and others in face-to-face and virtual environments

BOX 7.3 ▶ *(Continued)*

2. **Design and Develop Digital-Age Learning Experiences and Assessments**

Teachers design, develop, and evaluate authentic learning experiences and assessments incorporating contemporary tools and resources to maximize content learning in context and to develop the knowledge, skills, and attitudes identified in the NETS•S. Teachers:

   a. design or adapt relevant learning experiences that incorporate digital tools and resources to promote student learning and creativity

   b. develop technology-enriched learning environments that enable all students to pursue their individual curiosities and become active participants in setting their own educational goals, managing their own learning, and assessing their own progress

   c. customize and personalize learning activities to address students' diverse learning styles, working strategies, and abilities using digital tools and resources

   d. provide students with multiple and varied formative and summative assessments aligned with content and technology standards and use resulting data to inform learning and teaching

3. **Model Digital-Age Work and Learning**

Teachers exhibit knowledge, skills, and work processes representative of an innovative professional in a global and digital society. Teachers:

   a. demonstrate fluency in technology systems and the transfer of current knowledge to new technologies and situations

   b. collaborate with students, peers, parents, and community members using digital tools and resources to support student success and innovation

   c. communicate relevant information and ideas effectively to students, parents, and peers using a variety of digital-age media and formats

   d. model and facilitate effective use of current and emerging digital tools to locate, analyze, evaluate, and use information resources to support research and learning

4. **Promote and Model Digital Citizenship and Responsibility**

Teachers understand local and global societal issues and responsibilities in an evolving digital culture and exhibit legal and ethical behavior in their professional practices. Teachers:

   a. advocate, model, and teach safe, legal, and ethical use of digital information and technology, including respect for copyright, intellectual property, and the appropriate documentation of sources

   b. address the diverse needs of all learners by using learner-centered strategies and providing equitable access to appropriate digital tools and resources

   c. promote and model digital etiquette and responsible social interactions related to the use of technology and information

   d. develop and model cultural understanding and global awareness by engaging with colleagues and students of other cultures using digital-age communication and collaboration tools

(Continued)

BOX 7.3 ▶ *(Continued)*

5. **Engage in Professional Growth and Leadership**

   Teachers continuously improve their professional practice, model lifelong learning, and exhibit leadership in their school and professional community by promoting and demonstrating the effective use of digital tools and resources. Teachers:

   a. participate in local and global learning communities to explore creative applications of technology to improve student learning

   b. exhibit leadership by demonstrating a vision of technology infusion, participating in shared decision making and community building, and developing the leadership and technology skills of others

   c. evaluate and reflect on current research and professional practice on a regular basis to make effective use of existing and emerging digital tools and resources in support of student learning

   d. contribute to the effectiveness, vitality, and self-renewal of the teaching profession and of their school and community

ISTE's NETS for Students

All K–12 students should be prepared to meet the following standards and performance indicators.

1. **Creativity and Innovation**

   Students demonstrate creative thinking, construct knowledge, and develop innovative products and processes using technology. Students:

   a. apply existing knowledge to generate new ideas, products, or processes

   b. create original works as a means of personal or group expression

   c. use models and simulations to explore complex systems and issues

   d. identify trends and forecast possibilities

2. **Communication and Collaboration**

   Students use digital media and environments to communicate and work collaboratively, including at a distance, to support individual learning and contribute to the learning of others. Students:

   a. interact, collaborate, and publish with peers, experts, or others employing a variety of digital environments and media

   b. communicate information and ideas effectively to multiple audiences using a variety of media and formats

   c. develop cultural understanding and global awareness by engaging with learners of other cultures

   d. contribute to project teams to produce original works or solve problems

BOX 7.3 ▶ *(Continued)*

3. Research and Information Fluency

Students apply digital tools to gather, evaluate, and use information. Students:

a. plan strategies to guide inquiry

b. locate, organize, analyze, evaluate, synthesize, and ethically use information from a variety of sources and media

c. evaluate and select information sources and digital tools based on the appropriateness to specific tasks

d. process data and report results

4. Critical Thinking, Problem Solving, and Decision Making

Students use critical-thinking skills to plan and conduct research, manage projects, solve problems, and make informed decisions using appropriate digital tools and resources. Students:

a. identify and define authentic problems and significant questions for investigation

b. plan and manage activities to develop a solution or complete a project

c. collect and analyze data to identify solutions and make informed decisions

d. use multiple processes and diverse perspectives to explore alternative solutions

5. Digital Citizenship

Students understand human, cultural, and societal issues related to technology and practice legal and ethical behavior. Students:

a. advocate and practice the safe, legal, and responsible use of information and technology

b. exhibit a positive attitude toward using technology that supports collaboration, learning, and productivity

c. demonstrate personal responsibility for lifelong learning

d. exhibit leadership for digital citizenship

6. Technology Operations and Concepts

Students demonstrate a sound understanding of technology concepts, systems, and operations. Students:

a. understand and use technology systems

b. select and use applications effectively and productively

c. troubleshoot systems and applications

d. transfer current knowledge to the learning of new technologies

ISTE's NETS for Administrators and Coaches

Although teaching and learning occur in the classroom, school and district administrators traditionally have the responsibility for shaping and facilitating the vision for technology integration. Thus, technology standards for administrators ensure that schools provide leadership and resources that support the appropriate and effective use of technology to meet the needs of digital-age teachers and learners. However, the complexities of today's schools in terms of political issues, financial concerns, curricular demands, student diversity, and changing technologies mean that today's school administrators have less time to spend in classrooms—evaluating teachers and programs, identifying needs, and providing feedback and assistance. As a result, many schools have developed new positions: education coaches who have the in-school responsibility of facilitating better teaching and learning. While coaches often help teachers solve instructional issues with specific content or students, they can also help teachers create and implement technology-rich instruction. Box 7.4 lists ISTE's NETS for administrators and for coaches.

BOX 7.4 ▶ ISTE's NETS for Administrators and Coaches

ISTE's NETS for Administrators

Visionary Leadership

Digital-Age Learning Culture

Excellence in Professional Practice

Systemic Improvement

Digital Citizenship

© 2009 International Society for Technology in Education (ISTE), www.iste.org. All rights reserved.

ISTE's NETS for Coaches

Visionary Leadership

Teaching, Learning, and Assessments

Digital-Age Learning Environments

Professional Development and Program Evaluation

Digital Citizenship

Content Knowledge and Professional Growth

© 2011 International Society for Technology in Education (ISTE), www.iste.org. All rights reserved.

---

iNACOL Standards

Standards also aid school districts in planning for and implementing online course options at the K–12 level for online teaching and learning. According to the International Association for K–12 Online Learning (2011), online teaching and learning are increasing by 30% each year, with two-thirds of states having state-led virtual school programs, one-third having full-time online learning programs, and approximately three-fourths offering at least one online course. In response to this growth, the North American Council for Online Learning (NACOL) created a set of standards for K–12 online learning in 2007, and the International Council for Online Learning (iNACOL) released *Standards for Quality Online Programs* two years later (Pape & Wicks, 2009) that evaluate programs in terms of the institution, teaching and learning, support and evaluation. The standards for online courses were revised in 2011 by iNACOL. Box 7.5 outlines the main sections and key components of the second version (2011, October) of iNACOL standards, *National Standards for Quality Online Courses* (www.inacol.org/cms/wp-content/uploads/2012/09/iNACOL_CourseStandards_2011.pdf).

BOX 7.5 ▶ Outline of the iNACOL Standards for K–12 Online Learning

---

iNACOL National Standards for Quality Online Courses

Section A: Content
(Examines how a course helps learners engage in content, promotes content mastery, and aligns with state or national standards.)

Academic Content Standards and Assessments

Course Overview and Introduction

Legal and Acceptable Use Policies

Instructor Resources

Section B: Instructional Design
(Determines if a course engages students through active learning and facilitates interaction and communication among students and instructors.)

Instructional and Audience Analysis

Course, Unit, and Lesson Design

Instructional Strategies and Activities

Communication and Interaction

Resources and Materials

(Continued)

BOX 7.5 ▶ *(Continued)*

Section C: Student Assessment
(Analyzes if a course uses multiple techniques to assess student readiness for and progress in content as well as provides feedback on progress.)

Evaluation Strategies

Feedback

Assessment Resources and Materials

Section D: Technology
(Determines if the course maximizes the use of technology tools, provides a user-friendly interface, and meets accessibility requirements for students with special needs.)

Course Architecture

User Interface

Technology Requirements and Interoperability

Accessibility

Data Security

Section E: Course Evaluation and Support
(Evaluates course effectiveness in terms of currency of information and course design, preparation, and ongoing support of teachers and students for online environments, as well as how these findings are used for course improvement.)

Accessing Course Effectiveness

Course Updates

Certification

Instructor and Student Support

(iNACOL, 2011, October)

Curriculum Integration: Aligning ISTE's NETS with Subject Area and Common Core Standards

Certainly, most of today's schools have various quantities and qualities of technology available in classrooms, libraries, and labs for teaching and learning. In terms of curriculum integration, the question is not, "How much technology is available to support subject area knowledge and skills?" but, "How can technology foster subject area knowledge and skills?" The answer to the latter question involves the intersection of technology with specific subject-area standards, either as described in the Common Core State Standards or in standards created by professional organizations.

Thus, one way to view alignment is from the perspective of subject area standards and the ways they specify technology use. NCTM's Principles and Standards for School Mathematics do not address technology at all, but other subject area standards mention technology specifically. For example, the NCSS's Curriculum Standards for Social Studies' theme of Science, Technology, and Society appears to address technology; however, this theme really examines the role technology plays in society and science rather than how to use technology to learn about social studies. The NCTE Standards for English Language Arts are the most specific in the way they describe the application of technology to learning (see Box 7.2 on p. 152; standards 1, 6, 7, and 8).

A second perspective in alignment is to look at subject area standards in terms of the NETS. Because the NETS for teachers and NETS for students focus on the application of technology rather than knowledge about technology, NETS makes the most sense in terms of how it is used to facilitate achievement of subject area standards.

As the Common Core State Standards were developed to meet the needs of 21st-century learners born into an increasingly technological world, technology use is specifically identified as an integral part of the teaching-learning process. Indeed, its description of key points in the English language arts standards addresses media and technology in this context: "Just as media and technology are integrated in school and life in the twenty-first century, skills related to media use (both critical and production of media) are integrated throughout the standards." Here the question of whether or not to use technology is a moot point, but discussions about which technologies to use and how to integrate them still remain. Teachers are finding an increasing number of resources online that make integration easy and help students meet the standards. Table 7.1 shows examples of technology tools that align the NETS·S with Common Core or subject-area standards.

TABLE 7.1 ▶ Examples of Technologies that Align NETS·S with Common Core and Subject Area Standards

NETS·S	COMMON CORE OR SUBJECT AREA STANDARDS	TECHNOLOGY TOOLS
1. Creativity and Innovation	**Common Core ELA Standards, Writing, Grade 5 (Production and Distribution of Writing)** CCSS.ELA-Literacy.W.5.6: With some guidance and support from adults, use technology, including the Internet, to produce and publish writing as well as to interact and collaborate with others; demonstrate sufficient command of keyboarding skills to type a minimum of two pages in a single sitting.	Smories (www.smories.com) supports literacy by providing a forum for children to read aloud what they have written. BookR (www.pimpampum.net/bookr/) lets students publish what they've written in a flipbook format. ZooBurst (www.zooburst.com) takes flipbooks a step further by allowing students to create simple popup books.
1. Creativity and Innovation	**NCTE/IRA Standards for the English Language Arts** Standard 8. Students use a variety of technological and information resources (e.g., libraries, databases, computer networks, video) to gather and synthesize information and to create and communicate knowledge.	Fact Monster from Information Please (www.factmonster.com) provides references, activities, and homework resources as well as content for parents and teachers.

(Continued)

TABLE 7.1 ▶ *(Continued)*

NETS·S	COMMON CORE OR SUBJECT AREA STANDARDS	TECHNOLOGY TOOLS
2. Communication and Collaboration	**Common Core ELA Standards, Speaking & Listening, Grade 7 (Comprehension and Collaboration)** CCSS.ELA-Literacy.SL.7.1 Engage effectively in a range of collaborative discussions (one-on-one, in groups, and teacher-led) with diverse partners on Grade 7 topics, texts, and issues, building on others' ideas and expressing their own clearly.	VoiceThread (http://ed.voicethread.com) is a Web 2.0 tool for creating audio collaborative discussions. e-Pals (www.epals.com) is a resource for finding other K–12 classes around the world for collaborating on projects via Skype, video, email, blogs, forums, media galleries, and wikis.
2. Communication and Collaboration	**NCSS National Curriculum Standards for Social Studies** Theme 9. Global Connections	Global SchoolNet (www.globalschoolnet.org) engages teachers and students in project learning exchanges with people around the world to "develop science, math, literacy, and communication skills; foster teamwork, civic responsibility, and collaboration; encourage workforce preparedness; and create multicultural understanding."
3. Research and Information Fluency	**Common Core ELA Standards, Reading: Informational Text, Grade 11–12 (Integration of Knowledge and Ideas)** CCSS.ELA-Literacy.RI.11-12.7 Integrate and evaluate multiple sources of information presented in different media or formats (e.g., visually, quantitatively) as well as in words in order to address a question or solve a problem.	Encyclopedia.com (www.encyclopedia.com) is a compendium of more than 100 encyclopedias and dictionaries. It provides access to text, pictures, and video content for use in research and writing. The Wikimedia Foundation (http://wikimedia-foundation.org) operates collaboratively edited reference projects, including Wikipedia (free encyclopedia in different languages), Wikiversity (learning materials and communities), and Wikimedia Commons (freely usable media files).
3. Research and Information Fluency	**NCTM Principles and Standards for School Mathematics** Data Analysis and Probability (PK–12). Formulate questions that can be addressed with data; collect, organize, and display relevant data to answer them.	Utah State University's National Library of Virtual Manipulatives (http://nlvm.usu.edu) provides PK–12 activities for numbers and operations, algebra, geometry, measurement, and data analysis and probability.
4. Critical Thinking, Problem Solving, and Decision Making	**Common Core ELA Standards, Speaking & Listening, Grade 9–10 (Presentation of Knowledge and Ideas)** CCSS.ELA-Literacy.SL.9-10.5 Make strategic use of digital media (e.g., textual, graphical, audio, visual, and interactive elements) in presentations to enhance understanding of findings, reasoning, and evidence and to add interest.	Edjudo (http://edjudo.com/web-2-0-teaching-tools-links) features Web 2.0 tools (e.g., animation, blogging, video sharing, social media, and much more) that students can choose from for creating presentations or other visual content.
4. Critical Thinking, Problem Solving, and Decision Making	**National Science Education Standards:** Understandings about scientific inquiry	Apple Education: Middle and High School Math and Science (www.apple.com/education/k12/curriculumsolutions/midhimathsci.html) provides comprehensive content, tools, and activities that students can use to investigate complex math and science concepts.

TABLE 7.1 ▶ *(Continued)*

NETS·S	COMMON CORE OR SUBJECT AREA STANDARDS	TECHNOLOGY TOOLS
5. Digital Citizenship	**Common Core ELA Standards, Writing, Grade 6 (Research to Build and Present Knowledge)** CCSS.ELA-Literacy.W.6.8 Gather relevant information from multiple print and digital sources; assess the credibility of each source; and quote or paraphrase the data and conclusions of others while avoiding plagiarism and providing basic bibliographic information for sources.	The digital article "What Is Plagiarism?" (http://kidshealth.org/kid/feeling/school/plagiarism.html) explains plagiarism, looks at the consequences, and advises how to avoid it. Noodletools (www.noodletools.com/tools/free-tools.php) provides tools for correctly formatting citations and Internet search strategies. It also has resources for teachers (www.noodletools.com/debbie).
5. Digital Citizenship	**NCSS National Curriculum Standards for Social Studies** Theme 10. Civic Ideals and Practices	From Pokemon to Picasso, Art Rights and Wrongs (http://library.thinkquest.org/J001570) is a ThinkQuest about digital copyrights, piracy, and ethical use of information.
6. Technology Operations and Concepts	**Common Core ELA Standards, Speaking & Listening, Grade 11–12 (Presentation of Knowledge and Ideas)** CCSS.ELA-Literacy.SL.11-12.5 Make strategic use of digital media (e.g., textual, graphical, audio, visual, and interactive elements) in presentations to enhance understanding of findings, reasoning, and evidence and to add interest.	Web 2.0: Cool Tools for Schools' Presentation Tools page (http://cooltoolsforschools.wikispaces.com/Presentation+Tools) provides links and brief descriptions for Web 2.0 presentation, publishing, and broadcast tools, and for multimedia poster and page tools.
6. Technology Operations and Concepts	**NCTE/IRA Standards for the English Language Arts** Standard 1. Students read a wide range of print and non-print texts to build an understanding of texts, of themselves, and of the cultures of the United States and the world; to acquire new information; to respond to the needs and demands of society and the workplace; and for personal fulfillment. Among these texts are fiction and nonfiction, classic and contemporary works.	Computers for Kids! (http://library.thinkquest.org/5862) is a ThinkQuest about computer parts, definitions, history, and care; includes activities.

The ISTE Seal of Alignment (ISTE, 2012) presents another way to correlate technology with classroom content. Following a rigorous review process, a dated seal is awarded to products, services, and resources that meet ISTE national standards of excellence. The ISTE Seal of Alignment can be awarded for development (products/services/resources that prepare participants to meet standards) or assessment (products/services/resources that evaluate participants' attainment of standards) and can be attained independently or in partnership with ISTE. Examples of products/services/resources attaining the ISTE Seal of Alignment include Discovery Education (Seal of Development); Certiport Internet & Computing Core Certification (IC3) Program and Assessment (Seal of Assessment); Center for Technology at The Johns Hopkins University (Aligned for Partnership); and PBS Teacherline's PBS Capstone Seal for Development (Partner for Development).

Although the NETS Seal of Alignment provides answers for how technology contributes to subject area understanding, the real question is, "How well does technology contribute to the kinds of subject area understanding needed by 21st-century learners?" The answer, as given in a 2007 paper released by ISTE, the State Education Technology Directors Association (SETDA), and the Partnership for 21st Century Skills, at the SETDA Leadership Summit and Education Forum in Washington, D.C., was, "Not very well."

The paper reported that, according to the U.S. Department of Commerce, education ranks last (out of 55 industry sectors) in terms of technology usage (ISTE, SETDA, & Partnership for 21st Century Skills, 2007). The paper recommended the development of the Partnership for 21st Century Skills and a Framework for 21st Century Learning, as well as a three-pronged approach to improving technology integration in schools: (1) because knowledge of core subjects is necessary, but no longer sufficient in a competitive world, "technology should be used comprehensively to develop proficiency in 21st century skills"; (2) to keep pace in a changing world, "technology should be used comprehensively to support innovative teaching and learning"; and (3) for teachers and administrators to have training, tools, and proficiency in technology, "use technology comprehensively to create robust education support systems."

The action plan for stakeholders recommended in the paper included the following action principle for federal and state policymakers: "Require standards for educational uses of technology that facilitate school improvement, such as the National Educational Technology Standards (NETS) developed by the International Society for Technology in Education" (ISTE, SETDA, & Partnership for 21st Century Skills, 2007). Route 21 (Partnership for 21st Century Skills, 2007), the framework's site for 21st century skills-related information, resources, and community tools, identifies NETS·S as both a formative and summative assessment tool. Thus, alignment between ISTE's NETS for Students and subject-area content can also be evaluated by how well states are addressing the Framework for 21st Century Learning.

ISTE's NETS in the Classroom: Teachers and Students

Technology has always shaped and defined teaching and learning. Bolter (1984) suggests that a defining technology is a filter that structures and directs people's interpretations of their experiences. Applying ISTE's NETS to today's classrooms assures that what teachers do and what students learn with technology forms the kind of filter that can maximize student success as citizens of a digital age.

E-learning is an all-encompassing term generally used to refer to computer-enhanced learning, although it is often extended to include the use of mobile technologies, such as tablets, cell phones, and media players. It may include the use of web-based teaching materials and hypermedia in general, multimedia CDs or websites, discussion boards, collaborative software, email, blogs, wikis, and computer-aided assessment. Although students are the focus of e-learning design and delivery, teachers also learn from the design and delivery of e-learning lessons and activities. ISTE's NETS provide a structure that teachers can use to set, track, and evaluate their own technology goals. E-learning artifacts generated by teachers and students can be stored in electronic portfolios to demonstrate progress toward and attainment of specific standards.

Design and delivery of online, hybrid, and conventional courses can be used to meet ISTE's NETS for teachers. For example, NETS·T Standard 2 (Design and Develop Digital-Age Learning Experiences and Assessments) forms the foundation for the development and demonstration of other NETS through: (a) designing or adapting relevant learning experiences that incorporate digital tools and resources to promote student learning and creativity; (b) developing technology-enriched learning environments that enable all students to pursue their individual curiosities and become active participants in setting their own educational goals, managing their own learning, and assessing their own progress; (c) customizing and personalizing learning activities to address students' diverse learning styles, working strategies, and abilities using digital tools and resources; and (d) providing students with multiple and varied formative and summative assessments aligned with content and technology standards and use resulting data to inform learning and teaching.

For example, in meeting Standard 2, a teacher might provide a grade-specific or subject-specific rubric for evaluating technology resources for accuracy and suitability; however, it would be the teacher's reflection that would demonstrate his or her understanding of the knowledge, skills, and understanding of technology.

Of course, the real application of subject area and technology standards occurs in a teacher's classroom. Given that technology is essentially a tool in service of content, teachers can think about lessons they already teach and answer the following questions:

- ▶ **What technological sources are available for obtaining and delivering content that students will read and use?** Technological sources include information on the Internet, databases, spreadsheets, podcasts, audio files, video files, emails, blogs, and so on.

- ▶ **How can students use technology to manipulate or process content?** Answers might include word processing, spreadsheets, calculators, databases, or specialized software.

- ▶ **How can student outcomes be translated into digital form?** For example, papers can be written using word processors or presented via presentation software. Data can be organized into spreadsheets or databases and displayed in graphics. Art and music can be created digitally.

Box 7.6 shows how technology can be integrated into a math unit.

BOX 7.6 ▶ Sample lesson plan showing technology integration

Pizza Party Project (Geometry)

Subject Area Standards

Principles and Standards for School Mathematics
Math Content: Geometry, Measurement, Data Analysis & Probability

Math Process: Problem Solving, Communication, Representation

Standards for the English Language Arts
1. Students read a wide range of print and non-print texts to build an understanding of texts, of themselves, and of the cultures of the United States and the world; to acquire new information; to respond to the needs and demands of society and the workplace; and for personal fulfillment.

3. Students apply a wide range of strategies to comprehend, interpret, evaluate, and appreciate texts.

4. Students adjust their use of spoken, written, and visual language to communicate effectively with a variety of audiences and for different purposes.

7. Students conduct research on issues and interests by generating ideas and questions, and by posing problems. They gather, evaluate, and synthesize data from a variety of sources (e.g., print and non-print texts, artifacts, people) to communicate their discoveries in ways that suit their purpose and audience.

8. Students use a variety of technological and information resources (e.g., libraries, databases, computer networks, video) to gather and synthesize information and to create and communicate knowledge.

ISTE's NETS·S
1. Creativity and Innovation
   b. create original works as a means of personal or group expression.
2. Communication and Collaboration
   a. interact, collaborate, and publish with peers, experts, or others employing a variety of digital environments and media, and
   d. contribute to project teams to produce original works or solve problems.
3. Research and Information Fluency
   b. locate, organize, analyze, evaluate, synthesize, and ethically use information from a variety of sources and media.
   d. process data and report results.
4. Critical Thinking, Problem Solving, and Decision Making
   a. identify and define authentic problems and significant questions for investigation,
   c. collect and analyze data to identify solutions and/or make informed decisions.

BOX 7.6 ▶ *(Continued)*

Objective

After completing a unit on determining area, the class will order pizzas that (1) appeal to class members' preferences and (2) represent the best value in terms of cost per square inch.

Activities

Day 1. Anticipatory Set: Discovery Sheet: Let's have a pizza party on Friday!

Students will fill out the discovery sheet, listing at least three things the class needs to know or do so that the pizza party is successful and not too expensive. The teacher will collect the discovery sheets and read aloud and record the questions and needs on the whiteboard. If students don't identify the need to order pizza that everyone will like and/or list best value issues, the teacher should guide them to think of these issues. The class will be divided into groups, and each group will search online to identify local pizza places in order to order pizzas and have them delivered to the class. Each group will use a desktop publishing program to create a paper and pencil survey that the class will use to determine what kind of pizza to buy (e.g., thick or thin crust, toppings, etc.). For added incentive, the members of the group whose survey wins get 10 bonus points added to their grades.

Day 2. Group presentation and voting for survey.

At the beginning of class, each group has a maximum of two minutes to explain its survey and convince the rest of the class to vote to use its survey (Group members may not vote for their own group's survey). A class vote will be taken and copies made of the winning survey for the Day 3 class.

Day 3. Completing the survey and summarizing the results.

Each student completes the survey. Survey answers are given to each group. Groups use a spreadsheet to enter the results of the survey and create a representation of results based on random assignment of representation type (e.g., circle graph, bar graph, Venn diagram) to each group. Using the results, each group should determine what kind of pizza to order. Groups compare results in order to reach consensus.

Day 4. Analyzing the results.

Each group is assigned a different pizza place to use for the analysis. Using the Internet, each group will analyze the options (size, shapes, and special deals) available for the type(s) of pizza the class wants to order. The group must identify a minimum of three options (e.g., eight medium versus four large) and determine cost per square inch using an electronic calculator.

Day 5. Presenting the results.

Each group will present its results in a PowerPoint presentation of 3 to 5 slides, showing the calculations for the three options and a recommendation for ordering. The class will order the pizzas that most closely match class preferences and that mathematically represent the best value in terms of cost per square inch.

No matter how teachers choose to integrate technology, they must keep in mind that standards are flexible, in that there are many dimensions to a standard and multiple ways to demonstrate competency. Just as few, if any, lessons address all the standards in a subject area, and few, if any, lessons will address all of the NETS·S. However, the goal might be to address all of the standards at some point throughout the year. Table 7.2 shows how commonly used e-learning tools can be used in terms of NETS for students.

TABLE 7.2 ▶ Technology Examples and Artifacts Related to ISTE's NETS·S

STANDARD 1. CREATIVITY AND INNOVATION	
Technology Examples	**Sample Artifacts**
Concept Mapping Tools	Concept maps or other graphic organizers
Spreadsheets	Spreadsheets
Video	Podcasts
Podcasts	Blogs
Blogs	Computer assisted designs
Simulation software	3-D models
Graphing calculators	Photographs
Interactive books	Video
Instructional game software	Digital presentations
Problem-solving software	Web pages/websites
Computer assisted design (CAD)	Word-processed documents
Authoring tools	Newsletters or other documents created with desktop publishing programs
Virtual manipulatives	Computer programs
Digital storytelling	Avatar development and use
3-D modeling software	Virtual space development
Assistive technology	
Digital cameras	
Video cameras	
Web page development	
Presentation graphics software	
Word processors	
Virtual environments	

TABLE 7.2 ▶ *(Continued)*

STANDARD 2. COMMUNICATION AND COLLABORATION	
Technology Examples	**Sample Artifacts**
Chat rooms	Chat room or discussion board transcripts
Desktop publishing	Newsletters or other documents created with desktop or electronic publishing programs
Podcasts	
Digital video	Podcasts
ePals/key pals	Group projects: digital music, images, or videos
PowerPoint	Printed email or chat room communications
Blogs	Photos or videos of virtual world interactions
Discussion boards	Blogs
Electronic mailing lists (Listservs)	
Bulletin boards	
Email	
MUDs (multi-user domains)	
Avatar spaces	
MIDI tools: Music editors and sequencers	
Image editing software	
Electronic mentoring	
Electronic publishing	
Electronic translators	
Assistive technology	

STANDARD 3. RESEARCH AND INFORMATION FLUENCY	
Technology Examples	**Sample Artifacts**
Search engines and electronic research	Word-processed documents/reports
WebQuests	Reflections on WebQuest outcomes
Graphing calculators	Spreadsheets
Data collection and organization	Databases
Microcomputer based labs (probeware)	Lab reports
e-Books	Concept maps or other graphic organizers
Calculator-based lab (CBL)	Electronic outlines
Geographic information system (GIS)	Concept maps or outlines
Global positioning system (GPS)	Math problems
Electronic encyclopedias, atlases, dictionaries	
Graphing calculators	
Hypermedia	
Multimedia	
Concept mapping software	
Electronic outliners	
Group product development	
Electronic translators	
Assistive technology	

TABLE 7.2 ▶ *(Continued)*

STANDARD 4. CRITICAL THINKING, PROBLEM SOLVING, AND DECISION MAKING	
Technology Examples	**Sample Artifacts**
Programming languages	Word-processed documents
Spreadsheets	Analysis of data or information
Databases	Reflections on classroom response outcomes
Classroom student response systems	Charts/graphs
Charting/graphing tools	Reflections on problem-based learning or social action projects
Problem based learning	
Social action projects	
Assistive technology	

STANDARD 5. DIGITAL CITIZENSHIP	
Technology Examples	**Sample Artifacts**
Email	Printed emails
World Wide Web	Logs of web usage
Virtual learning and coursework	Analysis of graphic usage
Use of computer graphics/clip art	Reflections on virtual learning
Netiquette	

STANDARD 6. TECHNOLOGY OPERATIONS AND CONCEPTS	
Technology Examples	**Sample Artifacts**
Software use	Objective and subjective assessments
Programming languages	Outcomes of computer programs
Internet troubleshooting	

Similarly, a teacher's competencies in technology can also be demonstrated in multiple ways over time. Just as technology evolves, a teacher's understanding of it and its role in classroom instruction will be an evolutionary process. However, teachers need to be aware of which e-learning tools are available in terms of NETS. In addition to the technology tools identified in Table 7.2, e-learning tools that apply to the NETS·T include bulletin boards, electronic grade books, electronic mailing lists, puzzle generators, rubric generators, test generators, worksheet generators, and virtual field trips.

E-portfolios provide comprehensive opportunities to showcase individual achievement of NETS by teachers and students in conventional (face-to-face), hybrid, or online coursework. Helen Barrett's Electronic Portfolios page (2008; http://electronicportfolios.org/portfolios/howto) describes how to create different types of electronic portfolios and provides templates for teachers and students in HTML as well as Microsoft Word, Excel, and PowerPoint formats. No matter what format is used, a portfolio entry should contain the artifact (or a link to the artifact) that exemplifies the standard, an explanation of how the artifact demonstrates attainment of the standard, and a reflection that includes what was learned as well as future goals regarding that standard.

Teachers can use examples of student artifacts (e.g., student-created graphic organizers, word-processed documents, music, assessments) as well as artifacts that demonstrate their own instructional knowledge and expertise (e.g., lesson or unit plans, instructional games and activities, assessments, WebQuests). A blog of instructional endeavors in e-learning and their results throughout the academic year, an electronic or print file of new ideas and their references, and information from faculty meetings and professional conferences can be used to document teachers' competence and progress.

Teachers can also demonstrate their attainment of NETS·T competencies by completing the PBS Teacherline/ISTE Certificate program (Public Broadcasting Service, 2008). The program consists of three fee-based, facilitated online courses: an introduction and two 15-week courses.

ISTE's NETS Leadership: Administrators and Education Coaches

What teachers do and how students learn in their classrooms are shaped by their school's administrators, who identify the school's mission, set policies, allocate funding, and evaluate results, and by education coaches, who help facilitate classroom teaching and learning. Roblyer (2006) identifies seven essential conditions that contribute to technology integration. First, administrators, coaches, teachers, and students must share a vision for technology integration. However, the administration and education coaches often share responsibility for coordinating planning, involving personnel in decision making, allocating adequate funds, providing training, matching technology to academic needs, assuring that technology is up-to-date, and building in flexibility to meet changing needs. Second, both administrators and education coaches should ensure that the curricular content standards are aligned with technology standards. Third, while administrators set policies that define acceptable use for the Internet, legal and ethical use of technology, and equitable access to technology, education coaches implement and monitor the policies. Fourth, the administration ensures access to technology by allocating funding, creating and maintaining physical facilities, and purchasing hardware and software. Fifth, the administration must ensure that teachers know how to use technology by providing opportunities for training that is both hands-on and ongoing, as well as providing education coaches and other personnel that can model, mentor, and coach new users of the technology. Sixth, the increasing complexity of technology requires that schools provide technical specialists or coaches who are knowledgeable and readily available. Finally, school administrators and education coaches must ensure that teaching strategies correlate with curricular and student needs and that assessment methods correlate with both content and technology learning. Box 7.7 provides examples of technology resources to help administrators and other policy makers achieve NETS standards.

BOX 7.7 ▶ Technology Resources for Educational Administrators and Policy Makers

Standard 1. Visionary Leadership

Consortium for School Networking (CoSN): www.cosn.org
CoSN's mission is to advance K–12 technology leadership.

Education World, School Administrators Channel: www.educationworld.com/a_admin
Contains articles, archives, and resources.

U.S. Department of Education ED.gov for Administrators: www2.ed.gov/admins/landing.jhtml
Contains features and resources.

American Association of School Administrators (AASA): www.aasa.org
AASA's mission is to advocate for the highest quality public education for all students and to develop and support school system leaders.

Standard 2. Digital-Age Learning Culture

Mid-Continent Research for Education and Learning (McREL): www2.mcrel.org/compendium
Provides a collection of K–12 content standards and benchmarks that can be either searched or browsed.

Association for School Curriculum Development (ASCD): www.ascd.org
ASCD's mission is to develop programs, products, and services essential to the way educators learn, teach, and lead.

National Conference of State Legislatures:
www.ncsl.org/home/search-results.aspx?zoom_query=education%20finance%20database
Information concerning K–12 funding.

SmartBrief from ASCD: www2.smartbrief.com/ascd
Sign up to receive a free daily briefing on stories that impact K–12 education.

Technology Information Center for Administrative Leadership (TICAL): www.portical.org
Database for technology in education for administrators by administrators.

Standard 3. Excellence in Professional Practice

Microsoft in Education: IT Solutions for schools and universities:
www.microsoft.com/education/en-us/solutions/Pages/ education_analytics.aspx
Education analytics for K–12.

TechLEARNING: www.techlearning.com
Ideas and tools for ed tech leaders.

Google Docs: www.google.com/google-d-s/intl/en/tour3.html
Create documents, spreadsheets, and presentations online; share and collaborate in real time; edit and access from anywhere; safely store your work, and more.

BOX 7.7   ▶   *(Continued)*

Standard 4. Systemic Improvement

Clearinghouse on Assessment and Evaluation: www.ericae.net
Provides assessment, evaluation, and research information.

National Assessment Governing Board (NAGB): www.nagb.org
Independent, bipartisan organization that oversees the National Assessment of Educational Progress (NAEP), also known as the Nation's Report Card.

National Center for Research on Evaluation, Standards, & Student Testing (CRESST): www.cse.ucla.edu
CRESST's mission is to improve the quality of education and learning in America.

Standard 5. Digital Citizenship

National Education Association (NEA) School Crisis Guide: Help and Healing in a Time of Crisis: www.neahin.org/assets/pdfs/schoolcrisisguide.pdf
Step-by-step advice for schools and districts to use before, during, and after a crisis.

Education Law Association: http://educationlaw.org
A national, nonprofit, nonadvocacy member association that promotes interest in and understanding of the legal framework of education and the rights of students, parents, school boards, and school employees.

Digital Citizenship: www.digitalcitizenship.net
Identifies nine themes of digital citizenship as well as resources and publications.

Applying ISTE's NETS to Alternative e-Learning Environments

The NETS have the power to transform traditional classrooms and foster digital-age teaching and learning, but they also apply to alternative e-learning environments. Although some environments must, by definition, incorporate technology (e.g., podcasting, WebQuests), others do not (e.g., case-based learning, experiential learning). The key to achieving the standards—for teachers and for students—lies in teachers' use of technology. From teachers' perspectives, any of the following instructional strategies can use technology in various ways. Further examples of how you may use technology to facilitate learning in a variety of e-learning environments are provided in the second book in this series, titled *Online and Hybrid Learning Designs in Action*. In short, the ways in which a teacher creates and facilitates instruction can also be ways in which the teacher demonstrates NETS·T.

WebQuests. Inquiry-oriented lessons, in which most or all the information that students work with comes from the web, can be designed to meet most, if not all, of the NETS·S in a single activity. WebQuests (discussed further by Rogers in Chapter 2 of the second book in this series, *Online and Hybrid Learning Designs in Action*) promote critical thinking as students work collaboratively to complete a task. The online aspects of the task involve research and information fluency. The outcome of the task can be expressed in multiple creative or innovative ways, such as data representation, word-processed documents, graphic design, presentation software, and so on. Digital citizenship and technological concepts underlie any use of technology; however, these can also be illuminated more clearly as part of the WebQuest itself. WebQuests permit teachers to demonstrate all of the NETS•S.

5E Instructional Model. The 5E instructional model, developed by Biological Sciences Curriculum Study (BSCS) in the late 1980s (as discussed by Wyatt, Dopson, Keyzerman, & Daugherty in Chapter 3 of the second book in this series), is a mnemonic that helps students learn the sequence for constructing conceptual understanding: engage, explore, explain, elaborate, and evaluate. Although designed for the teaching and learning of science concepts, the model can also be applied to other content areas. This model easily lends itself to the demonstration of many NETS•S by teachers and students, in that a lesson's design and student work can utilize a variety of technology tools. For example, a teacher's use of a video clip, podcast, or digital simulation to engage students may facilitate and inspire student learning. The resources the teacher recommends for exploring the topic (e.g., online database, e-book, WebQuest) demonstrate the teacher's skill in designing digital-age learning experiences. The ways in which the teacher explains the topic could use electronic flashcards or an electronic presentation that demonstrates digital-age work and learning. The ways in which a teacher uses resources across the 5E model can demonstrate digital citizenship and responsibility. As students complete the exploration, elaboration, and evaluation stages of the 5E model, they have ample opportunities to demonstrate creativity and innovation, to communicate and collaborate, to conduct research and use information, to think critically and make decisions, to practice digital citizenship, and to use technology effectively and productively.

Case-Based Learning. Case-based learning is an instructional approach in which students discuss an authentic, real-world example of a content-specific problem. The group works together to analyze the facts, assumptions, and implications of the case in order to come to consensus about a solution. Although case-based learning was originally designed to engage learners in face-to-face classrooms, it is an ideal forum for application of NETS•S standards in hybrid or online courses. For example, learners can communicate and collaborate in synchronous (e.g., chat) or asynchronous (email, discussion) ways as they think critically about a problem and make decisions. The case may be presented online and involve online research and data collection. Like any real-life problem, searching for the solution requires creativity and innovative thinking. The case would need to specifically involve digital citizenship or technological concepts to address those standards.

Experiential Learning. Experiential learning, the process of making meaning from direct experience (Itin, 1999), can take many forms (e.g., service learning, cooperative learning) and be defined in many ways. David Kolb's model of experiential learning (1984) involves four learner abilities: (1) active involvement in the experience, (2) reflection on the experience, (3) analysis of the experience in order to conceptualize it, and (4) decision-making and problem-solving skills that allow the learner to use what was learned from the experience. If the experience involves technology (e.g., online service projects; development of a digital product to meet a need), it can then easily contribute to attainment of the following NETS•S: 1. Creativity and Innovation; 2. Communication and Collaboration; 3. Research and Information Fluency; and 4. Critical Thinking, Problem Solving, and Decision Making. As in the application of NETS•S to other alternative environments, digital citizenship and technology operations and concepts also could be incorporated, depending on the nature of the experience itself.

Podcasts. The use of podcasts (discussed by Curry in Chapter 2 of the third book in this series, *Online and Hybrid Learning Trends and Technologies*) to meet standards for students depends on the way the podcasts are used. Podcasting in itself is only a delivery format variation. That is, podcasts are merely digital audio or visual content distributed through the Internet by subscription. Downloading and listening to or viewing a podcast address the NETS•S because learners must understand technology operations and concepts (Standard 6) in order to do so. If learners have to search for the right podcast, using research and information fluency skills, they have demonstrated Standard 3. However, if the lesson involves development of a podcast by the learner, it could easily address creativity and innovation (Standard 1); research and information fluency (Standard 3); critical thinking, problem solving, and decision making (Standard 4); and digital citizenship (Standard 5) issues in the development and communication of the content for the podcast. Creation of the podcast would involve technology operations and concepts (Standard 6).

Although daily instruction can address NETS•S in many different ways, creating and teaching more traditional lessons may actually be better vehicles for demonstrating NETS•T for teachers. For example, Gagné (1987) identifies nine conditions for learning (discussed further by Hawkins in Chapter 1 of the second book in this series, *Online and Hybrid Learning Designs in Action*), including: (1) gaining attention, (2) informing learners of objectives, (3) stimulating recall of prior learning, (4) presenting the stimulus content, (5) providing learner guidance, (6) eliciting student performance, (7) providing feedback, (8) assessing performance, and (9) enhancing retention and transfer. Here, what teachers do at each stage of the lesson can become opportunities to demonstrate competencies. Creation of the lesson itself can be an exercise in designing and developing digital-age learning experiences and assessments. Certainly, gaining attention and presenting the stimulus content using technology should facilitate and inspire student learning and creativity. The way the teacher provides the content can be a model of digital-age work and learning, as well as digital citizenship and responsibility. Teachers' reflections on lessons and refinements of them in future instruction demonstrate professional growth.

Alignment to Standards for Teachers and Students

Alignment can be defined as the act of adjusting a method of teaching or learning to match a standard. In some cases, alignment may be achieved by comparing students' comprehension of an instrument used as part of a lesson (e.g., a thermometer) with the standard to ensure accuracy. Alignment also applies to teachers' and students' efforts to meet educational standards. Standards are not points on a checklist to be met and then forgotten. Rather, standards form a kind of continual goal of learning and professional development. As students and teachers reflect on their attainment of NETS•S or NETS•T, the questions they ask themselves should not focus on completion: "What did I do to meet the standard?" or "Did I meet the standard?" Instead, the questions should be ones that address continual adjustment and readjustment of actions and thinking: "How well did I meet the standard?" What could I have done differently to better meet the standard?" "In what ways do I want to extend and refine my thinking and actions in terms of this standard in future teaching or learning activities?"

Rubrics presented in the *NETS for Teachers,* 2nd ed. (ISTE, 2008) help teachers answer these questions by showing attainment of a specific standard on a continuum with the following stages: beginning, developing, proficient, and transformative. For example, in demonstrating competency in Standard 1a (promote, support, and model creative and innovative thinking and inventiveness), a teacher at the beginning stage might research and discuss ways in which students could use digital tools in innovative and creative ways, whereas a teacher at the transformative stage would work with students as the lead learner in exploring, creating, and evaluating the use of digital tools for creativity and innovation. Sample student profiles in the *NETS for Students* (ISTE, 2007) exemplify ways in which NETS·S can be attained by learners at early childhood (PK–3), elementary (3–5), middle (6–8), and secondary (9–12) levels.

Standards, in general, form the maps for teachers and students to follow in reaching their learning destinations. Some destinations will be reached quickly and easily. The route to others may, at times, be difficult to traverse. Because technology is always changing, new teaching and learning destinations will always appear on the horizon, necessitating different standards and new ways of reaching them.

References

Adler, S. (2010). *National curriculum standards for social studies: a framework for teaching, learning and assessment.* Silver Spring, MD: National Council for the Social Studies.

American Association for the Advancement of Science. (1993). *Benchmarks for science literacy* (Project 2061). New York, NY: Oxford University Press. Retrieved from www.project2061.org/publications/bsl/online/index.php

Barrett, H. (2008). electronicportfolios.org. Retrieved from http://electronicportfolios.org

Beglau, M., Craig-Hare, J., Foltos, L., Gann, K., James, J., Jobe, H., Knight, J., & Smith, B. (2011). Technology, coaching, and community: Power partners for improved professional development in primary and secondary education [White paper]. Eugene, OR: ISTE. Retrieved from www.instructionalcoach.org/images/downloads/ISTE_Whitepaper_June_Final_Edits.pdf

Bolter, J. D. (1984). *Turing's man: Western culture in the computer age.* Chapel Hill, NC: University of North Carolina Press.

Gagné, R. (1987). Instructional technology foundations. Hillsdale, NJ: Lawrence Erlbaum.

International Association for K–12 Online Learning (iNACOL). (2011, October). National standards for quality online courses. Retrieved from www.inacol.org/cms/wp-content/uploads/2012/09/iNACOL_CourseStandards_2011.pdf

International Society for Technology in Education (ISTE). (1998). *National educational technology standards for students.* Eugene, OR: author.

International Society for Technology in Education (ISTE). (2000). *National educational technology standards for teachers.* Eugene, OR: author.

International Society for Technology in Education (ISTE). (2001). *National educational technology standards for administrators.* Eugene, OR: author.

International Society for Technology in Education (ISTE). (2007). *National educational technology standards for students* (2nd ed.). Eugene, OR: author.

International Society for Technology in Education (ISTE). (2008). *National educational technology standards for teachers* (2nd ed.). Eugene, OR: author.

International Society for Technology in Education (ISTE). (2009). *National educational technology standards for administrators* (2nd ed.). Eugene, OR: author.

International Society for Technology in Education (ISTE). (2011). *NETS for coaches.* Eugene, OR: author.

International Society for Technology in Education (ISTE). (2012). NETS seal of alignment. Retrieved from www.iste.org/standards/seal-of-alignment

ISTE, Partnership for 21st Century Skills, State Educational Technology Directors Association (SETDA). (2007). Maximizing the impact: The pivotal role of technology in a 21st century education system. Retrieved from www.setda.org/c/document_library/get_file?folderId=191&name=P21Book_complete.pdf

Itin, C. M. (1999). Reasserting the philosophy of experiential education as a vehicle for change in the 21st century. *The Journal of Experiential Education, 22*(2), 91–98.

Kolb, D. A. (1984) *Experiential learning.* Englewood Cliffs, NJ: Prentice Hall.

National Commission on Excellence in Education (1983, April). A nation at risk: The imperative for educational reform. Retrieved from http://datacenter.spps.org/uploads/SOTW_A_Nation_at_Risk_1983.pdf

National Committee on Science Education Standards and Assessment & National Research Council. (1996). *National science education standards.* Washington, DC: The National Academies Press.

National Council of Teachers of Mathematics (NCTM), Commission on Standards for School Mathematics. (1989). Curriculum and evaluation standards for school mathematics. Reston, VA: Author. Retrieved from www.fayar.net/east/teacher.web/math/standards/previous/CurrEvStds

National Council of Teachers of Mathematics, NCTM Commission on Teaching Standards for School Mathematics. (1991). Professional standards for teaching mathematics. Retrieved from www.fayar.net/east/teacher.web/math/standards/previous/ProfStds

National Council of Teachers of Mathematics, Assessment Standards Working Group. (1995). Assessment standards for school mathematics. Retrieved from www.fayar.net/east/teacher.web/math/standards/previous/AssStds

National Council of Teachers of Mathematics. (2000). Principles and standards for school mathematics (Standards 2000 Project). Retrieved from www.fayar.net/east/teacher.web/math/standards/document

National Council for the Social Studies, Schneider, D., & others. (1994). Expectations of excellence: Curriculum standards for social studies. Washington, DC: Author. Retrieved from www.eric.ed.gov/PDFS/ED378131.pdf

National Council of Teachers of English, & International Reading Association. (1996). Standards for the English language arts. Urbana, IL: National Council of Teachers of English. Retrieved from www.ncte.org/library/NCTEFiles/Resources/Books/Sample/StandardsDoc.pdf

National Governors Association Center for Best Practices & Council of Chief State School Officers. (2012). Common core state standards. Washington, DC: Authors. Retrieved from www.corestandards.org/the-standards/download-the-standards

NGSS Lead States (2013). *Next generation science standards: For states, by states.* Washington, DC: National Academies Press.

Pape, L., Wicks, M., & the International Association for K–12 Online Learning (iNACOL) Quality Standards for Online Programs Committee. (2009). National standards for quality online programs. Washington, DC: iNACOL. Retrieved from http://gsehd.gwu. edu/documents/gsehd/resources/gwuohs-onlineresources/standardslegislation/inacol_ nationalstandardsonlineprograms-102009.pdf

Partnership for 21st Century Skills. (2007). *Route 21.* Retrieved from http://route21.p21.org

Public Broadcasting Service. (2008). PBS teacherLine. Retrieved from www.pbs.org/teacherline

Roblyer, M. D. (2006). *Integrating educational technology into teaching* (4th ed.). Upper Saddle River, NJ: Pearson/Merrill Prentice Hall.

Rutherford, F. J. , & Ahlgren, A., (1991). *Science for all americans.* Washington, DC: American Association for the Advancement of Science; New York, NY: Oxford University Press.

APPENDIX A

ISTE's National Educational Technology Standards

ISTE's NETS for Students (NETS·S)

All K–12 students should be prepared to meet the following standards and performance indicators.

1. **Creativity and Innovation**

   Students demonstrate creative thinking, construct knowledge, and develop innovative products and processes using technology. Students:

   a. apply existing knowledge to generate new ideas, products, or processes

   b. create original works as a means of personal or group expression

   c. use models and simulations to explore complex systems and issues

   d. identify trends and forecast possibilities

2. **Communication and Collaboration**

   Students use digital media and environments to communicate and work collaboratively, including at a distance, to support individual learning and contribute to the learning of others. Students:

   a. interact, collaborate, and publish with peers, experts, or others employing a variety of digital environments and media

   b. communicate information and ideas effectively to multiple audiences using a variety of media and formats

   c. develop cultural understanding and global awareness by engaging with learners of other cultures

   d. contribute to project teams to produce original works or solve problems

3. **Research and Information Fluency**

   Students apply digital tools to gather, evaluate, and use information. Students:

   a. plan strategies to guide inquiry

   b. locate, organize, analyze, evaluate, synthesize, and ethically use information from a variety of sources and media

   c. evaluate and select information sources and digital tools based on the appropriateness to specific tasks

   d. process data and report results

4. **Critical Thinking, Problem Solving, and Decision Making**

   Students use critical-thinking skills to plan and conduct research, manage projects, solve problems, and make informed decisions using appropriate digital tools and resources. Students:

   a. identify and define authentic problems and significant questions for investigation

   b. plan and manage activities to develop a solution or complete a project

   c. collect and analyze data to identify solutions and make informed decisions

   d. use multiple processes and diverse perspectives to explore alternative solutions

5. **Digital Citizenship**

   Students understand human, cultural, and societal issues related to technology and practice legal and ethical behavior. Students:

   a. advocate and practice the safe, legal, and responsible use of information and technology

   b. exhibit a positive attitude toward using technology that supports collaboration, learning, and productivity

   c. demonstrate personal responsibility for lifelong learning

   d. exhibit leadership for digital citizenship

6. **Technology Operations and Concepts**

   Students demonstrate a sound understanding of technology concepts, systems, and operations. Students:

   a. understand and use technology systems

   b. select and use applications effectively and productively

   c. troubleshoot systems and applications

   d. transfer current knowledge to the learning of new technologies

ISTE's NETS for Teachers (NETS·T)

All classroom teachers should be prepared to meet the following standards and performance indicators.

1. **Facilitate and Inspire Student Learning and Creativity**

   Teachers use their knowledge of subject matter, teaching and learning, and technology to facilitate experiences that advance student learning, creativity, and innovation in both face-to-face and virtual environments. Teachers:

   a. promote, support, and model creative and innovative thinking and inventiveness

   b. engage students in exploring real-world issues and solving authentic problems using digital tools and resources

   c. promote student reflection using collaborative tools to reveal and clarify students' conceptual understanding and thinking, planning, and creative processes

   d. model collaborative knowledge construction by engaging in learning with students, colleagues, and others in face-to-face and virtual environments

2. **Design and Develop Digital-Age Learning Experiences and Assessments**

   Teachers design, develop, and evaluate authentic learning experiences and assessments incorporating contemporary tools and resources to maximize content learning in context and to develop the knowledge, skills, and attitudes identified in the NETS·S. Teachers:

   a. design or adapt relevant learning experiences that incorporate digital tools and resources to promote student learning and creativity

   b. develop technology-enriched learning environments that enable all students to pursue their individual curiosities and become active participants in setting their own educational goals, managing their own learning, and assessing their own progress

   c. customize and personalize learning activities to address students' diverse learning styles, working strategies, and abilities using digital tools and resources

   d. provide students with multiple and varied formative and summative assessments aligned with content and technology standards and use resulting data to inform learning and teaching

3. **Model Digital-Age Work and Learning**

   Teachers exhibit knowledge, skills, and work processes representative of an innovative professional in a global and digital society. Teachers:

   a. demonstrate fluency in technology systems and the transfer of current knowledge to new technologies and situations

b. collaborate with students, peers, parents, and community members using digital tools and resources to support student success and innovation

c. communicate relevant information and ideas effectively to students, parents, and peers using a variety of digital-age media and formats

d. model and facilitate effective use of current and emerging digital tools to locate, analyze, evaluate, and use information resources to support research and learning

4. Promote and Model Digital Citizenship and Responsibility

Teachers understand local and global societal issues and responsibilities in an evolving digital culture and exhibit legal and ethical behavior in their professional practices. Teachers:

a. advocate, model, and teach safe, legal, and ethical use of digital information and technology, including respect for copyright, intellectual property, and the appropriate documentation of sources

b. address the diverse needs of all learners by using learner-centered strategies and providing equitable access to appropriate digital tools and resources

c. promote and model digital etiquette and responsible social interactions related to the use of technology and information

d. develop and model cultural understanding and global awareness by engaging with colleagues and students of other cultures using digital-age communication and collaboration tools

5. Engage in Professional Growth and Leadership

Teachers continuously improve their professional practice, model lifelong learning, and exhibit leadership in their school and professional community by promoting and demonstrating the effective use of digital tools and resources. Teachers:

a. participate in local and global learning communities to explore creative applications of technology to improve student learning

b. exhibit leadership by demonstrating a vision of technology infusion, participating in shared decision making and community building, and developing the leadership and technology skills of others

c. evaluate and reflect on current research and professional practice on a regular basis to make effective use of existing and emerging digital tools and resources in support of student learning

d. contribute to the effectiveness, vitality, and self-renewal of the teaching profession and of their school and community

ISTE's NETS for Administrators (NETS•A)

All school administrators should be prepared to meet the following standards and performance indicators.

1. **Visionary Leadership**

   Educational Administrators inspire and lead development and implementation of a shared vision for comprehensive integration of technology to promote excellence and support transformation throughout the organization. Educational Administrators:

   a. inspire and facilitate among all stakeholders a shared vision of purposeful change that maximizes use of digital-age resources to meet and exceed learning goals, support effective instructional practice, and maximize performance of district and school leaders

   b. engage in an ongoing process to develop, implement, and communicate technology-infused strategic plans aligned with a shared vision

   c. advocate on local, state, and national levels for policies, programs, and funding to support implementation of a technology-infused vision and strategic plan

2. **Digital-Age Learning Culture**

   Educational Administrators create, promote, and sustain a dynamic, digital-age learning culture that provides a rigorous, relevant, and engaging education for all students. Educational Administrators:

   a. ensure instructional innovation focused on continuous improvement of digital-age learning

   b. model and promote the frequent and effective use of technology for learning

   c. provide learner-centered environments equipped with technology and learning resources to meet the individual, diverse needs of all learners

   d. ensure effective practice in the study of technology and its infusion across the curriculum

   e. promote and participate in local, national, and global learning communities that stimulate innovation, creativity, and digital-age collaboration

3. **Excellence in Professional Practice**

   Educational Administrators promote an environment of professional learning and innovation that empowers educators to enhance student learning through the infusion of contemporary technologies and digital resources. Educational Administrators:

   a. allocate time, resources, and access to ensure ongoing professional growth in technology fluency and integration

b. facilitate and participate in learning communities that stimulate, nurture, and support administrators, faculty, and staff in the study and use of technology

c. promote and model effective communication and collaboration among stakeholders using digital-age tools

d. stay abreast of educational research and emerging trends regarding effective use of technology and encourage evaluation of new technologies for their potential to improve student learning

4. Systemic Improvement

Educational Administrators provide digital-age leadership and management to continuously improve the organization through the effective use of information and technology resources. Educational Administrators:

a. lead purposeful change to maximize the achievement of learning goals through the appropriate use of technology and media-rich resources

b. collaborate to establish metrics, collect and analyze data, interpret results, and share findings to improve staff performance and student learning

c. recruit and retain highly competent personnel who use technology creatively and proficiently to advance academic and operational goals

d. establish and leverage strategic partnerships to support systemic improvement

e. establish and maintain a robust infrastructure for technology including integrated, interoperable technology systems to support management, operations, teaching, and learning

5. Digital Citizenship

Educational Administrators model and facilitate understanding of social, ethical, and legal issues and responsibilities related to an evolving digital culture. Educational Administrators:

a. ensure equitable access to appropriate digital tools and resources to meet the needs of all learners

b. promote, model, and establish policies for safe, legal, and ethical use of digital information and technology

c. promote and model responsible social interactions related to the use of technology and information

d. model and facilitate the development of a shared cultural understanding and involvement in global issues through the use of contemporary communication and collaboration tools

Index

A

abbreviations, 120

accessibility, 140–143

action and expression, multiple means of, 138, 141

action verbs, 18–19, 35–37

activities, creating. *See* materials and activities, creating

adaptive instructional design, 70

ADDIE (analysis, design, development, implementation, and evaluation) model, 3–4

advance organizers, 140

American Association for the Advancement of Science (AAAS), 150, 151

American Association on Intellectual and Developmental Disabilities (AAIDD), 132

analytic assessment rubrics, 24, 28–29

assessment. *See also* assessment items/criteria; assessment rubrics; learner assessment alignment tables

  conventional criterion-referenced testing, 12, 13–14, 24

  criterion-referenced tests, 12–14, 24

  entry-behavior tests, 23

  norm-referenced tests, 12

  performance-based assessments, 12, 13, 14

  performance/product checklists, 24, 27, 39

  posttests, 23

  practice tests, 23, 40–41

  pretests, 23

assessment items/criteria

  assessment rubrics, 27–30

  conventional CRT assessment items, 26–27, 40–41

  defining, 26–33

  health and wellness instructional unit, 38–41

  performance/product checklists, 27, 39

  portfolio assessment, 30, 170

assessment rubrics

  analytic, 24, 28–29

  descriptors and scale, 27–28

  for elaborating on what you learned, 74–75

  holistic, 24, 29–30, 38

attention deficits, 128, 131

Attribution (Creative Commons condition), 79

autism, 131–132

B

behavior, 18–20

behavioral objectives, 11

Biological Sciences Curriculum Study 5E model. *See* 5E instructional model

blogs, 99–100

Bloom's Taxonomy, 36–37

brain-based principles for universal design. *See* universal design for learning (UDL)

brainstorming, 97, 101

Brokers of Expertise (BOE), 85, 88–90

BSCS 5E model. *See* 5E instructional model

C

California Brokers of Expertise, 85, 88, 89–90

Career Technical Education (CTE) Online, 85

case-based learning, 174

case-based reasoning, 70

Center for Applied Special Technology (CAST), 134, 137, 138

Center for Science, Mathematics, and Engineering Education (CSMEE), 151

checklists

  email communication skills, 123–124

  performance or product, 24, 27, 39

collaboration, 97, 99, 100–101, 142–143

collaborative problem-solving, 69

Common Core standards, 160–163

communication

  email, 123–124

  written, 114–115, 120

concept mapping, 101

conditions, as element of objectives, 18

confidence, 99–100

Connexions, 87

constructivist learning, 70

content, student-generated, 113

conventional criterion-referenced testing

  about, 12, 13–14, 24

  assessment items, 26–27, 40–41

cooperative groups, 142–143

copyright, 125

CPALMS, 84–85, 89

creating, 98

Creative Commons licenses, 78–79

criteria, as element of objectives, 18